KENNETH

The **Given Day**

A Reconstructed Life

First Published in Great Britain 2021
By Twinlaw Publishing
Kirkcairn, Westruther, Gordon
Scottish Borders TD3 6NE

A CIP catalogue record for this title is available from the
British Library

ISBN: 978-1-9164558-2-5

www.twinlawpublishing.co.uk

The Given Day

A 'Reconstructed Life' by Kenneth Hall

The day thou gavest, Lord, is ended:
the darkness falls at thy behest;
to thee our morning hymns ascended,
thy praise shall sanctify our rest.

We thank thee that thy Church unsleeping,
While earth rolls onward into light,
through all the world her watch is keeping
and rests not now by day or night.

As o'er each continent and island
the dawn leads on another day,
the voice of prayer is never silent,
nor dies the strain of praise away.

The sun that bids us rest is waking
our brethren 'neath the western sky,
and hour by hour fresh lips are making
thy wondrous doings heard on high.

So be it, Lord; thy throne shall never,
like earth's proud empires, pass away;
thy kingdom stands, and grows for ever,
till all thy creatures own thy sway.

John Ellerton (1826-1893),
To the tune St Clement by Clement Cotterill Scholefield (1839-1904)

Charcoal sketch for portrait: Anton Beaver, Liverpool

Acknowledgements

First and foremost I acknowledge the very strong assistance provided by my dear wife Dorothea (Dorle) who has managed this project so efficiently, and Anthony Powell who has acted as proof-reader with a real eye to detail and most of whose recommendations I have followed. With my sight impairment, there are so many slips I have missed. It has been very much a collaborative effort, and I do appreciate all the help I have received.

I am particularly indebted to my late sister Vine, who was an avid record-keeper, and to my brother-in-law Stuart who made sure these records were retained, and who produced a wealth of photographs, films and videos relating to their life together, which also impacted on Dorle and me..

I have, fortunately, an enormous archive of photographs, due to the fact that I bought a Voigtlander camera on the advice of a colleague in Nürnberg, who generously also acted as official photographer at our wedding, free of charge. I later converted to a digital camera, with the possibility of sending images electronically, which has proved to be a real bonus.

I re-joined the Old Bedfordians, prompted by the list of 'Lost Sheep' published by the school. I was sent a complimentary copy of *Bedford School, a History*, written by Michael De-la-Noy. The volume was of particular interest to me as I had been involved in the re-publication of *Newport Free Grammar School, a Brief History* by Fred Thompson, a wonderful record by a meticulous historian and much-loved schoolmaster, whose whole career, ending as Deputy Head, was at Newport. Bedford, founded in 1552, is even older than Newport, which dates from 1588.

When researching points of fact or history, I have been much helped by online information on Google or Bing. Formerly I would have searched in a public or institutional library or on my own very limited book shelves. Now, information is instantly available. I am grateful to the compilers and maintainers of such sites.

I am very grateful to my publishers Russell and Dorothy Bruce for their co-operation and their willingness to take on my book, and also to my cousin John Belton who gave permission to reprint a chapter of his father's short biography of my brother James.

Finally, I wish to pay tribute to the staff of Sight Scotland Veterans, formerly the Scottish War Blinded, who have shown enormous generosity towards my main disability, my sight impairment. I admire all those who served their country in different ways, and I have a strong empathy with those who struggle with their eyesight. It is when you start to lose a faculty that you realise how precious it is.

For those who have received this book as a gift, I would ask you to make a donation to Open Doors, a charity founded by Brother Andrew, which defends the right to freedom of belief. A suggested amount, which can be Gift Aided, might be £10.00. Details are enclosed.

Contents

CHAPTER	TITLE	PAGE
	The Given Day	iii
	Acknowledgements	v
	Foreword	1
	Alms for Oblivion	5
1	In the Beginning	9
2	The Valley of the Shadow	25
3	Shaping the Mind	43
4	First Forays Abroad	69
5	On His Majesty's Service	83
6	Alma Mater	95
7	European Residence	105
8	Epiphany	117
9	Scotland, our First Home	135
10	Onward and Upward	145
11	The Garden of England	155
12	Top of the Ladder	169
13	Accompanying Pleasures	181
14	Twilight Career	195
15	Alpha	211
16	Dream Studio	217
17	Going West	223
18	Chelsea Bypass	231
19	A Taste of Heaven	237

Contents cont.

CHAPTER	TITLE	PAGE
20	Back in Scotland	255
21	Behind the Curtain	261
22	Battles Royal	277
23	Australia, again	283
24	Round the World	289
25	Lockdown	299
26	Rowing Across the Sahara	305
27	To Each a Season	313
28	Epilogue	317

Appendices

1	Farewell to James	323
2	Reflections on the End of a World War	329
3	*Corporate Identity in Secondary Schools*, Abstract of PhD Thesis	335
4	A Day in the Life of a Senior Volunteer	337

Bibliography	343

Foreword

Life is a gift. We don't ask for it: we get it, whether we like it or not. It is gone in a flash: we are but grass that withers and disappears. Our bones may last a while longer, but the bodily essence of ourselves is finite. We arrive: we leave.

This is why I have chosen the title *The Given Day*. Life is a gift from God, a factor which determines how I live what has been given – and it lasts but a day. The gift, which doesn't come easily, due to the difficult nature of birth and growth, comes via an act of love between our parents, but it still remains, to my way of thinking, a gift from the Lord, the origin of all creation. I cannot dismiss it as just a phenomenon of animal reproduction: I rate human beings higher than that. I believe that every human being, however imperfect, has a purpose in living and every person has a soul which outlives physical death. With that purpose comes a code of behaviour, which for me is outlined by Jesus Christ, as recorded in the Bible. To exist without a purpose and without a guide as to how we should interact with our fellow humans seems complete nonsense.

I have called this 'A Reconstructed Life' because of my defective memory (more about this later) and because I am lacking in sources for much of my life. I am by nature a note-taker and recorder. I regard each day as significant, not to be cast onto the scrap-heap. I have kept a log scrupulously for a large chunk of my life, and for other parts, much to my current regret, imperfectly and sporadically. Having done research, I am conscious that every statement needs a source. For many days there is no record of what I did and for many others only a hint. And so, for much of this, I have to rely on my recall of past events and, maybe, the dreams which reflect them.

Since the last year of my full-time employment, I have written a daily log, with certain elements recorded in each entry. However, I have earlier diaries which record events erratically and which are becoming mouldy. I also have a daily log which I gave my secretary to type throughout my last job as Headmaster of Newport Free Grammar School (1981-1990). I also kept a daybook so that I had a record of all my visitors and phone calls. In addition, quite often when we went on holiday, whether abroad or in the UK, I would write an account of what we did, because I enjoyed looking back over the experiences we had. I have been a prolific photographer, taking mostly slides for many years which have now been digitalised and transferred to data sticks by Dorle. I have boxes of prints, too, which I have been too lazy to place in albums.

In some cases I have avoided naming names, in order not to cause offence and in recognition that in any disputes I have had with others the fault may have lain with myself. However, if you are reading this and are a friend or member of the family and expecting to find your name mentioned and it is missing, I do apologise. I have been blessed by so many people in my long life and I am immensely grateful to them for their love and friendship, but, as I have indicated, my memory is defective; I can only apologise if you have been omitted.

I enjoy writing, even though I struggle to find the right word and the right expression. I live in a world of words, being a linguist, but words, whether spoken or written, do not come easily to me. I quite often have difficulty with spelling and frequently look up a word to check that I have not misspelt it.

I am an academic by nature, but without the ability to be called erudite. I love foraging for facts and then assembling them together to make a narrative. I have done many courses of study and was happiest when I gathered material, under guidance from my supervisor at Liverpool University, for a MPhil which turned into a PhD. I am very creative, but a poor improviser: I have ideas but I usually need images to work from. In music I am – or have been when my vision allowed it – a good sight-reader but a very poor extemporiser. I am an unashamed romantic and attracted to flights of fancy and strong emotional pulls, whether it be in an attractive landscape or seascape, a moving piece of music, an inspiring building, an intriguing or colourful work of art, or an exotic culture. I shall elaborate on all of this later.

We are the sum of the parts which have made us. In this I was very fortunate to be born of loving parents with high standards, and to have arrived on the scene in 1932, an auspicious year in history, but not one which would require me to endure the horrors of battle. I had the great fortune to live in the UK, which, although bombed, did not have the terrifying experience of living with the compromises and oppression of a cruel occupying military force. Although we were not affluent we enjoyed the privileges of private education and, for three of us, the chance to go to the best universities. Our parents were active Christians and encouraged us to follow suit. My place of birth, Bedford, was unspectacular, but had a lovely, sauntering river, some distinguished schools and a fine hero in John Bunyan, who represented nonconformist independence from the ruling classes. Within easy reach of London by train, it opened up the excitement of a large, bustling city, which for us at the time was the centre of the civilised world.

So, in all of this I consider myself to be a child of privilege: being born in Bedford at this time had every promise. 'The Given Day' had an optimistic, prospect-full dawn.

Alms for Oblivion

A phrase from *Troilus and Cressida* by William Shakespeare is a legacy from my education which sticks in my mind:

> *Time hath, my lord, a wallet at his back*
> *Wherein he puts alms for oblivion.*
> *A great-sized monster of ingratitudes.*
> *Those scraps are good deeds past; which are devour'd*
> *As fast as they are made, forgot as soon*
> *As done.....*
> Ulysses in *Troilus and Cressida* Act 3

Ulysses is talking to Achilles who has referred to a good deed he performed, which is now forgotten. I have always, since I studied the play at Bedford School as a set text, thought that the subject matter was memory alone, but the context implies that it really refers to the forgetting of good deeds, implying that most people hold the bad deeds of others in their minds rather than the good ones. However the quotation is interpreted, I am reminded that the passage of time eradicates much of what I have done, both good and bad, and much of what has been done to me. When I review my 'archives', as I call them, I am amazed at what came my way and how I coped with it. Documents, letters, computer files, recordings, programmes and photographs reveal a myriad of encounters, meetings, conferences, interactions and performances, of which time has erased the memory and senility has eroded the capacity.

To continue on the subject of Shakespeare's play, Dorle and I did 'manage to see a magical performance of *Troilus and Cressida* by the Royal Shakespeare Company in Stratford in 1969. It was in the old theatre and our seats were far removed from the stage. We were with my Aunt Mildred (Auntie Moo), an elder sister of Gracie, my mother. We wondered whether she might be shocked by the performance, as it was rather 'near the bone', but she loved it just as we did. The cast included Michael Williams, Judi Dench, Helen Mirren, Alan Howard (very much the leading man in those days), Norman Rodway, Patrick Stewart, John Shrapnel, Susan Fleetwood and Ben Kingsley. Most of these later became household names in the film and theatre world.

Many of the past years are imperfectly remembered due to the passing of time, but I have to admit that I have always had a defective memory, in terms of instant recall at least. I remember a very embarrassing general knowledge quiz at Bedford School when I was about 12 or 13 and in the Junior School. I got a low score – probably the worst of the class – and my form master made fun of me as I had stated that I wanted to be a schoolmaster as my chosen profession. I do not blame the member of staff [1]: it was a boys' school, after all, where you had to take the rough with the smooth, and he was a kindly man who had lost a leg in the war. However, the poor memory was a fact which stuck with me throughout my professional career and from which I still suffer. I have done an enormous amount of study and have come through many tests and examinations, so maybe my condition could be put down to an 'absent-minded professor' syndrome. Despite all this, I will attempt to give a true account of my life, using whatever documentation I have where I am in doubt.

However, before leaving the topic of 'Alms for Oblivion' I will record what most octogenarians experience due to the natural ageing process. I frequently start an action and then lose my way in the middle of it. I take out a document, place it somewhere and then forget where I have put it. This is partly a sight problem: I have advanced glaucoma. My right eye is practically useless and my left eye – the better of the two – has a developing cataract and a very limited field of vision. Spotting where I have placed an object 'in the corner of my eye' just does not happen. However, it is also a memory problem against which I have to invent a series of mnemonics. These work quite well and are certainly very useful when using pin numbers (which I rarely forget). However, trying to remember names of people is a nightmare, especially when the person you meet is a well-known friend. If you use a mnemonic, which might be a physical characteristic, and then call the person by that name, e.g. 'Tubby', instead of his/her real name, this could cause serious offence! One other mnemonic device for numbers is to sing the musical intervals and make them into a tune.

So, all in all, life has become a strategy for countering my age-related shortcomings.

1. Jack Carlton, a Lower School Master, later Housemaster of Sanderson's.

For, having now my method by the end,

Still as it pulled, it came; and so I penned

It down: until at last it came to be,

For length and breadth, the bigness

which you see.

John Bunyan, extract from *The Pilgrim's Progress*

CHAPTER 1

In the Beginning

I was born at 59 Goldington Avenue, Bedford, on 10 July 1932. My father was Herbert Nathaniel Hall and my mother was Emma Grace Hall, née Belton. I am told I was born during the night so I assume it was in the early hours of the 10th. Goldington Avenue was a quarter-mile straight road with Victorian housing climbing slightly from Goldington Road, in the east of the town which led to the village of Goldington and continued in a generally north-eastward direction towards Cambridge via St Neots. Our house, attached on either side, was on the corner of Richmond Road and had a bay window which faced the corner. I was named Kenneth, recalling an uncle who died as a child from diabetes (untreatable in those days), Grant Matthews, from ancestors of those names. My father was born at Fox Hall in 1887 in the small village of Kelshall, on the top of the Royston Heath downs, Hertfordshire, surrounded by huge arable fields. He was the son of Nathaniel Hall, a tenant farmer, who died at the early age of 30 from the effects of rheumatic fever, leaving my grandmother Mary (née Matthews) to manage the farm with her staff. Fox Hall was a large property, in the grand manner, with a pond in front of it. Like the other farms in the village, it was owned by Francis Fordham. Nathaniel had a high reputation as a bailiff farmer. Today (2021) it is worth nearly £1,230,000. With a direct rail connection to Cambridge and King's Cross from Royston it is in an ideal

KENNETH HALL

59 Goldington Avenue

position and can only be occupied by people of some wealth. My father came from this rather genteel background, even though his parents were tenants and not owners of the farm. He did not attend the local primary school - or elementary school as it must have been when he was a child. He had a private tutor, who was the Rector. He did, however, attend Hitchin Grammar School. David and Ann King were later owners and residents of Fox Hall. We kept in touch with Ann right up to shortly before her death. She and David moved to a house in the grounds of the farm, which was a barn conversion called Little Foxes. We attended David's funeral at St Faith's. David, who was a church warden, was a seed merchant. Ann, who studied at Newnham College Cambridge, was an expert on the historical fiction writer George Alfred Henty and wrote a book about him. She was a great character and we loved her dearly. When we last visited the church, there was a glass door at the south

Father's family: Herbert, Frank, Stanley

Fox Hall (2021), Kelshall, Herts

entrance engraved with David's and her names, a fitting and architecturally suitable memorial to their contribution to St Faith's and the village of Kelshall. The Hall family graves, enclosed with a low marble rail, stand alone in the old graveyard, where the other graves have been moved to the perimeters.

My mother, born in Hastings, Sussex, was the daughter of the pastor of an evangelical chapel in Welwyn, also in Hertfordshire, Herbert Belton, whose previous employment had been as a commercial traveller. Before she married, my mother, who had studied at a secretarial college, was private secretary to a Conservative MP, Major Guy Molesworth Kindersley (1876 – 1956) MP for Hitchin 1923 - 1931. When she married she gave up her job and did not have paid employment again. They met at Wymondley Hall, Hertfordshire. She was born in 1900 and was therefore 13 years younger than my father. They started their married life in Faversham, Kent, even though my father's career had started in Hitchin, and their first child, Vine, was born there in 1928. Vine derived her name from the Vine family who were millers in Sussex. So, in my background there was a strong element of cereal production.

There was also a tradition of Nonconformity. My father was a trustee of the Congregational Chapel of Therfield, the nearest village to Kelshall, and my mother came from an evangelical family. Nevertheless, the family graves of the Halls and Matthews' are in the old churchyard of St Faith's Parish Church in Kelshall. An annual visit to these graves was a family ritual when I was a child and constituted an exciting trip by train to Royston, changing at Hitchin, and completing the journey to Kelshall either by bus or on foot via the King's Highway from Royston Heath. Both my parents were lay

Family Graves, St Faith's Churchyard, Kelshall, Herts

preachers, at a time when much social life centred on churches and chapels.

I cannot remember much of my early days. We moved from Goldington Avenue to St Augustine's Road, which was close to Bedford's impressive main park. This road led off from Kimbolton Road. Our house was again Victorian in style and semi-detached. At the far end of our road was Park Road, where the Headmaster's House of Bedford School was situated: from here we had a fine view of the playing fields and distinctive main building of the school. Farther along was De Parys Avenue, considered to be the best address in Bedford at the time. This does not imply that we were well-to-do. My father had a good job, as a solicitor's clerk, but that was the only income. We had no car and we lived quite frugally.

Nevertheless in my infant years we had a nanny. My earliest memory is being sent away from home on the birth of my brother James, who was two years younger than myself. I am pretty certain that Neil and I were sent to Mildred's home in Barnet but I have no evidence for this. Suffice it to say that at the age of less than two being removed from my parents was a significant, even traumatic, event. However, a far more dramatic event was to follow a few years later. I caught scarlet fever. In those days there was only one option: to go to an isolation hospital. I was placed in a hutted establishment a few miles out of Bedford, at Clapham. My parents could visit but not enter the hospital: they had to stand outside the window. We were well cared for, no doubt, but it was like being in prison. I was heartily glad to be released. In those days, before the NHS, you had to put up with such privations, and with catching diseases such as mumps, measles and chicken pox, against which there were no vaccinations.

One really exciting event of my early years stands out. When we lived in St Augustine's Road Neil and I had our first real adventure. This was to take off for the day on a trek, armed with refreshments supplied by our mother. We were very young, possibly 6 and 5 years old. We walked through the park and then on to Putnoe past the Laxton orchards, which were famous for their own species of apple, Laxton Superb. These orchards have long since disappeared and housing has been built on the land released. At one stage we saw a little cottage down a lane: we were convinced that a witch lived there. No doubt we were recalling the fate of Hansel and Gretel! When a woman appeared we ran away as quickly as our little legs would carry us! Such is the imagination of small children! These days parents would think twice before they allowed their children to go off like this. It was a more innocent, less suspicious age, although the dangers may have been just as great in reality. We survived, and the experience helped us to mature. The impending war was to bring far greater dangers.

While we were at St Augustine's Road we used to take walks in the beautiful town park, in the north of the town close to the cemetery. It had a sizeable lake, with an island and the inevitable ducks and swans. There were also peacocks, with colourful fans of feathers and eccentric, squawking cries which matched their strange behaviour. There was a prominent bandstand. One day my father was out with Vine in the park when a cyclist ran into Vine, causing a serious injury. My father lobbied the borough council to ban cycles in the park, but to no effect. He decided that we needed to relocate to Woburn Sands, a large village on the railway line to Hitchin, to allow Vine to recuperate. My father could commute daily from the station to his work at the Bedford solicitors' firm of Sharman and Trethewy, close by St Paul's Church and the town bridge. We were very young and did not attend school in Woburn Sands. However, I can remember going to Miss Moore, for pre-school tuition with other children. She was an extraordinary maiden lady with a bonnet, like a character out of an Ealing comedy.

Woburn Sands was aptly named: it has a pine woodland with sand dunes. Under Vine's leadership we would go for walks in the woods and slide gleefully down the sand slopes. One day we met a tramp, who warned, 'Yoor'll get lawst'! We didn't, and we came to no harm! For worship on a Sunday we went to a local Methodist church.

This interlude only lasted a year and we returned to Bedford. Our new home was another semi-detached house but this time closer to the river. It was at 12 Kingsley Road in a group of streets named after English writers: opposite our house was Tennyson Road. We were right by Russell Park, which was pleasant but lacked the flamboyance of our previous park. It was at the end of a bus route, which was withdrawn while we lived there. We walked to school, down George Street, lined with terraced garage-less houses, crossing Castle Street, our local shopping area, and then the main thoroughfare of Goldington Road and thereafter via a couple of backstreets to our hutted school, the Training College School, or TCS, commonly known as the Tom Cats School. This was a Froebel institution, with links to the Teachers' Training College in the west of the town, the principles of which were based on child-centred learning. This did not suit James, who needed a firm hand. On one occasion he was naughty and was ordered to leave the room. He refused to do this and consequently the teacher took out the whole of the rest of the class instead. Personally, I could have done with a more disciplined regime myself, even though I was a sensitive child. One of the life-long influences I gained from my years there was from the reading to us by one of the teachers of Bunyan's *Pilgrim's Progress*. This was a

The Hall Family - Front row: Herbert, Vine, Grace. Back row: Kenneth, Neil, James (Photo: Parrish, Bedford)

vicissitudinous adventure, an allegory of the Christian life, which grabbed our excitement-hungry imaginations. Further than that, many of the fictional locations in the pilgrimage were derived from local sites, and the story of John Bunyan himself - an ordinary tinker defying the authorities and writing an English masterpiece in prison – fanned our feelings of justice and equality.

One of the joys of this early part of my life was visiting the country. We lived a very humdrum existence in those dull, flat, dusty Victorian terraces, despite the fascination of the river and boating lake nearby. Certain streets signalled danger: in our smart private-school uniforms we were easy pickings for rough bullies. To get away to the country, with its smells, its sounds (particularly the busy clucking of hens and

Miss Moore's Kindergarten, Woburn Sands: Kenneth on Miss Moore's knee, Vine on her right

Elsvic Thatch (2021), Stevington, Bedfordshire

Bunyan Meeting, Stevington, Bedfordshire

the exalted crowing of cocks, accompanied by the slow squeak of wooden steel-rimmed wheels with the regular clopping of horseshoes on hard surfaces) and, above all, the slow pace of life, was sheer heaven. My parents hired a thatched cottage in Stevington, a truly idyllic settlement with a shop, a bakery, a stone cross and a forge. The river and the parish church were a little removed from the centre and on the way to these was a spring, huge 'wild-rhubarb' plants and a place where we could bathe. At the other, far end of the village, up a hill, was a Baptist chapel, a Bunyan meeting-house, defying the royal edict that forbade the preaching of the Gospel within a six-mile radius of a town and, at the other end, the ecclesiology of the Anglican-gothic sanctuary by the river. This meeting-house is where we worshipped on Sundays and where my father preached on occasions. But that was not all. In a field near the cottage was a massive, heavy windmill, a roofed construction mounted on a turntable so that it could be swivelled to face the prevailing wind with its huge sails. From time to time it actually produced flour. There was also a railway nearby with a halt. Steam trains would occasionally pass, chugging, whistling and smoking, on their way to Northampton. Back at the cottage there was a deep well from which our parents – we were forbidden to move the heavy stone on the cover – could draw water. We drank unpasteurised milk which came warm from the cows at the farm nearby and shamelessly ate rich cream. Stevington really was the ideal get-away for us town children. I can remember lying in the windmill field gazing at the blue sky and cumulus clouds thinking, and hoping, that life would go on forever. It was a moment of childish bliss. In the same field there were haystacks. One of these caught fire one evening. We joined a crowd of villagers who gathered to watch this spectacle, as the

Stevington Windmill

fire brigade arrived: a memorable occasion to our young impressionable eyes.

Farther away, at Oakley, trains thundered up and down the LMS main line, travelling between St Pancras, London, and Leicester and Sheffield. Whereas the Northampton line was benign and comical, the main line was awe-inspiring, fascinating and even threatening. We were used to these trains as they passed through Bedford Midland Road Station, sometimes stopping at the platform and sometimes roaring through on a bypass track. Trains were very much part of our lives and our allegiance to LMS (London, Midland and Scottish), rather than LNER (London and North East Railway), was strong. But there was another line closer to our homes and closer to the river. This was the LMS line running into St John's Station on the south side of the town. It wound its way westwards to Oxford via Bletchley where it crossed the

LMS main line from Euston to Glasgow, and eastwards to Cambridge via Sandy and Gamlingay. St John's was our local station, accessible on foot by crossing the new cut of the Ouse over the suspension bridge. It often carried freight in small coupled wagons, which at night could be heard pinging up and down the train's length as it shunted, causing the buffers to impact on one another. Of the aural memories on sleepless nights in my early years this was one of the most indelible.

At Stevington at the end of the summer holidays on Sunday evening 3 September 1939 my father announced solemnly to the family that we were at war with Germany. Neville Chamberlain, the British Prime Minister, had issued an ultimatum to Adolf Hitler, after the invasion of Poland two days previously, that German forces had to be withdrawn by 11.00 am that day otherwise Great Britain would honour her commitment to Poland and declare war. In fact, the declaration came at 11.15 am. I was seven years old. We had little idea of the seriousness of the situation, nor of the horrors to come. Had we known what danger we were in and how hazardous the course of the war would be, we would probably have burst into tears. However, as far as I can recall, we accepted the situation, and no doubt there was a frisson of adventurous excitement in our hidden reaction. My parents accepted it stoically, and subsequently, through the long six years of its duration, played their patriotic, community-supporting part. Fortunately my father was not eligible for military service: he was 52.

YEA, THOUGH I WALK THROUGH THE VALLEY

OF THE SHADOW OF DEATH,

I WILL FEAR NO EVIL; FOR THOU ART WITH ME;

THY ROD AND THY STAFF THEY COMFORT ME.

David Psalm 23 – King James Version

CHAPTER 2

The Valley of the Shadow

The good thing about World War Two was that there was a clearly-defined, really evil, villain in Adolf Hitler. We were brought up to admire the British Empire and regarded it as our wider family: the injustices which were perpetrated in conquering and subjecting a third of the world's surface were glossed over. After the invasion of the Soviet Union by Germany the murderous rule of an even worse tyrant, Josef Stalin, was forgotten. Hitler remained the arch-devil. A study of the history of the war reveals bestiality of the most heinous kind. The invasion of neutral countries, plus the deportation of Jews, the disabled, and political opponents, to the concentration camps and gas chambers - not only from their own country but also from the states they subjugated – plus the philosophy of racial superiority, and the political system of dictatorship, all added up to a challenge which had to be met full-on. Someone had to stand up to this evil. David, with meagre resources amounting merely to five stones and a sling had to meet the huge, armed Goliath[1], even though the odds were unmercifully stacked against him. For us children this was a righteous cause and also one which carried the smell of adventure. The historians disclose how close we were to disaster, but we, perhaps too full of optimism and defiance, were unaware of this at the time.

One of the strongest memories of the run-up to the war and its early stages was putting on a gasmask, with its suffocating

KENNETH HALL

Bromham Baptist Chapel Congregation: Father in the middle, seated

smell of rubber and its protruding nose-piece, and, when not in use, carrying it over my shoulder in a cardboard box as we walked to school. We had homes of friends, designated by our parents, on the way, in which we could shelter in the event of an air raid. Fortunately we rarely needed to use these. However, we did have raids from time to time. These were preceded by sirens. The rising and falling wail of these sirens, filling us with foreboding, remains indelibly in my catalogue of spectral memories. Perhaps an ice-cream van's jingle would have put us in a more positive mood to withstand the fire from above! The relief of the single-note all-clear was the most glorious antidote, even though the relief lasted just until the next raid. Part of the horror was the distinctive throb of the German Heinkels and Messerschmitts above, amongst the far-reaching, shafting searchlights which provided the backdrop to the enfolding drama. We were spared the worst: Bedford was regarded as relatively safe – safe enough to become the base for the morale-boosting BBC orchestras and the daily broadcast service. However, an early bombing experience for Neil and me happened when we were at Bedford Modern School one morning. There was an air-raid warning and we sat at our desks in our form rooms waiting nervously for the worst. A German bomber, clearly spotted through the window, flew over and shortly after we heard a deafening crash. We were terrified. A building next to the station just down the road had been hit and we watched as the dust settled around us in the classroom. Maybe it was an attacker just releasing his weapon having not found a worthwhile target. Later in the war there was a much worse attack. We were at home, at night. The siren went and the whole family gathered under the stairs. Flares lit up the sky. There were explosions happening all round us, or so it seemed. One caused the whole house to shake and the front-door knob to rattle, like the arrival of the Grim Reaper. No harm came to us and on the following day we saw the bomb debris in Russell Park, evidence of the night before. We were aware of the London Blitz and the terrible bombing of other British cities, including Coventry. If anything, these raids served to strengthen the will of the British people rather than demoralise them. Our parents played their part: my father took his turn doing fire-watch duty at his office by night, and my mother became air-raid warden for our street, wearing (no doubt with pride) a white helmet. We were called to 'dig for victory', so we dug up our back lawn and planted vegetables, in patriotic response. Some households acquired an Anderson shelter, half-submerged outside in the garden, but we had, in the later stages of the war, a Morrison shelter, a steel construction the size of a table into which we would crawl when the siren sounded and which, in theory at least, would withstand the collapse of the house above us.

Aware of the danger of the London area, we took some evacuees. Aunt Mildred's family lived in Barnet, North London. Rosemary, the younger of my two Barnet cousins, lodged with us for a while and attended the Girls' Modern School (later, the Dame Alice Harper School) on the south side of the river. Her elder sister Barbara used to visit us in the holidays and came with us when we went away but she remained at Barnet High School during the term. Another family, the Sayers (Uncle Herbert and Aunt Irene) lived in Streatham, South London. There were four children and in this way they mirrored our family. Marion, the only girl, would visit us quite often. Another cousin, Maurice, the only son of Uncle Leslie and Aunt Ethel, was old enough to join up: he, very sadly, was killed near the end of hostilities and this caused terrible sorrow to his parents. He was a brilliant young man, who when still at school published a hand-written newspaper, a copy of which was regularly passed to us. He had the intellectual qualities of his parents, both graduates of Liverpool University. Peter Renouf was another evacuee, but he came via the relocation of Victoria College, Jersey, to Bedford School, upon the occupation of the island by the Germans.

My father's family was more enigmatic. I have mentioned elsewhere his brother Stanley, whose wife Kitty we adored because she was eccentric, unpredictable and unconventional. She appealed to us because she was constantly urging us to break the rules of good behaviour! They had no children and lived at St Mary's Bay, Kent, which took us, and our 'adopted family' to that area on holiday, usually at Easter. My father was very loyal to Stanley, a pharmacist, but he had nothing to do with his elder brother Frank, who was very much the 'black sheep' of the family. We did, however, meet up with Frank's wife Beatrice, who was blind and we got to know their children, our cousins, Sylvia and Rodney.

Because we lived in the east of England there were airfields all around us. The sky was constantly filled with aircraft. The local airfield was Cardington, but, although an RAF station, it did not house aircraft: it had two huge airship hangars, very visible from some distance away. The fated R101 was based here. By then airships were out of fashion and aircraft were far more effective as fighting weapons. Also prominent were barrage balloons whose function was to prevent enemy aircraft from landing. The nearest airfield of any importance was Therleigh which was run by the RAF until the US Air Force took it over in 1942, a base for B-17s, or 'Flying Fortresses'. Similarly the same year Bassingbourn in Cambridgeshire, near Royston, was adopted by the USAAF using the same aircraft. Other notable RAF airfields were at Cranfield,

12 Kingsley Road, Bedford

Henlow, Duxford and Waterbeach. One of my vivid memories of the latter part of the war was the roar of squadrons of B-17s returning to base in the morning after a night raid over Germany – obviously this was when the Americans had changed to night raids, abandoning the earlier policy of daytime raids . My thoughts turned to the danger of what they had been doing and how many of the squadron passing over us were missing. As the war grew towards its end, Hitler developed rockets, the V1 and the V2: the V stood for '*Vergeltungswaffe*' or 'Vengeance Weapon'. Although the V2 was more menacing in that it was a rocket missile which landed without warning, the more terrifying was the V1, or the 'doodlebug' as it was called by the British public. Armed with a bomb of 850 kg, this flew like an aircraft, but was pilotless and was driven by a pulse-jet engine with a staccato-throbbing, throaty roar. When the roar stopped, after a sickening pause of about 15 seconds, you knew it was going to drop and explode on the ground. If the engine stopped after passing over you, you were safe as it dived at an angle. However, if the pause started away from you the fear was that you might be its target. One night after the siren had sounded we heard this fateful roar: suddenly it stopped. A girl who was billeted on us screamed. Would it be us this time? There was an enormous crash when it landed and we gave a huge sigh of relief that it was somewhere else. Undoubtedly, uncertainty was one of the tortures of war. The RAF had strategies for dealing with the V1s, either by shooting them down or tipping their wings so that they dived into an unpopulated area. Anti-aircraft guns also destroyed some; RAF raids and the advance of the allies after D-Day destroyed the launch sites. The V1 raids lasted from 13 June 1944 till March 1945.

The community prepared for any eventuality. Staggered trenches were dug in open areas to prevent aircraft from landing; sandbag defences were set up. At home all windows were taped, so that shattered glass would not spread causing injuries, and were blacked out at night. The black-out, a potent symbol of dark and gloomy times, was very strongly enforced by air-raid wardens prowling around in the murk of the distinctly yellow street lighting, to check that we had complied. We took this very seriously, particularly as our white-helmeted mother was part of the team enforcing the rules. The slightest slither of light could betray the presence of inhabitants below to the menacing German bombers.

Our father was appointed Lay Pastor of Bromham Baptist Chapel which he used to visit one Sunday a month - Bromham is a village near to Bedford: to reach it you have to cross the River Great Ouse via a 'pack-horse' bridge. This Sunday visit was an opportunity (which lasted beyond the war) to bring along all the family and the adopted boarders. We would spend the whole day there, using the wooden chapel hut as a dining-hall and play-space and attending the morning service, afternoon Sunday School and the evening service in the same space transformed into a stove-heated sanctuary. We did not object: this was an opportunity to get into the country and spend our Sunday in a different way amongst ordinary, good-hearted folk, who, in those days, respected Sunday observance as a day for the worship of God rather than football stars.

The headlamps of cars, of which there were very few privately owned in those days, had to be masked with slitted deflectors. Driving in those conditions was extremely hazardous. We experienced this when our taxi-driver from Castle Street, who had a lumbering old Rolls-Royce, took my father, often accompanied by members of the family, out to country preaching engagements on winter evenings. We used to wonder how on earth he got us there.

There were some very positive effects of the war. We were all suffering together – some more than others, inevitably – and this brought us together and encouraged people to serve one another. There was still a central philosophy of Christian values and church-going, with Sunday observance still the norm. We had national Days of Prayer for the success of the war effort. We followed the progress of the war avidly, fed by BBC news bulletins and by daily papers: my father took the *Daily Telegraph*. We were buoyed by the stirring speeches of Winston Churchill, a magician of inspiring word-spinning. Maps indicated the course of the different campaigns, and cartoons, notably by David Low, a New Zealander whose parents came originally from Scotland, boosted our spirits. As the war progressed the tide turned. The Battle of Britain was fought and won by a few audacious pilots against the overwhelming power of German bombers. The unreliable and morphine-ridden Luftwaffe chief Hermann Göring switched from destroying British aircraft at their bases to bombing cities instead, and, as the window of opportunity evaporated, the invasion of Britain was postponed. Undoubtedly Hitler's decision to open up an eastern front with the Barbarossa Campaign helped to shift the emphasis away from the west. Through felicitous channels of supply and deft leadership the war in North Africa steered away from the previously thought to be undefeatable 'Desert Fox' Field Marshal Erwin Rommel (1891 – 1944)' towards the more confident Allies, led by the charismatic Montgomery, which was followed by the invasion of Sicily and the 'underbelly of Europe', Italy. The entry into the conflict by the USA was of crucial importance and the self-sacrifice and tenacity of the Red Army and Soviet citizens at Leningrad and Stalingrad plus the severe Russian winter halted the German invaders. Hitler's manic, stubborn decisions were a grave disadvantage to the Axis side, but the

Raising the Flag on Iwo Jima, Joe Rosenthal, Public domain, via Wikimedia Commons

outcome was never a foregone conclusion until very near the end in May 1945. Both sides fought ferociously and there was senseless loss of life and limb. The D-Day landings in June 1944 evoked great excitement and we followed the slow progress of Allied ground forces through France, Belgium and Holland with anxious anticipation. We empathised with the disaster of the Arnhem parachute campaign, our imaginations fired up by radio reports from the crisp public-school tones of Richard Dimbleby, caught up in the midst of battle, to the accompaniment of explosions. He and Winford Vaughan Thomas, a very Welsh Welshman, brought the war to life for us adventure-hungry children.

The end of the European War on 8 May 1945, known as VE Day, came quite suddenly. We were on holiday and warned at school that if VE Day was declared we would automatically have our holiday extended. There was unhinged rejoicing in London, which was shared in Bedford, where, as was the tradition for special events, lights were rigged up on the river. After six weary years of conflict we all breathed a huge sigh of relief.

We were less conscious of the Pacific war, although we knew that British forces in Burma under General William 'Bill' Slim, were suffering through the humid climate and difficult terrain, as well as relentless, ideology-driven Japanese opposition and cruelty. This theatre of the war was long drawn-out, extending from 1941 till 1945. What we did not realise was the vulnerability of India, with which we in Bedford had strong ties through Foreign Service parents posted there, some children of whom actually boarded with us. We knew about the Gurkhas, from Nepal, whom we greatly admired – in fact Slim, although British, was a member of the Gurkhas himself. War in the Pacific was very much an American affair, sparked off by the disaster of Pearl

Harbour on 7 December 1941. Nevertheless, our experience of American forces was strong because we had so many of their airmen serving from local airbases and because their presence as part of the D-Day force brought them to prominence. They were known for being better paid, more softly treated as serving men and also, in their off-duty moments boosted by alcohol, extremely rowdy. We admired them for their bravery, often reinforced by Hollywood films, and enjoyed their gifts of chewing-gum. We were inspired, too, by the photo published in the newspapers, of the raising of the Stars and Stripes on Mount Suribachi, Iwo Jima, Japan. It is an iconic photograph, about the most famous of all time, but it is a fake. In fact, it had to be staged, after the original was deemed inadequate. It was the second attempt and made by another photographer, John Rosenthal. It nevertheless expresses the original moment of conquest, which was achieved under fire from the Japanese. It expresses struggle: the fact that the flag is not yet vertical makes it all the more effective, reminding us of struggle and danger. It also emphasises the steep nature of the mountain, the highest point of Iwo Jima. So in this sense it is an expression of the truth of the moment. Perhaps it illustrates the nature of great photography: a mixture of truth and dramatic reconstruction.

We were freed from the effects of war, in Britain, but the conflict was not over. In the summer of 1945 we went on our first real family holiday, to the Lleyn Peninsular in North Wales, where we had bed and breakfast in an old Welsh farmhouse for one week near Llithfaen and a week's self-catering in a terraced house in Pistyll. Coming from flat, dull Bedford, it was the height of exoticism for us: a 'foreign' country, surrounded by hills and close to the sea. To get there we had to undertake an exciting train journey, travelling via Leicester, Crewe, Chester and Caernafan to Pwlleli. From there we travelled by taxi to Llithfaen. At Caernafan we were intrigued that the railway actually passed through the castle. Our first glimpse of the sea was from the train south of the Dee Estuary as we sped towards Rhyl. Our accommodation was an isolated small farm, Tanyfael, outside the village. The farmer, who had returned from the war, in which he had served as a soldier, lived in the cottage with his wife, their children and their collie dog. We slept in the family bedrooms while they slept above the cows. To us this was just perfect. It was a statement of down-to-earth oneness and integration. It was here on 15 August that we celebrated the final end of World War Two on VJ Day. We had heard about the dropping of two atomic bombs, on Hiroshima and Nagasaki, which forced the Japanese to concede a very reluctant defeat but we were unaware of the official day until our father brought the news from Llithfaen. We celebrated with the farm children who were Welsh-speaking, and their dog: we could not communicate with each other verbally but we could rejoice vocally and play with one another, in a way that children of different cultures do universally. I remember playing 'Queenie, Queenie, who's got the ball?' which we all enjoyed in equal measure.

There were, despite horrific suffering, good outcomes of the war. It had been an opportunity to re-examine our social structure. We were still very class-conscious and the elite institutions, notably the public schools, dominated the whole of society. The rest of the education system was faulty and it was a chance to give children of all classes the opportunity to go to a school which would develop their abilities to the full. The Butler Act of 1944 installed a tripartite system of free primary, secondary modern and grammar schools - the elementary schools were gone. So, bright children from working-class families now had an easier chance to receive

Family VJ Day Celebration in North Wales with the farm's sheepdog,
15 August 1945

the best education and to go to university. There was a general election on 5 July 1945, with the results published on 26 July, and largely due to the overseas service vote the Conservatives, led by the inspirational Winston Churchill, lost and a left-wing Labour Party (led by a public school old boy, Clement Atlee) took power, even before hostilities ended.

We were generally healthier through rationing and the free supply of milk to schoolchildren (1/3 pint daily), orange juice and cod-liver oil (in the form of sticky malt). However, due to poverty there were still many cases of rickets, and tuberculosis was still rife. The development of penicillin was a great step forward in dealing with disease. The National Health Service and welfare system, the brainchild of a Liberal economist William Beveridge, was instituted, and so health care and other services became free at the point of delivery. Although there were black market merchants taking advantage of the chaos of war, there was a greater sense of self-sacrifice and mutual altruism due to its challenges. The character of the nation was tested and, generally, rose to the occasion.

The post-war period was nevertheless a time of great austerity. We still had ration-books and the economy was sluggish. The British Empire was still intact but India gained its independence, as a state split by religious allegiance, Muslim and Hindu, into Pakistan and India. Pakistan was itself split geographically, as East Bengal, far to the south east, was predominantly Muslim. East Pakistan finally broke from its parent in the north-west with a war of independence in 1971. The chief bone of contention was a matter of language. West Pakistan tried to impose Urdu on Bangla-speaking East Pakistanis. Today the Bangladeshis look upon the War of Independence with awe and, notably, honour the martyrs. They remember the murder by the police of 5 students on 21

February 1952 at Dhaka University for protesting about the imposition of Urdu. This is celebrated on Mother Language Day, or Ekusherey. Martyred Intellectuals Day is celebrated on 14 December, when the country remembers the brutal murder by the Pakistani Army of intellectuals and professionals who opposed the regime, even though Pakistan was already losing the war.

The British Empire continued to decline after the initial break-out in the forties: one after another, like bolting horses, the subject nations of the Empire galloped off into the promised land of independence: a few in the fifties, but accelerating into a stampede in the sixties. Sadly, in many cases the oppressed became the oppressors and the victims of injustice became tyrants, the most notorious of whom being, perhaps, Idi Amin. A whole way of life for colonial civil servants, as described so vividly and acerbically by Somerset Maugham, disappeared. For us in Bedford with its strong links to the Empire, and particularly for our family, who gave the children of such personnel a home, this was a significant adjustment. Fortunately most of the escapees were rounded up to form the Commonwealth, in an attempt to restore a self-belief in British values. One of the unifying elements is the general common use of the English language.

In 1951, well after the end of the war but still within the period of austerity, the Labour Government decided to have a Festival to mark the centennial anniversary of the Great Exhibition in 1851 in Hyde Park, when the huge ecology-friendly greenhouse structure which housed it was designed by Joseph Paxton. After that the building was removed to Sydenham in South London and is known today as Crystal Palace. The 1951 exhibition was very different and was located on the South Bank of the Thames on a derelict industrial site, which had been badly damaged by bombing. The emphasis was on discovery and fun. The central construction was the Dome of Discovery and its accompanying Skylon, a thin, high needle pointing upwards, as it were to the future. The architecture and exhibitions showcased the very best in British architecture and design. The only permanent structure was a brand-new concert hall, the Royal Festival Hall, which was a reminder of the importance of music in British culture. There was also a landing-stage on the Thames, inviting visitors to take a boat trip on the water and, in particular, to proceed to the Funfair at Battersea Park upstream.

I visited the exhibition with my father and we also attended a concert in the Royal Festival Hall. It was a tremendous morale-booster at a time of economic depression and national diminution with the loss of Empire. It proved that, despite everything, 'Britain could make it'. I loved it.

1. 1 Samuel chapter 17: 1 - 58

I NEVER LET MY SCHOOLING

INTERFERE WITH MY EDUCATION

Mark Twain

CHAPTER 3

Shaping the Mind

I have alluded to the beginning of my education, both nursery and preparatory. I transferred to a secondary school at the age of 9, not 11. I was given an interview and a test at the Bedford Modern School, a boys' fee-paying secondary which was supported by the Harpur Trust, one of four schools, the other 3 schools being The Girls' High, Bedford School (for boys) and the Girls' Modern (which became the Dame Alice Harper School). I was accepted. The school was situated right at the heart of the town near the Library, and Corn Exchange and the main shops, and close to the Parish Church, St Paul's. It was housed in a crenellated stone building looking like a castle: severe and forbidding. It enclosed a large quadrangle. It was adjacent to a secondary modern school, the Harpur Secondary which was regarded by ourselves, in our selective institution, as the 'riff-raff'. There were no grammar schools in Bedford at the time. Neil joined at the same time. I was, obviously, in the Lower School.

As expected, it was a tough environment. I remember fights in the quad during break time. It was usually between two boys, battling it out with fists or, worse still, grabbing their opponent's private parts. A crowd would gather round the contestants. Cheering would ensue, and eventually a member of staff would emerge from the staffroom to quell the brouhaha and deal with the warring couple. No doubt, for the contestants, involvement in such a confrontation brought

Bedford School

great prestige and was treated as a badge of honour. Violence was not confined to pupils, however. Offences would frequently be punished with a beating, or 'six of the best', as it was called. But for some this brought even more kudos and could be regarded as evidence of toughness, earning a further badge of honour. Corporal punishment was rife in those days and some staff prided themselves in the efficacy and pliability of their canes. 'Public' chastisement, in front of the whole school or class, was also common, executed as a warning to others.

Against all this, the school had a much-vaunted teenage treble, within a fine musical tradition, capable of 'wowing' an audience with his fluty tones. So, the image of Bedford Modern had another, high-cultural, facet. We had a revered Head of Music, Mr Colson, who was also organist of St Paul's Church. He became my piano teacher and introduced me to the organ. There were memorable concerts, undoubtedly boosted by the presence of the evacuated musicians from the BBC orchestras and singers. I was not a soloist in those days, but with Neil, my brother, I joined the school choir. I was introduced to unfamiliar music, written by Thomas Dunhill, George Dyson and Charles Stanford and I had the great joy of singing with other vocal parts, although I was a treble at the time. What later became my great passion for singing was born here. With BBC Music based in Bedford, the school was tasked with providing a junior choir for the BBC Schools Services. I was invited to join this choir and we would broadcast regularly from St Paul's Church.

One other interesting feature of the war period in this school was the fact that it hosted Owens School, Islington, another boys' school, which took over the building in the afternoon, so that we attended only in the morning, till 1.00 pm. We understood that the boys from Owens School were of the Jewish faith[1]. In those days we knew nothing of the Holocaust and the concentration camps.

At the Modern School Neil and I were placed in East House, because our home lay in that area of Bedford. I was reasonably academic, and I received the form prize in 1944, for which I chose a copy of *Flight Today* by Naylor and Ower (members of the Aeronautical Research Committee), published by Oxford University Press (1936, revised 1942). The fact that one of the chapters is entitled *Balloons and Airships* gives a flavour of the era in which it was written. I can remember little of the teaching, but I do recall that English included parsing (an analysis of the structure of a sentence). This fitted well with Latin, where an understanding of the type and function of words in a sentence (as in certain other languages, such as German) is vital.

One of the disadvantages of the Modern School was that it was situated right in the middle of the town and without a surrounding sports field, as at Bedford School. The playing-fields were in Clapham Road on the edge of the town, but at least there was a covered swimming-pool there (whereas at Bedford School the pool was open-air and therefore more limited in use). Rugby football was the winter game, and this fitted the ethos of Bedford which had a top-class rugby club. Cricket and tennis would be located out there, but the other main summer sport was rowing, based on the clubhouses on the River Ouse. This again accorded with the Bedford profile, as it was a sport for which the town and both boys' schools had a reputation. I did not participate in rowing, the only sport I really loved as a teenager, until I transferred to Bedford School.

The decision to transfer Neil and myself to Bedford School was vital to our subsequent development and life chances. Although I do not recall all the arguments for this decision, I do know that my father was not happy with the amount of corporal punishment at the Modern School, whilst at the latter we regarded Bedford School as posh and snobbish, evidenced by the way the pupils talked. I cannot remember adapting my speech to an upper-class accent, even though I enjoyed — and still do — acting a part. There were scholarship boys there, too - especially important as there was no grammar school in Bedford — and they usually kept their local, Cockney-tinted drawl, which was sometimes an amusement to the sons of the majority upper-middle-class parents. In those days Bedford had prestige and was classed with Haileybury, Aldenham and Uppingham, and had a very large boarding section.

The transfer coincided with my family's removal to 60 Bushmead Avenue, next to Russell Park, in 1944. This was a large, detached house with 13 bedrooms and 5 garages in a very desirable road leading to the Embankment which runs along the river. At that time the house had been requisitioned for use by the Ministry of Defence, but my father still managed to secure it for the price of £3,000, I was told. The size was put to good use, as my parents ran a boarding-house for pupils at the local schools and young people of different nationalities needing somewhere to stay in the holidays because their parents were abroad. The house was later split into flats and my family was based on the ground floor. After a few years, my father bought a second house, in Goldington Avenue. This was semi-detached, no. 44. Sometimes we would decamp there. Quite why he did this I am not sure. Maybe it was to get away from the flats.

Bedford School was an interesting experience, which did much to shape my character, although there were aspects of it which I did not appreciate. I transferred at the age of 12, whereas the normal transfer from preparatory school was at 13.

I was put into the Lower School: Neil went straight into the Upper School. Strangely enough we were both known as K. Hall; I was K. Hall(ii) and Neil, K. Hall(i)! As my birthday is 10 July I was young for my age group. I was placed in the second stream by ability, but when I reached the Upper School I was deemed clever enough to take my first public exam (School Certificate). I was placed in the 4th Year, or Remove as it was called, and I actually sat it when I was still 14. Because I did not do particularly well (even though I passed my Matriculation, as it was called) I was put into Form 5, rather than straight into the Sixth Form: in this way Neil and I both landed up in the same form. Two years later I sat the Higher School Certificate but decided to stay an extra year to take the new Advanced Level. In this way I left school when I was just 19.

The general ethos of the school was Christian Anglican, with assemblies held in the 3-storey Great Hall at the beginning of the day and, on certain days, at the end of school. Morning assemblies included a hymn, Bible reading and formal prayer. Monitors, each carrying a cane, were placed in the aisles to maintain order and to ensure that no boy was chatting or reading a book. Non-compliance was met with a swipe on the boy (sometimes even on his head!) or the book. If we were given time off unexpectedly, the school bell would ring and we would all go, euphorically, to the Great Hall for an extra assembly. Assemblies were part of a formal ritual, a ritual which was somewhat foreign to my background, but I do not remember feeling any resistance to them. I accepted them as part of the rhythm of school life and found the singing of hymns by a huge body of boys most inspiring, even though none of the hymns were the CSSM (Christian Special Service Mission) chorus so familiar to us at Crusader meetings.

There was a school chapel in the grounds, where I used to go and practise the organ in a high loft. In the winter when it was dark this was a decidedly spooky experience. Because of my interest in singing I really should have been in the chapel choir. However, with decidedly High-Anglican theology and style of worship this would not have accorded with my family ethos of evangelical Nonconformism, and I would not have been able to worship with the rest of the family. I missed out on a valuable training ground for singing in parts and sight-reading, but I think this was the better way for my spiritual development. As a family we worshipped at Russell Park Baptist Church and here I had many opportunities to play the organ for services. However, I joined the Crusaders, boys and girls meeting separately, and this filled our Sunday afternoons. I was fortunate enough to be appointed pianist for these meetings, where I learnt the art of congregational accompaniment. We felt a strong allegiance to this organisation — now called, rather mysteriously, Urban Saints — and we boys loved our leader, William Northwood, to whom the term 'saint' really did apply. He was utterly dedicated to his task but sadly neglected his health and met a comparatively early end. Being evangelical, we regarded ourselves as slightly subversive in the context of the accepted religious practices of Bedford School, although this was never expressed through subversive behaviour. John Bunyan was a thorn in the flesh of the Anglican establishment in his time, but Bedfordians gave him the utmost respect. In fact, there was a strong evangelical Anglican presence in Bedford in St John's Church, on the south side of the river. Several of us would frequently gather there, under the fatherly eye of Rev Guinness, the Rector, with other young people on a Sunday evening.

Another important influence on Neil and me was a local

resident, Basil Clarkson, who ran Christian holidays for boys. Through this organisation we went on a couple of cruises on the Norfolk Broads. These were staffed by university students, apart from Basil himself. One of these, John Hapgood, many years later became Archbishop of York. These cruises, on sailing boats without motors, introduced us to the supreme, completely flat, windmill-punctuated beauty of Norfolk, to the water world of the Broads, with its narrow rivers and channels and its stretches of reed-surrounded lakes, and to the completely new and very exciting activity of sailing. We also had the opportunity of trying out a gaff-rigged dinghy, towed behind the larger vessel. On my first attempt at small-boat sailing, on a gusty day, I capsized — probably because I pulled the tiller towards me instead of pushing it away, causing the dinghy to jibe. This introduction to sailing gave me a taste for the sport, which I later took up and of which I became an RYA Instructor. It was all very primitive: every effort was made to avoid using the 'heads', or toilets, where all waste matter was pumped into the water. If you wanted to pass water you would just do so over the side. If you wanted to empty your bowels you had to ask to be put ashore and you were given a trowel, so that you could perform amongst the reeds and bury the proceeds. We were re-victualled extremely well, and in the evening the crews of all the boats would gather together ashore for an evening meal around a bonfire, a singsong and a Christian message with prayer. I loved it. We sang mostly devotional songs, but the chorus of *Good night, ladies* still rings in my ears.

The School was designed round a tall, spacious Great Hall from which classrooms emanated. There were balconies on three sides and heavy beams crossing. This gave a vertiginous feeling of height. One intrepid and agile young boy used to edge across the beams — obviously when there were no staff around. Such an act, if detected, would no doubt have resulted in suspension or even expulsion. It was a unique space, much loved for its superb acoustics as a studio by the BBC orchestras. We had the great privilege of hearing them rehearse and also being invited to a broadcast or recording. This Hall was very nearly destroyed by fire on the night of 28 February 1945. This was not due to enemy action. In fact the European war was drawing to an end, with nine weeks only to go, and the Allies had very much the upper hand. The last great push of the German army in the Ardennes had ended by January. An attack by the Luftwaffe was highly unlikely: the cause of the fire was unknown. The roof of the main school building was very badly damaged, but fortunately the beams of the Hall survived. All the classrooms on the top gallery, including my own, were affected, more by water than fire, and I can remember the awful smell of damp plaster when we resumed our lessons there. The fire is mentioned in the official school history peremptorily, probably because the disruption was very brief and every effort was made to carry on as normal. For us boys (i.e. Neil, Malcolm Gale and Peter Renouf), eager for excitement, it was a major event and the stimulus of much comment. Amazingly enough, there was to be another, far more damaging, fire in 1979, which was caused by arson. The main school building this time was gutted, and the Headmaster's Study and the so-called Bell Room (school office) were badly affected. Fortunately the main walls survived but a complete reconstruction of the 1891 building was necessary. The arsonist probably did the school a great service: the redesign of the interior by Arup Associates was inspired and the iconic exterior, with a little modification, preserved.

This was the era of eccentric schoolmasters, many of them at that time having come from serving in the forces, after demobilisation. In those days teaching was regarded as a calling, not a profession, and no doubt some staff had had no teacher training, and probably an accelerated university course because of their service in the war. It was not compulsory to have training in independent schools, anyway. Some of the older generation had served in the First World War. My Latin master was reputed to be suffering from shell shock from that war. Certainly, I was terrified of him and did my utmost to stay in the background out of the line of fire! Most of them had nicknames and oft-repeated turns of phrase or acts of eccentricity. One was called Dudley Davenport, from a radio comedy programme, starring Kenneth Horne and Richard Murdoch, called *Much Binding in the Marsh*, played by the multi-charactered Maurice Denham. This master used to say, in a very upper-class accent, 'Don't yer know or won't yer say, eh boy?' He also had another much-used and much quoted phrase: 'Who did thet?' Another master had a unique method of learning history which he called *Dotty Ditties*. Events and trends in history would be reduced to a comic rhyme and repeated by the class. I was poor at the subject – which I came to love later in life — and this method helped me enormously. Another master was called Panhandle Pete! He was tall and thin. Another, in fact the Headmaster's brother Geoffrey, lined us all up against the lockers one day and charged past us with a drawn sword. Another, who was my Form Master in the Lower School, would have friendly fights with the boys, but would also lose his temper badly and on one occasion slapped a boy's face. I am certain that we were no worse off for these eccentricities which today would provoke parental court actions.

The Headmaster himself, a much respected and revered personage, with the extraordinary name of Grose-Hodge, was a retired officer in the Indian Army and had bushy whiskers growing out of his ears. He acted as if he were still commanding a battalion and was an unrepentant snob. On one occasion I was at Bedford Station about to board a train for London (undoubtedly with members of my family), and he arrived but found the first-class carriage locked. He yelled at the top of his voice 'Stationmaster!' as if expecting all the assembled passengers to come to attention. The Stationmaster duly arrived and opened the carriage. Mr Grose-Hodge was a VIP and people, especially an employee of the London Midland and Scottish Railway, had to recognise his status! To be fair, he was a strong leader and ran one of the country's top public schools well. I never had cause to cross swords with him.

Part of the routine at Bedford was PE in the morning break. We would form up in ranks outside and perform a number of physical exercises, supervised by a Monitor. In fact there was no lack of exercise in the school's syllabus. Sport played a most important role. We had no afternoon school on Wednesdays or Saturdays and had to do Games, as it was called. In the winter this was rugby, which was considered a higher form of sport than football, which had no place in those days at Bedford. Cross-country running, athletics, cricket and tennis all played an important part, but what I really enjoyed was rowing. I rowed on the port side, at 4 or 8 depending on the size of the crew, and on a few occasions I took out a scull, a very narrow boat, delicately balanced, with two oars which served to keep the oarsman upright as well as to propel the boat in a backward direction. With no rear-view mirror and no outriggers this was a delicate operation. Sadly, I had to abandon active participation in the only sport I really loved as I did not have the physical strength to continue. After rowing in the House Rowing Championships, which were raced in fours, I developed heart palpitations, which caused great anguish until they calmed down each time of their own accord. I was advised to stop rowing, much to my chagrin. Nevertheless, I was allowed to train others. So I coached a junior eight, sitting, and sometimes standing, in the cox's position. For this I won a school award 'for the Promotion of Sport'. Our two PE masters were in fact military men with military ranks, teaching in the uniform of army PE instructors. They were men who demonstrated amazing feats on the gym bar and would organise the annual gym show called *Call to Arms*. We all had to do a minor sport and there were four of them: boxing, gymnastics, fencing and fives (a form of squash played against walls using a glove rather than a racquet). I was poor at all of them.

One of the features of Bedford, and other public schools at the time, was a Combined Cadet Force. We met on Monday afternoons, for which we had to wear uniform for the whole day, and blanco our webbing, shine our brasses and polish our boots. Staff officers had to do the same. Our playground was our parade ground and the school became an army base. We had a CO, a Sergeant-Major and a Staff Sergeant. There was a CCF office, an armoury and a rifle range. The school staff member who commanded the CCF would sometimes be called away to answer the phone by the Sergeant-Major in the middle of a lesson. Cynically, the boys used to say that the real reason was to give him the chance to have a fag! I cannot say that I enjoyed the CCF, but it has to be remembered that World War Two was still in progress, or just metamorphosing into the Cold War, and that senior boys were leaving school to join up and maybe meet an untimely end in Europe, the Far East or Korea. All of us, with very few exceptions, were destined to do two years' National Service, and personally I subsequently served for ten years as a CCF officer, ending up in command of the army section of one school with the rank of Captain.

Even though I often felt alienated from the ethos of the School, certainly its huge emphasis on team sport and my lack of ability in this respect, there was much to savour in its life. There was a strong cultural tradition, particularly in drama and in music. I remember a magnificent production of *Julius Caesar* and the sparkling portrayal of Cassius by a senior boy who really had that 'lean and hungry look'. Music was encouraged no doubt by the presence of so many brilliant BBC artists based in the town. We would see the chief conductor of the BBC Symphony Orchestra Adrian Boult wandering along the pavement, as well as other very famous players. Top vocal soloists would sometimes participate in our school concerts, e.g. Stanley Riley, or Rene Soames. My father would often attend a lunch-time orchestral broadcast performance in another hall, the Corn Exchange, next to his office and much used by the BBC, and invite me to come with him. They were wonderful occasions.

The river played a prominent part in my life in that part of Bedford. I used to visit the swimming-pool in the summer, which in those days was a millpool at the end of the new cut of the river near our home, with tented changing facilities and a gravel bottom to the pool. I remember vividly the aroma of male flesh as we changed, men with boys, with no inhibitions or reservations, before and after bathing in the murky, uneven pool, usually accompanied by whistling, which was what ordinary working men did frequently on such occasions. It was here that I learnt to swim, at the age of nine. I decided to launch myself forward and take my feet off the ground and it worked: I was water-borne. We would also from time to time swim in the river itself, regardless of mud and pollution. I remember on one occasion taking part in the school's Long

Swim. This started on the main river, nearer Bedford Bridge. We had to swim three-quarters of a mile, which I had never before achieved. Would I drown, I mused? There were, of course, safety boats accompanying us. I completed it and felt very proud of myself for doing so. Perhaps one of the benefits of attending such a school was being persuaded to push oneself beyond one's limit - part of the 'Guts and Dash' philosophy of one of our military PE masters.

On Sundays I had to wear a suit with a tie, even at home. There were strict rules during term-time, even for dayboys. There was a curfew and we were not allowed out after a certain time in the evening. This would be policed by Monitors riding round the town on bikes. I remember being punished by them once when I infringed this curfew. Certain places were out-of-bounds, which included cinemas. It was the heyday of films, many of them from the USA, and of film stars who were the equivalent of pop stars these days. They represented an adventure world to which we would escape for a few blissful hours. We were able to experience wartime battles, cowboys' fights, exotic locations and larger-than-life heroes portrayed by actors such as John Wayne, as well as dastardly villains, often played by foreign actors with a German accent. Conrad Veidt was a magnificent, hiss-able villain whom we loved to hate. My favourite film of all time, even now, was *The Thief of Bagdhad* in which he played a treacherous calif who ended his days on a flying clockwork horse which collapsed in the sky. The hero was played by John Justin, a very upper-class actor portraying a very unlikely Arab prince who was struck blind by Jaffa, the calif. The thief was played by Sabu, an Indian child actor, who enjoyed great fame for a time, and brought life and humour to the role: his *deus ex machina* entry in the final scene on a flying carpet to kill the executioner just before the prince's head was chopped off was an unforgettable moment. The film, produced by Alexander Korda, won an Oscar for special effects. These were revolutionary at the time. It was more than a children's entertainment like *Over the Rainbow*. The scriptwriter was Miles Mathieson, a serious playwright and actor, who also played a role in the film himself. I first saw this in the Empire Cinema in the town centre—obviously in the school holidays.

There were four cinemas in the town. They all allowed smoking and all our films were watched through a cloud of smoke. The Grenada even displayed, through a window at the side, how the air was cleansed with water spray. At each showing there was a full programme, with a subsidiary 'B' film and a newsreel. At the Grenada we would also be treated to an organ recital: cinema organs were a unique vibrato sound in themselves but had all sorts of stops which would play drums, a glockenspiel and even the keys of a nearby piano. Cinema organists enjoyed a high reputation. Very fortunately my parents, who considered films and their stars worldly, were indulgent about my attendance at cinemas. I would have lost so much if they had been banned. My father was a great admirer of Shakespeare and a lover of Dickens, so perhaps this formed the bridge between performance art and piety. My mother was also a practitioner of acting in sketches and plays — something which I inherited from her. In fact, we were a performing family. This was very much part of church life. My father would frequently lead a service from a local village pulpit, without a microphone - and that in itself was an art, both of vocal delivery and content, for which he would often prepare late into the previous night. He had distinct mannerisms, often swapping and brandishing his glasses, favourite ideas, references, phrases and biblical quotations. However, my father was not a born actor and his delivery, unique as it was, stemmed from his training as a lay preacher,

*Kenneth as Sganarelle in a Bedford School production, in French,
of Le Médecin Malgré Lui (Molière)*

as well as from his convictions. My mother was different: apart from preaching or leading women's meetings she had a repertoire of recitations and sketches. She had studied elocution and knew how to deliver according to the book. We as children took part in playlets. My favourite was *The Bathroom Tap*, in which the story of an overflowing bath is related in three different cultures: English (very matter-of-fact), Irish (melodramatic) and Russian (full of *Angst* and self-questioning and ultra-slow, in the manner of Chekhov). There were three dramatis personae: Father (myself), Mother (my mother) and Daughter (Vine). Such productions were a delight to both performers and audience. I have performed this sketch on a number of occasions since those blissful teenage years. As budding musicians we were expected to play, and sometimes Vine, Neil and I would perform trios six-handed on the piano.

To compensate for the ban on visiting cinemas in term-time, the school purchased a 32 mm film projector and gave regular Saturday-night shows. We loved these and went eagerly to them. These Saturday-night shows were an exciting antidote to the humdrum business of school attendance and homework. The films were, of course, vetted. However, on one occasion the supplier sent the wrong classification of film and we watched a production, *The Lost Weekend,* which was considered *risqué.* There was no harm done and as far as I know no heads rolled. I have to admit that the memory of the adventures we saw on a Saturday night would live on in my imagination as I sat through a sermon on the following day!

Neil and I, attending the same Secondary School and separated by only fifteen months in age, were great buddies, although very different in character. Neil was personable; I was shy. Neil was a sportsman, particularly in rowing; I struggled. He was extrovert; I was introvert. There is no doubt that my mother felt closer to him, as he was more like her in character. However, I loved both my parents: I was more like my father in character but I had great affection for my mother's eccentric and ebullient nature. I had the misfortune to be in the middle of the family. My sister Vine was the first-born and the only girl. She was worshipped by my parents and given the name of Treasure, a name which we all used for her for a time. James was the baby, the fourth child, and as such had a very special place. Neil was the eldest boy. I was the odd one out. However, I bear no grudge, because life has been very kind to me. It was James who in his late teens and early twenties had to bear terrible suffering. A strong, robust lad with an easy nature, he had a brain tumour. He had to endure the pain and upheaval of an operation to remove the tumour and then all the anguish and disappointment of having it return.

James was educated at St Andrew's School, in Kimbolton Road, Bedford, after sharing the same preparatory school with Neil and myself. As he did not qualify for Bedford School my parents sent him away to a boarding-school, Goudhurst, Kent. As far as I am aware, he enjoyed the experience. The school had a strong Christian ethos and my father preached there on at least one occasion. So, James' life was somewhat different from ours. For the other three of us life was much more centred round the academic and sporting aspects of independent secondary day schools. Vine attended the Bedford Girls' High School, which was situated right next to Bedford Prison and, unlike Bedford School, had no playing field around it. Sometimes the High School girls would use our swimming-pool. Viewing their aquatic exercises from one of the upper floors was a source of great pleasure for us.

One activity which we all shared, boys and girls from a certain age, was doing paid postal duty at Christmas. Boys meeting with girls was part of it, but no doubt the fact that we were treated as responsible young people, entrusted with the public's correspondence and greetings cards, and paid for it, was a tremendous boost to our self-esteem. Getting up early on cold mornings and sticking our already frozen hands into scratchy letter-boxes was painful but it all added to the magic of Christmas. Neil and I discovered another aspect to this festive time: singing carols in a mixed teenage choir. Through our mutual friend Malcolm Gale we joined a small group from Bunyan Meeting, one of three nonconformist churches in Mill Street. Our source book was *The Oxford Book of Carols*: we came across settings we had never discovered before and we formed friendships which were missing from our own church, Russell Park Baptist. To this day I love all the aspects of Christmas and this springs very much from those early days — which also included traipsing round local streets singing carols, rather badly, and collecting at doors.

With a birthday in July I was young for the year and I had secured a place at Cambridge for three years hence, 1953, which would give me time to stay another year at school and do my two-year military service before going up. The place was at Downing College. I got in with an interview: no doubt having been at Bedford School gave me credibility and, maybe, my decision to become a schoolmaster. It was the most modern of the mainstream colleges in those days (founded in 1800), and therefore less prestigious but, as it turned out, I am delighted I got my place there. It was the college of F R Leavis, the English lecturer at Cambridge with the most colour and maverick nonconformity, who edited the famous review *Scrutiny*. He would cycle into the college without a tie (which was considered impolite in those days) and with unkempt hair, looking every inch a rebel eccentric. An exact contemporary of mine was the illustrator Quentin

*Bedford School Monitors 1951, with the Headmaster, Humphrey Grose-Hodge.
Kenneth middle row, first from left*

Blake, famous for his collaboration with Roald Dahl. Subsequent undergraduates were Trevor Nunn, who became Artistic Director of the Royal Shakespeare Company and the Royal National Theatre, Mike Atherton, the international cricketer, and the comic author and actor John Cleese. The college also had a reputation for Medicine and Law. I gained my place to read French and German (within Modern and Medieval Languages), but in the end, after my National Service, I read French and Russian.

I was happy to have this breathing-space before leaving home. It gave me an opportunity to develop my own character and spread my wings. Neil went off to the Signal Corps, and was subsequently posted to the Sudan. At school I blossomed, although I never became a front-runner. I was promoted to the position of Monitor (i.e. Prefect), something I had desired for some time. At last I was valued by the powers-that-be and I was extremely grateful to the master, or masters, who recognised my particular contribution to the life of the school. I also helped to direct the physical exercises during morning breaks. My other award was for piano-playing, when I won the school competition with a performance of an atmospheric piece by Sibelius, called Serenade. I took the new examination Advanced Level Certificate before I left school.

I am grateful to various adults who guided my cultural and intellectual development. My Uncle Leslie took a genuine interest in me, as I was doing German at school. He had been drafted into the army in World War One and captured by the Germans. He had suffered badly in a prisoner-of-war camp and this had affected his digestion. Despite this, he had studied Theology at Leipzig University after the war. I was to discover in my retirement that we had something else in common: his British university education was at Liverpool,

Our extended family at St Mary's Bay, Kent, in August 1949

where I did my PhD. He was a real intellectual and was a role model for me at a young age. Another relative, Aunt Enid, took a keen interest in Neil and me. We used to enjoy visiting her at St Albans, where she lived. On one visit she took us to the cinema to see Laurence Olivier's *Henry V.* The mixture of an Elizabethan theatre, set in a model of London in Shakespeare's time, the obvious studio/theatre locations in many scenes and the outdoor sequences, particularly the charge of the French army at the Battle of Agincourt with the devastating effect of the English archers - together with William Walton's magnificent, varied score reflecting each mood as the drama progressed - had a huge effect on both of us, even though, at our tender age, we might not have understood every word. Another aunt, Nellie Grant, who lived in Melbourn, on the A10 road near Royston, gave us a taste of typical village life, with a Nonconformist chapel flavour. She was a single woman who had inherited enough money to run a modern Arts-and-Crafts-style house with a gardener and a maid, whom she regarded as her 'staff'. Her main contribution to our early years was to take us in her Austin 10 car (which she managed to keep running through the Second World War) to visit Cambridge. Her driving was of comical eccentricity, as she assumed that other vehicles would give her passage if she sounded her horn loudly enough! In Cambridge she would park at the Lion Yard, before its redevelopment, and tour the Colleges with us – in the days when members of the public had open access. I must admit that at that age I was somewhat overawed by Cambridge University, feeling (unjustly, as it turned out) that this seat of learning was beyond my capability.

Another adult, this time a member of Bedford School staff, did me an enormous service by taking me, with a group of other sixth-formers, to the Cambridge Arts Theatre to see my first opera. It was sung in English and could well have been performed by Sadler's Wells Opera, precursor to English National Opera. It was the finest opera of all, *The Marriage of Figaro*, by Mozart, based on the play by Beaumarchais. It has everything: gorgeous melodies with superb orchestral accompaniment, the most exciting ensembles, characters from different levels of society - with the lower echelons gaining the upper hand - comedy and tragedy, superb stage 'business', an intriguing mixture of personalities, complete with a young man (sung by a female) who is in love with love itself and a mad music master.

All this set fire to my sensibilities and started a passion which has never been extinguished. I have seen operas of all eras, from Monteverdi to Webern, from Handel to Benjamin Britten, on the most prestigious stages, at the Royal Opera House Covent Garden, the Paris Opéra, the Bayreuther Festspielhaus and Glyndebourne. I have sung and danced on the stage of Sadler's Wells Theatre, where I took part (as a member of the chorus) in the first London production of Stravinsky's *The Rake's Progress* and (as an extra) in the première of Arthur Benjamin's *A Tale of Two Cities*. I regard opera as the finest of all art forms, because it uses them all (dramatic, poetic, musical, choreographic, textual, visual) often in extravagance, and allows more than one character to express what he or she feels simultaneously (in a duet, trio, quartet or ensemble), which still makes sense and fits the dramatic situation. This dutiful schoolmaster was doing his job properly and passing on a cultural heritage which he treasured himself, and I am eternally grateful to him. That, after all, is what teaching is all about.

1. I was under the impression that it was a Jewish school at the time. There was probably a strong Jewish element to it but I can find no evidence for it being a Jewish foundation.

FAR AWAY PLACES

WITH STRANGE-SOUNDIN' NAMES,

FAR AWAY OVER THE SEA,

THOSE FAR AWAY PLACES

WITH STRANGE-SOUNDIN' NAMES

ARE CALLIN', CALLIN' ME

Joan Whitney & Alex Kramer 1948

CHAPTER 4

First Forays Abroad

At Bedford School I was given some strange option choices: Science or German at School Certificate level, and Art or German at Higher Certificate level. In both cases the course of my subsequent life benefited from my choice of German, which destined me for a career in Modern Languages, but I still feel I missed out on some important study related to the sciences and to my artistic talents. When I was still seventeen, in March-April 1950, I undertook my first visit abroad and my first flight. I made an exchange visit to my penfriend, Jean Millet, in Versailles, and to get there I flew for the first time.

At the end of March I took the Birch[1] coach to Hatfield and then another bus to the De Havilland Flying School to board a Douglas Dakota DC3 aircraft destined for Gatwick Airport. The Dakota was the 'workhorse' aircraft of WW2, used for all sorts of purposes, and this was the current passenger version before the new generation of airliners (e.g. the British Viking, Viscount, and, later, Comet). Two of these aircraft landed at Hatfield. Aircraft of this vintage were not level when not in flight, and tipped backwards towards the tail wheel, making boarding very different from today. Our school was merging with a party from three Hertfordshire schools (Baldock Secondary Modern, Hertford Grammar and Hitchin Grammar) exchanging with the Lycée Hoche in Versailles, near Paris. I was with a school friend, Michael Squibbs. We boarded one of them: there was a passenger cabin of 32 seats arranged in pairs either side of a single aisle. The weather was not too good but we got a fair view of London below as we flew towards Gatwick. What impressed me was the roaring power and lift of the aircraft when it took off after revving on the runway. It was a thrilling sensation. We landed with a bump at Gatwick. After a visit to the café and a wait, Michael and I boarded one of the Dakotas for the next leg of this journey, to Le Bourget Airport, Paris. We had a better view this time, with seats close to the window. Cruising at 150 knots (so we were informed) we could see Brighton below us, the flat coast of the Pas de Calais and the River Seine, in northern France. We boarded a coach at Le Bourget and drove to the Lycée Hoche in Versailles. We were welcomed by the *Proviseur* (academic head) of the Lycée, and the Headmaster of the Baldock School, who was also in the party, responded. We were given refreshments, which included wine, which I did not appreciate! Jean and his father approached us and took us to their flat in the narrow Rue de Vergennes via the famous Palais which was lit up. I was treated very civilly by Jean's parents and given a meal and a bedroom. What struck me straight away on that first night was the loud busyness of the street, due to its location at the centre of the city and the French lifestyle of night activity. It was utterly different from Bushmead Avenue in sleepy, characteristically-English Bedford.

Jean was a typical teenager, although obviously bright enough to attend a selective state lycée. When his parents asked him what he would like to do during the emerging day, he would reply 'J'ai pas', or 'Je ne sais pas' (the equivalent of 'Dunno!'). When I was asked, I had a very extensive programme of visits to the sights of Paris, above all, but also to the famous Château de Versailles. I wanted to use this opportunity to the full, and fortunately Jean and his parents were very understanding. We took the train on many days to Paris and, from the Gare de Montparnasse, the Métro. The latter, with short trains fitting onto short platforms, was inevitably crowded. The buses, on the other hand, were green, ancient and open-ended – a very French phenomenon, very different from the red double-deckers of London. In fact, the whole French style was very different from Great Britain, deliberately so, like the language and the '*kepis*' of their '*flics*' (policemen) and military. The smell of France from their tobacco (of 'Camel', 'Gauloises' and 'Gitanes') was totally different and was noticeable as soon as you arrived. Most men in those years smoked and this very French smell permeated everything. Another feature which was very distinctive was their attitude to public conveniences. The *urinoirs* (urinals) were extremely public, and men could be viewed relieving themselves exhibitionistically, as though they were exercising their right to do so. Far worse were their WCs, which were no more than a hole in the ground with a couple of places for the feet. Balancing oneself whilst performing was a very delicate business! It was as if the French were saying that they were proud of their differences from 'Americans' and the 'Anglo-Saxons'. The fact that Paris was the very heart of European civilisation made the paradox even more palpable. Perhaps the essence of civilisation is art rather than plumbing!

We visited the main sights of Paris: the Champs-Elysées, the Arc de Triomphe, the Louvre, the Panthéon, Montmartre, the Sacré-Coeur, Notre-Dame, the Opéra, the Rive Gauche of the Seine and its Quartier Latin. The boulevards gave the city dignity and grandeur, and the Seine intimacy and romance (compared to the Thames) and the overall impression was stunning and very exciting. Added to this was the sound of French accordion-accompanied popular songs by such artists as Charles Trenet, Georges Brassens and Yves Montant, often

Crussol Castle, Valence (Drôme), France, 1957

in a minor key, about the sadness and joy of love. We had some really memorable trips to the opera. We saw a marvellous production of the jewel of the French repertoire, Bizet's *Carmen*, at the Opéra, and also, at the same house, Berlioz's *La Damnation de Faust*, which whetted my appetite for the music of this very individualistic and very French composer for whom I now have a great admiration, having seen *Benvenuto Cellini, Béatrice et Bénédict and Les Troyens*, and having sung in the oratorio *L'Enfance du Christ (The Childhood of Christ)*. As far as I recall, we also went to the Opéra-Comique where we saw *Mignon* (1866) by Anbroise Thomas (1811-96). The composer and the opera were totally unknown by me but *Mignon*, based on Goethe's novel *Wilhelm Meisters Lehrjahre*, proved to be a delight. It is known mainly for its aria *Connais-tu le pays*?

We explored, thoroughly, the Château, built in the reign of the Roi Soleil (Sun King) Louis XIV (1638-1715) on the site of a former hunting lodge. This was splendour on a grand scale, with fountains to match. We visited the famous *Salle des Glaces* (Hall of Mirrors) where the Treaty of Versailles was signed on 28 June 1919, in the presence of David Lloyd Jones, George Clémenceau, Woodrow Wilson and Vittorio Orlando (of Italy). We also had an insight into the mentality of the Louis XIV courtiers, who liked to play the part of peasants in the hamlet situated in the grounds of the palace, where there are two smaller palaces, the Grand Trianon and the Petit Trianon. Perhaps they were overwhelmed by the size and magnificcncc of the large Palais and dreamt of a simpler life unburdened by wealth and responsibility. They did not realise what was in store for their descendants in 1789 when the feudal system would be brutally reversed. Versailles is a symbol of two sorts of *maladie*: poverty and injustice, in the face of wealth and privilege, and revenge and stupidity, in the

Rhône River, Valence (Drôme), France, 1957

face of generosity and wisdom. The French Revolution arose out of its extravagant splendour, and World War Two arose out of the folly of its 1919 mirror-surrounded treaty.

As far as I was concerned, this first visit to France was a great success. Later, I was to have much longer to appreciate the beauty and diversity of this great country, through two years of residence but also various school trips. The second visit of my late teens was to Germany. In 1951 I undertook a magnificent trip to Essen, the Rhineland and Hamburg with my friend Dolf. His name was a shortened version of Adolf. He was a pupil at Bryanston School, near Blandford Forum in Dorset. He, with his sister Trixie, stayed with us during the holidays. Their father was a judge in India. Dolf had a German relative living in Essen.

We took the train to London and from Victoria to Dover, then the ferry in the early evening to Ostend, arriving about 2130. We boarded a train to Köln, where we alighted. We asked a porter to tell us where the train to Essen was and we followed his instructions. I dosed off in the train we boarded and was woken by the ticket collector. He said we were on the wrong train, going south, in the opposite direction! We had to get out at Brühl and return to Köln and then take a train going north to Essen. It was early morning and misty: We caught the 0530 back to Köln and changed to another train which was destined for Essen, a 2-hour journey away. Having ascertained where our host, Herr Funke, lived, we took another train to Kettwig, a suburban village. From the station there we took a bus to Annahof, a most attractive villa situated in a beautiful area – very unlike my concept of industrial Essen – where Herr Funke lived. We were met by his daughter. After breakfast we were taken in Herr Funke's luxurious Buick car, driven by his chauffeur, to Düsseldorf. I was not used to such a salubrious way of life! We sat on the terrace for our evening meal and savoured the feel of luxury, enjoying the gorgeous, rural view.

The following day we were taken, again in the same Buick, to Duisburg, where there was a massive dock for barges plying up and down the Rhein. We were delivered to a tug from the Raab Karcher Lines. The commodity transported in five barges attached to our tug was coal, as the shipping line stemmed from the Raab Karcher mining company. We were installed in the comparative comfort of the captain's quarters from which we had superb views of the river and settlements along it. We were guests of the captain and his daughter Anne, who did the catering and housework on board. The Rhein does not only provide a means of water transport: it provides a flat route, like many other rivers worldwide, for roads and railways, in this case on both sides of the river in both directions. On the water, progress speeds upstream and downstream are very different. The journey to Mannheim, our furthest point south, took five days and the return journey took only two.

At first the landscape was very flat, but from Königsberg, site of the ruins of *Drachenfels* (Dragon Rock), reached by funicular railway, steep hills rose up, covered in vineyards and woodland. We saw the Niederwalddenkmal, near Rüdesheim, commemorating the unification of Germany under Bismarck, in 1871 at the end of the Franco-German War. This stretch, known as *Die Rheinschlucht* (Rhine Gorge) stretches from Bingen, on the west bank, to Koblenz. It is a steep gorge and is highly picturesque with frequent, marvellously romantic castles perched on or above the slopes, redolently lyricised by the music of Wagner.[2] We disembarked at Oberwesel whilst the captain took the tug and barges further upstream to a mooring at Niederheimbach and returned by train. The beautiful old town of Oberwesel - captured in an atmospheric watercolour by Joseph Turner - was the home of the captain. We visited the Schönberg Castle, now a hotel, and the Catholic church, the Liebfrauenkirche, where I briefly (and amateurishly) played the organ. The captain and his wife invited us into his home and gave us a meal, which consisted of raw mince mixed with raw egg (!).

I had a long chat with him – how I managed this with my limited grasp of the spoken language, I don't know, but I have a record of our wide-ranging conversation. He said he was not a supporter of Hitler and believed in a united Europe, which should include the UK. He predicted, prophetically, that the USSR would eventually collapse (as it did in 1989). He had two sons who went to war, one of them only sixteen: the latter was stabbed to death fighting the Russians and the other son just disappeared. He told us that employment in Oberwesel was 60% in the shipping trade and the rest were wine producers and slate workers. In fact, slate was very prominent in the buildings of the Rhein and gave them a rather dismal aspect. For us, to get back to the boat we had to take the train. It was extremely wet, as it can be in those parts at that time of year, and we got thoroughly soaked. The captain had to wake up a ferryman to take us to the ship: we reached it at midnight. His wife came on board, to replace their daughter and look after him and us. We stopped again at Koblenz. At the *Deutsches Eck* (German Corner), where the Mosel joins the Rhein. There was only a plinth where the equestrian statue of Kaiser Wilhelm I, dating from 1897, once stood. (Since the reunification of Germany in 1990 a replica statue has been placed there and so this monument has been restored to its old, dramatic, triangular glory).

We then negotiated the most exciting part of the Rhine Gorge. We passed *Die Pfalz,* the former toll island of Falkenau – tolls ceased in 1897. Walt Disney could not have invented

Oberwesel, Rhein, at the Schönburg Castle, 1951

any castle more fantastic and imaginative. It is the most unexpectedly beautiful and colourful building on the Rhein, much as I love the other more mystical castles and churches. It positively sings with beauty! However, the singing was to come shortly afterwards. We passed the Lorelei Rock along the narrowest and most dangerous stretch of the Rhein. Here the rush of water sings with a murmur as it passes through its hazardous rocks and it is this which has given Lorelei its name. The legend has it that a beautiful maiden threw herself into the Rhine because of an unfaithful lover. She was transformed into a siren who lured fishermen to their deaths. She sat on the Lorelei Rock singing, and sailors would look up to her rather than keep their eyes on the dangerous rocks below and were shipwrecked. In our case the captain was obliged to take on a pilot before these rapids. The Lorelei Rock was steep and high but we saw no siren and we came through without incident: the pilot embarked and disembarked and no doubt received his fee for doing so.

Heinrich Heine wrote a beautiful poem about the legend which Franz Liszt set effectively to music.

We passed Mainz, where the Main joins the Rhein, enters a flatter area and reaches Mannhein, our destination. Here the barges were unloaded and we set off again downstream, at more than twice the speed. No doubt travelling downstream, with less rudder effectiveness, was more dangerous. We left the tug at Duisburg Dock, thanking the captain and his wife for their hospitality. This trip up and down the most prestigious river in Europe had been the experience of a lifetime.

Our next visit was to Hamburg. The trip included a short cruise on the Elbe. This was fresh, green, expansive and flat – delightful, but very different from our Rhein experience. What shocked me was a view of a working-class area of

Cassis, Côte d'Azur, France, 1957

Hamburg which looked as if an atom bomb had fallen on it. This city district was totally destroyed. Post-war accounts tell of incendiary bombs dropping on the houses from RAF aircraft and forcing people out into the open, where they were suffocated by the upward draught of air. It is difficult to assess whether this inhumane action had an effect on the outcome of the war. It was a strategy promoted by 'Bomber Harris' (Air Chief Marshall Sir Arthur Harris), who, we are told, had an obsession that RAF bombing of Germany would win the war.

Dolf and I returned to Bedford presumably3 by the same route as our outward journey. Later, in September, the family decamped to a first-floor sea-front flat in St Leonard's, Hastings. My father's intention was to help my mother recover from a hysterectomy. The prospect of doing National Service, starting in October, dampened my spirits, although there was also great pleasure in being by the sea at this time of year, and there was plenty to do in Hastings (birthplace in 1900 of my mother, and also, strangely enough, the location - in a nursing-home - of her death in 1981) and in that lovely part of East Sussex. The summer was over, but not quite, and there was a bitter-sweet feel about that month in 1951.

1. A coach company which operated regular services from Bedford to St Albans, Hatfield, and London
2. Richard Wagner (1813 – 1883) creator of *Der Ring der Nibelungen* (1876)
3. I have no record of how we got back to Bedford

Suffer and Serve

*Motto of Newport Free Grammar School
(founded 1588 by Dame Joyce Frankland)*

CHAPTER 5

On His Majesty's Service

I knew that I would be called up around the beginning of October. I no longer have my call-up papers, but I was due to report to Woking on 04 October. I had a natural feeling of dread that I would be totally subject to the whim of the Army. This idea of control weighed heavily on me. However, in no way do I regret doing my National Service. I was doing what other young men like me were forced to do, serve my country. The run-up to my service was unreal. September 1951 was a strange month of waiting. I knew what was coming and I viewed it with trepidation. Weather-wise it was a typical autumn month: fresh and cool, and I was nostalgically wishing that the summer would not go away, particularly as the sea lay before us. Along the front, trolleybuses hissed past on their way to Cooden Beach, a supposedly sandy alternative to the pebbles of our St Leonard's beach.

During our time at St Leonard's, Edward Cunningham, a young man my parents looked after while his parents were serving overseas, visited us. He was a typical public schoolboy who had a Morris sports car. We took great delight in riding on the back seat in the cool air, sitting up on the seat without belts – there were none in those days - or any restraint, and expressing our freedom and flamboyance. Edward had a place at Cambridge but, like me, had to do his National Service. Sadly he was drafted to the Korean War and returned without one of his legs. This did not alter his Cambridge career, however.

There was also another tragedy lurking. James experienced dizziness whilst swimming. He went to the doctor, who diagnosed a brain tumour. This was a terrible blow to James, who seemed to be so healthy and had such a happy manner. He was operated on but the tumour returned and he died at the early age of 21.

I duly reported to Woking on 4 October, taking the train, and drew my uniform, boots and webbing. I was officially in the Education Corps but was passed on to the Queen's Royal Regiment at Stoughton Barracks, Guildford, for my basic training.

The main outdoor activity, apart from marching on the parade ground, was a daily trip to the Hampshire heathland for military manoeuvres. The weather during the day was warm and the heathland attractive. This, however, did not lift my spirits. We were transported there in a 3-ton lorry, sitting under the back awning on uncomfortable wooden benches. The ride was bumpy and unpleasant. On the exercise we had to crawl around like crabs among the heather trying to avoid imaginary bullets. I could see no sense in this, but I just had to comply as there was no alternative.

I counted the days to 'demob' right through my service, even though here, in this prison, a miraculous escape was on its way. I do not know how the Army found out that I was a linguist, but this was my salvation. I was selected to join a Russian course at Bodmin, Cornwall. This was at the beginning of November, so the basic training lasted only a month. The location was exciting: as a family we had been to Cornwall, even as far as Land's End, and this was very much a holiday area. I remember the romantic train journey as the hills and dales became higher and deeper. I disembarked at

Bodmin Lines (now Bodmin Parkway) and from there boarded a branch-line train to the town station. On the way we passed Walker Lines, where my new hutted camp home was to be found. Once I was installed there the train would puff past regularly, although it did not stop at the camp, and trips into town, wearing army boots, were lengthy, downhill and uphill. When it rained my hairy, heavy uniform became sodden and most uncomfortable, if I had no cape. This was the extension of the Duke of Cornwall's Light Infantry barracks, on a hillside overlooking a valley. I was allocated to a wooden barrack-room with an iron stove. I had amenable, intelligent hut-mates, who in this case were not obsessed with copulation! Mornings were very cold, as before, until we could light the stove, and there was a walk to the ablutions, and, obviously, the cookhouse. I remember looking across the valley and watching a bird, which fluttered and chirped in abundant freedom and thinking how lucky it was, but this was infinitely better than Stoughton Barracks. A place of refuge was the Church Hut, which was also used for choir practices and regular Christian gatherings – we had Bible studies and prayer meetings there. The son of a local bank manager, Bill Andrew, took me under his wing and invited me out: he was a Christian and was trying to put his faith into action.

The demands made on us intellectually were considerable. We had to learn a new orthography, many unfamiliar words and grammatical constructions. Nouns had three genders and six cases, so a knowledge of German and Latin was helpful. The worst part of verbs was 'aspects' – whether an action was complete or not - but perhaps the hardest thing to understand was stress, which influenced the sound of vowels and in this respect we were fortunate in that our texts were marked with stresses. The tutors, who often looked homesick, were mostly from Soviet satellites and thus not ethnic Russians themselves. We were training to be translators. However, there were two university courses running, in London and Cambridge. I was selected to join the latter, to my amazement and infinite joy, the following January. We were attached to the university, under Professor Dame Elizabeth Hill, as civilians. We had to draw civvies from the depot at Woking: an ill-fitting suit, a shirt and tie and, even, shoes. We received sergeant's pay and we had the status of officer-cadets. We were based at Salisbury Villas in Station Road. As a serving soldier I could not have asked for more. My first billet was at the RAF station at Waterbeach, where the routine, using a tannoy, was very different from an army camp. I would hear every morning 'The correct station time is 0700 hours' and this still rings in my ears. We were transported to Cambridge by coach. The second billet was accommodation at Newmarket, where the clatter of horses' hooves reminded us of the real purpose of that East Anglican town. The third billet, in the Long-Vac Term, was at Foxton Hall, close to the railway station. In the Michaelmas Term we were housed in a former maternity home, Douglas House, on the Trumpington Road. This was sheer luxury: ensuite bathrooms and private lodging of a high standard, from where we could get into Cambridge easily. We revelled in everything Russian: we attended lectures and saw films at the Arts Cinema; we sang Russian songs and read Russian poetry. I just loved it. However, there was always the prospect of being thrown off the course: we had to learn 30 words a day and were tested once a week. To fail the test meant being sent back to Bodmin. Fortunately, although most other *Kursanti* (members of the course) were a lot brighter than I was I never suffered that fate.

Living in Cambridge enabled me to go home frequently, which was a great privilege, and I made the best of it.

Sometimes, if I was having a weekend in Cambridge I would attend Emmanuel Congregational Church. Strangely enough I don't think I ever went to the Baptist Church in St Andrew's Street, which later became my regular place of worship when I was at Downing and a member of the Robert Hall Society. Peter Renouf, who used to live with us, was at Downing in that year and I met up with him frequently. He was an active member of the College's Christian Union and also CICCU (Cambridge Inter-College Christian Union).

All good things eventually have to come to an end, and so in the Michaelmas Term I had to leave this idyllic life of ease and comfort and return to the rigours of service life in Bodmin. I took the train down to Cornwall. As before, I alighted at Bodmin Lines and took the connecting train to the town station. I made my way back, in a taxi, to Walker Lines, my hutted camp. I had swapped our en-suited private room at Douglas House for a wooden barrack room, my civilian lifestyle for military routine. Sad, but inevitable!

The much-feared Black Jack, the Irish RSM with the cocked hat, was still there, reigning supreme, but even though we were back in the military wearing uniform, this was a more relaxed time and no doubt our status as officer-cadets helped. We were able to explore the tourist spots around us, accessible by train, such as the picturesque estuary harbour of Fowey to the south and the north-coast resort of Padstow. However, I went one better: with two buddies I bought a 1931 Austin Seven. I believe we gave £30 for it. The carriage work was dodgy but it was waterproof. To start it, you had to swing a handle below the front grille. You made sure the handbrake was firmly on, set the throttle and then moved to the front. You gave a mighty swing, watching that you were not caught by any kick-back and, if you were lucky, the vehicle sprang to life. The brakes were very sluggish and almost led to disaster.

I had to learn to drive and one of my fellow-owners acted as instructor. On one occasion we were rolling down a hill towards a narrow bridge. Another car was approaching the bridge towards us. I decided that we would stop before the bridge to let the other car pass. However, I had miscalculated the stopping distance and the efficacy of the brakes. My friend grabbed the steering-wheel at the very last moment, jerked us onto the bridge and the two vehicles passed one another without incident. His presence of mind saved us from a potentially lethal crash.

Other journeys under my friend's tutelage were more successful but I was still not a qualified driver: I had to pass my test. I applied and was given a date and a venue. The main part of the test was due to be on the busy A30 High Street in Bodmin. I did it in the Austin Seven. The examiner was pleasant and undemanding. I performed all the requirements adequately until we reached the Emergency Stop. The examiner called out 'Emergency Stop' and we were doing about 15 miles an hour. The vehicle ground to an unenthusiastic halt which was anything but 'emergency'. The examiner commented on my brakes! He said I should get them fixed. Nevertheless, he did not fail me. I passed, on probably the busiest road in Cornwall, at my first attempt in a clapped-out, ancient car and I was heartily thankful, and grateful to a very indulgent examiner! This certainly opened up Cornish resorts around us, particularly those inaccessible by rail. This was July 1953 and I celebrated my twenty-first birthday there.

At that time I attended the Methodist Church in the High Street in Bodmin. I sang in the choir there and was joined by my friend Keith Howard. Keith and I had followed the same path, starting in Bodmin on the 'B' Course and transferring to Cambridge, then back to Bodmin. Keith was musical and played the 'cello. We both sang in the Bodmin *Messiah*, in St Petroc's, the Parish Church. Keith was also a great rugby player. After his service he was given a place at Christ's College, Cambridge. His subsequent career was a lot more prestigious than mine and no doubt the National Service spell in Cambridge opened up possibilities for him which he might otherwise have missed. It was with great sadness that I heard of his death in December 2020, via a reply from his wife Elsbeth to a Christmas card we had sent. He was a great character and a great friend, although latterly we saw him and his family rarely.

The next step for us both was an OCTU (Officer Cadet Training Unit) selection and a short officers' training course at Mons, lasting a fortnight. Keith preceded me and at one stage I had to call him 'Sir'! At the selection the Commanding Officer was an Old Bedfordian, who even hailed from the same house as me, Paulo-Pontine. I often reflect that this helped me to be selected. I was somewhat apprehensive of the training course, but there was no need to be. I performed perfectly well and there was no problem about passing out as Second Lieutenant Hall. We had manoeuvres as in Basic Training but they were more acceptable. The officer in charge was Captain West and he was a pleasant man. He would often talk about the tactic of advancing past the enemy with a right-hand movement and then 'snookering him up the a*se'! We had to do a night exercise with firework bangers going off around us. I did not enjoy this but I survived it without letting the side down.

The rest of my service was incredibly boring. I was sent to Maresfield, the depot of the Intelligence Corps (to which I was transferred). We had to translate Russian training manuals, which were pedestrian and stodgy. However, we were on the road to Brighton and the coast and this had a lot

Officer Cadet Training Unit course, Mons, Hants, 1953: Kenneth is third from left in front row, seated next to Capt. West

of exciting possibilities. There was a famous cafe on the main road, which attracted the local soldiery, run by a stout man called John and his mother, which became a favourite eating-place for a night out.

During this period we did an exercise in the Guildford area, in which we were supposed to be stopping enemy agents from getting through our lines. I was allocated to a signals unit and given an army radio to operate. Needless to say, the radio broke down and, without proper equipment, I proved to be utterly useless. One of the strongest messages to come through, when the radio was still working, was from a fellow signaller who kept broadcasting to all and sundry, 'Where the h*** are my f****** blankets?' I never knew whether he retrieved them. If he had blankets he was fortunate: I had to kip down on a road bridge with only dead leaves as my mattress and blanket, which meant that I had a full week with no sleep at all. In the coach back to base I realised how dead tired I felt! The exercise, called 'Corn Crake', was an utter failure and we learnt nothing from it, apart from the need to find blankets and a suitable sleeping-place at night.

As might be expected, we had men of talent amongst the members of the course. One such was Michael Frayn, who later became a well-known playwright. Another was an actor who, despite early promise, never quite reached the heights of his profession, Peter Woodthorpe. He was at Magdalene College, Cambridge and a member of *The Footlights*. He was spotted by Peter Hall at Cambridge and cast as Estragon, one of the two central characters in his production of *Waiting for Godot* by Samuel Becket at the Arts Theatre in the West End of London. At Bodmin we staged Pushkin's Shakespearian-style drama *Boris Godunov*. This is known these days in its operatic form by Modest Mussorgsky (1839 – 1881) and most British people are unaware of what a brilliant straight play it is. Aleksander Pushkin (1799 – 1837), poet, dramatist and short- story-writer is regarded as the founder of Russian literature. The true story of the impostor tsar Boris Godunov is a huge role in its original dramatic form and requires immense vocal and acting power. Peter Woodthorpe fitted the part wonderfully. In every word and gesture he was the very epitome of Boris Godunov.

One event in the first year of my service sticks obsessively in my memory. In the summer of 1952 a friend of mine, Roland Brown, and I decided to go to the Farnborough Air Show. We agreed to meet at the station but we missed each other. One of the thrills of air shows at the time was to watch and hear a fighter go through the sound barrier. John Derry was piloting a De Havilland DH 110 twin-fuselage jet. He broke through the sound barrier with a loud bang, but then as he straightened out after his dive his aircraft disintegrated. The engines flew on while the cockpit followed at a slower pace. The engines crashed into the crowd and killed eighteen people, near to where Roland was watching, and the place we had intended both of us to be. I can only be thankful that I was not with Roland, who was fortunately unhurt, because the sight of those spectators being killed would have been traumatic.

Service in the Army Reserve at Crail, 1955, – Left: Kenneth Hall,
Right:Keith Howard

My first car: 1931 Austin 7

KENNETH HALL

Hᴵɴᴄ ʟᴜᴄᴇᴍ ᴇᴛ ᴘʀᴏᴄᴜʟᴀ sᴀᴄʀᴀ

Hᴇʀᴇ ᴡᴇ ʀᴇᴄᴇɪᴠᴇ ʟɪɢʜᴛ

ᴀɴᴅ ᴘʀᴇᴄɪᴏᴜs ᴋɴᴏᴡʟᴇᴅɢᴇ

Motto of Cambridge University

CHAPTER 6

Alma Mater

I took the Civil Service Interpreter's exam before I finished my service and also sat A Level Russian. I decided to change to Russian from German at Cambridge. I was finally demobbed and could get on with my real Cambridge career. The experience of National Service had been very rewarding in most ways, and I was both glad I had done it and relieved that it was over. Faced with other undergraduates who had not yet done their service I certainly felt more mature. I was given a shared room on 'J' Staircase and my name was duly inscribed on the list at the bottom of the stairs. I did not like sharing but at least I was in college. During the other two of the three Tripos1 years I was lodged in 'digs' on the other side of Parker's Piece in Guest Road. Very fortunately my friend and former classmate Malcolm Gale was with me. We were great pals and did a lot together. In fact, one day when the Chaplain, George Woods, who had a high voice, spotted us he called out in sing-song tones: 'Ah, Hale and Gale'! We both auditioned for the university chorus. The man who conducted the audition, who was the stand-in organ scholar – the Chapel was only just constructed – asked us if we would like to join an octet who were due to perform Brahms' *Liebeslieder Walzer* (Lovesong Waltzes). The piano duet parts were played by the Master's wife, Lady Whitby, and an undergraduate. It was a most exciting project, in which we were thoroughly at home, as we were familiar with the language. We sang bass, although my voice was developing towards baritone/tenor. We were accepted for the Cambridge University Musical Society (CUMS) chorus, under the direction of the very vigorous and irascible Boris Ord, Director of Music at King's College. We were also invited to sing in our own college chapel choir: the new chapel was opened that year, 1953, completing the west side of the quadrangle.

Singing in such a large chorus (CUMS) and rehearsing in the Music Department main hall (which was a well with four sides), with the choir sitting upstairs, was thrilling indeed and we did some memorable works: *Verdi's Requiem, The Peaceable Kingdom* by Randall Thompson[2], Albert Roussel's wonderful, arching *Psaume 80* (Psalm 80), and, most exciting of all, Vaughan Williams' 'opera/morality' *The Pilgrim's Progress* which had a lot of choral passages. I remember, after struggling with some difficult harmonies of the latter, we sight-read Buxtehude's wonderful *Missa Brevis* (Short Mass). What a joy that was! Boris Ord raged at us at times but we loved him. Sadly he had a fall and damaged his shoulder, so that he had to retire, which included finishing at King's. We then had Alan Percival who became Principal of the Guildhall School of Music in London. We did some lovely music but it was never the same. One of the works was Berlioz's evocative *L'Enfance du Christ* (The Childhood of Christ). I auditioned for the very minor part of a Centurian and got the part: this was an encouragement. The tenor narrative role was taken by Kenneth Bowen, from St John's College Chapel Choir, who was very much the star singer at Cambridge in those days. However, there was also a baritone star, John Noble, also of St John's, who sang the part of Pilgrim with great dignity and with dulcet tones. He later sang the role for Sir Adrian Boult's recording. This Late-Romantic music, based on an adaptation of John Bunyan's allegory, had an enormous effect on me.

Vaughan Williams came to the rehearsals and took a personal interest in the Cambridge production, which was in the Guildhall: we were in the offstage chorus, so I was able to watch it. However, I was to have an even greater experience of Vaughan Williams a couple of years later[2].

I cannot say that my academic studies at Cambridge were a success. I think it was right to change to Russian. I was interested in Russian literature, notably Tolstoy, whose philosophy of non-violence attracted me. I read *Resurrection* (in English) in the army, but I identified most with the character of Levin in *Anna Karenina*, who was an echo of Tolstoy himself. Above all, I loved Chekhov's plays: the unstable psychology of his characters, unsure of what to say next or how to react to their interlocutors. I suppose my favourite play is *The Seagull* (Chaika), after which I named my sailing boat when I retired. However, what really turned me on was history: I opted for a period of Russian history, from the Emancipation of the Serfs in 1861 to the Reign of Stalin, for the second part of my Tripos. The overall class was a 2ii, but I did very well in Russian Part 1: I was told I nearly got a First. I had little interest in French literature, although I was attracted to Stendhal. I had little time for Classical plays and found Corneille and Racine extremely stuffy and quite overshadowed by Shakespeare. As for learning to speak the French language, or even to write it effectively, this was not part of the discipline of the course.

What was missing for me was the will to work. Terms were very short and distracted by other pursuits, and vacations were filled with short-term jobs rather than background reading. I transported vegetables in the earliest version of the VW Transporter, picked tomatoes, tended pigs and drove caravans to the Farnborough Air Show. It was only in my retirement that I discovered the joy of study and the revelation it opened up, based on research, although during my professional career I attended and enjoyed many courses, notably one in Kent and Essex on Management (Diploma in Management Studies). I even enjoyed a section on study skills, on the latter.

The big moment in my Cambridge career was being selected to sing in the Cambridge Opera Group's production of *Sir John in Love*, a version of Shakespeare's *The Merry Wives of Windsor* by Vaughan Williams. I attended singing lessons from Robert Rowell who had once performed at Glyndebourne. I sang a lot of songs and arias with him, but I did not develop vocally. When he heard about the opera audition, he suggested I sing Giorgio Gernont's baritone aria *Di provenza il mar* from Verdi's *La Traviata*. This was a good choice: the producer and musical director liked it, and I was selected to play the part of John Page. This was not a huge part, but at least I was a member of a Cambridge team performing opera on stage. Vaughan Williams and his wife Ursula came to many rehearsals. We wore Elizabethan costumes against a cut-out style of decor: we were at the Arts Theatre. The singer who played the part of Falstaff was Christopher Bishop, who later produced the EMI recording of *The Pilgrim's Progress*. He was a choral scholar at Gonville and Caius College. He fitted the part wonderfully, both vocally and dramatically.

Many years later[3] *Sir John in Love* was given a production by English National Opera at the Colisseum, London. I wrote to the company and told them I was in the Cambridge production. They showed some interest. Dorle and I attended a performance at which Ursula Vaughan Williams was also present (the composer had died in 1958). The management arranged for us to meet her in the interval. We regarded this as a great honour.

My other main activity at Cambridge was the Robert Hall Society, representing the Baptist community at the university. We met before the service at St Andrew's Street Church, close to Downing, on Sunday mornings. I eventually became a committee member. Very fortunately a lecturer at Downing, John Biggs, was heavily involved and this was a great encouragement to me. John was also a great supporter of Downing Chapel and an advocate of the early-morning BCP[4] communion there. The service was somewhat alien to Nonconformists like Malcolm Gale and me and turning out at 7 am was not easy, but we stuck it out and delivered the choral responses diligently. No doubt the prospect of breakfast in John's rooms next-door was an attraction. Robin Proctor was appointed Organ Scholar and we did a lot of singing under his sympathetic direction: this included, of course, evensong on Sundays, when the Master would often be present. Keeping the time opposite each other on both sides were Malcolm and I. I was allocated solos from time to time and I particularly remember the thrill of singing *The Three Kings* by Peter Cornelius, arranged by Ivor Atkins, at a carol service. I was elected President of the Musical Society, and I initiated several concerts myself, taking the conductor's baton on a few occasions, the most prominent of which were outdoor performances of Henry Lawes' masque *Comus*, based on Milton. One of the difficulties for any choral concert was the lack of women. So we imported them from the Saffron Walden and Hockerill (Bishop's Stortford) training colleges. Some of these young ladies would also come to the Robert Hall Society meetings on Sundays, as well. No doubt the prospect of linking up with a male Cambridge undergraduate played a part in their motivation. We much valued the contribution they made, as females were in short supply in the male-dominated Cambridge of the day.

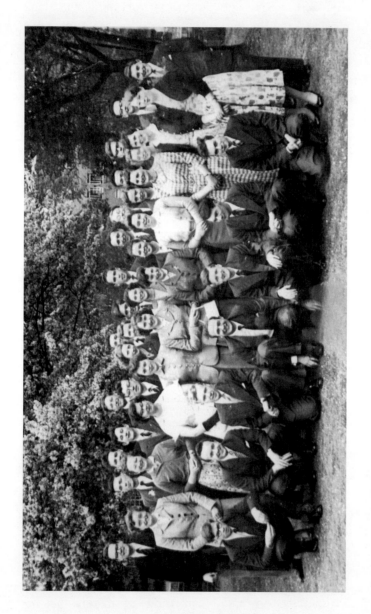

Robert Hall Society 1954. Kneeling: John Biggs 3rd from left, Peter Naylor right.
Standing back row: Nigel Phillips 2nd from left, middle row: Hazel Chesterman 2nd from right

I formed some strong friendships in the Robert Hall Society. My greatest pal was Peter Naylor who was reading English at Fitzwilliam Hall, but was also an excellent pianist and composer. He, as accompanist, and I formed a very productive partnership. We would often rehearse Fauré[5] songs. On visits to Bedford Peter would make some recordings with me. He was also very fond of Vaughan Williams' music. Other good friends were Nigel Phillips and Hazel Chesterman (studying Education at Homerton College), whose father was once Medical Officer for the BMS (Baptist Missionary Society). They later married. From the Robert Hall Society I took part in three student missions, to Upminster, Kingston and Luton.

My brother James died in March 1955. My parents were quite rightly angry with me for not taking his suffering seriously enough by visiting him. I did go to see him in hospital, but only once. The fact is, I was too preoccupied with my university career. I regret this deeply to this day and I wish I could reverse my lack of compassion. I remember the day he died. I cycled to a tutorial somewhere along Trumpington Road. Whilst there I experienced a wrenching feeling as if power were being taken out of me. I later discovered that this was just about at the moment he died. James' funeral was at Russell Park Baptist Church, Bedford, and he was buried in the family grave at Kelshall, near Royston, where my parents' ashes also lie. His death was a shattering blow to my parents. I still visit these graves, as I used to on our annual family outings years ago. (*cf* Appendix *Farewell to James*)

My Tripos years came to an end, but I was happy to stay on and do a year at the Education Department, maintaining my link with Downing College. I had to find digs in Cambridge, the first of which was in Jesus Lane. I joined the Cambridge University Rugby Referee Society (partly because I liked the

Cambridge University Opera production of Sir John in Love
(Vaughan Williams). Kenneth (John Page) in centre

Robert Hall Society mission at Upminster:
Hazel Chesterman distributing leaflets

tie!), and I refereed a few very low-level games during the Michaelmas Term. I had to revise the rules each time, as I was no great authority on the game! I lived at home during the Lent Term as it was my teaching practice term. I was appointed to Luton Grammar School and travelled there on the train. I was 'pitched into the deep end' from the start as my head of department had to withdraw sick. This was no doubt good for me, although I did struggle with one class.

When I returned to Cambridge for the Easter Term, I took up residence in a room guarded by a very fierce Alsatian dog in one of the backstreets of East Cambridge. Arriving home at night was a dangerous experience! I was able to continue various activities and this was a factor in staying on and doing the extra year. In fact, having started in January 1952 my whole time at Cambridge stretched out for almost six years. Malcolm did the extra year with me as he was destined for school teaching as well.

1. The system of awarding a BA (Bachelor of Arts) degree at Cambridge
2. Randall Thompson (1899-1984) American composer and academic
3. When I was cast in the Cambridge University Opera Group's production of his opera *Sir John in Love*
4. Book of Common Prayer (1549)
5. Gabriel Fauré (1845-1924), composer whose *Mélodies* were the equivalent in the French repertoire to Schubert's *Lieder*

LOVING LIFE

IS EASY WHEN YOU ARE ABROAD.

WHERE NO ONE KNOWS YOU

AND YOU HOLD LIFE IN

YOUR HANDS ALL ALONE,

YOU ARE MORE MASTER OF YOURSELF

THAN AT ANY OTHER TIME.

Hannah Arendt
German born political theorist

CHAPTER 7

European Residence

It is common for universities to include a period abroad as a part of their language courses, but this did not happen at Cambridge in my day. A year as an English assistant in the country concerned, after the degree course, was more usual, so I applied to go to France. I was sent to Valence, on the River Rhône in the north of Provence, to the Lycée Émile Loubet. My experience of France was limited to the north. I had an exchange with Jean, a schoolboy in Versailles, in 1950 (see above), while still at Bedford School, and then another exchange arrangement with Françoise Lesur in Lambersart, Lille who attended the Catholic University there. Her parents were both pharmacists. There were five girls and one boy in the family. They had a typical Flemish brick farm at Sailly-sur-Lys, near Béthune, which was used as a meeting point for the family and their offspring. The second-eldest daughter Monique and her husband Jean took over the farm when the parents died, and I later visited them there. I maintained a firm link with the Lesur family and later with Françoise's family in Lapugnoy, near Lens. Françoise married a doctor, Gérard Quénon, and they had nine children. They were a strong Catholic family.

Valence seemed a very exotic place to go to. It was near the Massif Central, not too far from the Alps and had exciting prospects. However, when I got there I found the climate and the culture of the school very strange. I was accommodated in the school, which like many others in similar parts of France were boarding establishments – because of the size of the *départments* (county areas), the nature of the school (selective), and the distances for some pupils to travel. The pastoral staff, called pions, were students who needed the money to fund their studies, which they did not seem to take too seriously. They put the boys to bed and slept near enough to supervise them overnight. They were a crude bunch and they obviously found me very odd. My spoken French was appalling but I soon learnt their slang, such as '*dégueulasse*' (disgusting, or vomiting), and '*vachement*' (like mad, extremely). With practically everything they added '*putain*' (whore): being from the south they had a particular ring to the second syllable, which gave the word an ugly kick. This was not a word that I used personally! There were far worse obscenities which came from the rich vocabulary of French *argot* (French slang), of which there were specialist dictionaries. Despite their crudity they were friendly folk and full of fun and humour. The other assistant was German and his grasp of spoken French was much better than mine. He and I formed a strong bond and we did an unforgettable tour of the *Côte d'Azur* together.

On Sundays I went to the local *Église Réformée* (the main Reformed Church in France). Apart from this, my main activity was the Chorale Universitaire de Valence. This was conducted by the local *Inspecteur Général* (Director of Education), a man of somewhat fiery character who would sometimes describe us, in frustration, as '*incroyable*' (incredible). We sang Fauré's *Requiem* which we took on tour to Paris, where we performed in the famous Conservatoire de Musique. To keep up my solo singing I found a teacher. Her name was Nelly Draussin. She was in her nineties and had lost her own voice, but she was a real treasure. I explored the

French repertoire with her and she introduced me to the wonderful composer of French *mélodies* (songs, the equivalent of German Lieder), Henri Duparc (1848-1933). We also explored the lighter side of French opera. Another important activity was the *Jeunesses Musicales* (music clubs for young people), a French national organisation which encouraged the appreciation of classical music amongst teenagers. In terms of composers and performers, France was such a creative country, in this sphere, but there was a lamentable lack of musical education in state schools. The Valence branch of this was very active and vigorously supported: concerts and talks would be held in the local theatre. One of the most interesting evenings was a visit by the composer Francis Poulenc (1899-1963, a member of Les Six[1]). He was promoting a book he had written. After his talk – with musical examples - I bought a copy and he autographed it for me: in this way I met one of the most influential composers in France. His eclectic style, combining off-key elements of Mozart and Richard Strauss in a delightful, witty French *mêlée*, was a true delight.

I was very active in a number of fields, but I was different from the *pions*. I had the very embarrassing experience of overhearing them discuss me at one stage. I believe my German colleague was there, too. They described me as unintelligent. In terms of my speech in French I was inadequate, but in terms of my activities I used my time in Valence very profitably, and in many ways my lifestyle was very different from theirs. However, I do not hold a grudge against them: they were telling the truth. I never fitted in, and I was never really at peace in their company, nor in the French way of life. I was much better integrated into the lifestyle of Germany, which was to be my next residential project.

As my time in Valence drew to a close, I was asked if I

Côte d'Azur tour from Valence, Drôme,

Nürnberg from the Castle. The two Hallenkirchen, The Sebalduskirche in the foreground and the Lorenzkirche in the background, are visible

would sing with the Chorale Universitaire de Lyon, who needed help with a tour to the Llangollen International Festival. I obliged and got to know a new bunch of British and French students. It was here that I met Geoff Drought[2], who featured in a later period in my life. We sang Elgar's *As Torrents in Summer*, which was a very English piece for a French choir to tackle and, competitively, we got nowhere with it, apart from the joy of singing it.

At the end of my time in France I decided I wanted to revive my German. I also wished to extend my free-and-easy life, with part-time employment, in Europe which I loved so much. So I applied for a similar post in Germany, as an *Englischer Assistent*. I had no connections in Germany and did not specify where I wanted to go. The only experience I had had with the country was the trip with my friend Dolf, described above. A stroke of an administrator's pen with an invitation to go to Nürnberg turned my life round completely. I was assigned to the Realgymnasium in the city, to which was added another school in the nearby town of Fürth, the Dürer-Oberrealschule, when I got there. I had the name of the Head of Department at the Realgymnasium, Studienrat Kurt Wetzel, but no other contacts whatsoever. My spoken German was very limited. I arrived at the *Hauptbahnhof* (main station) and had no idea what to do or where to go. Fortunately Herr Wetzel had earlier made contact. Clutching the sandwiches my mother gave me for the journey I installed myself in the *Bunkerhotel,* which, windowless, was part of the city wall opposite the station. A miserable place to start! I was there for a few nights and lived off my sandwiches, which started going mouldy! I just did not have the confidence – or the language – to go to a restaurant.

However, eventually I made my way to the school, by tram. At that time parts of the city, right to its centre, were linked by a highly efficient network of trams, radiating out from the *Hauptbahnhof*. Herr Wetzel was very kind and sorted out my duties and responsibilities. He even suggested accommodation. I lodged in a suburb along the Sulzbacherstrasse on the No. 8 tram line, at Erlenstegen with Frau Herzog. She was a very kindly, motherly woman who looked after a small child. My main reservation with her was the way she made my tea: she would let it continue to simmer on the hob, which ruined it! Because of the child, she asked me to move on to another lodging, where I was also very happy. My new landlady, Frau Sorsche, had a lively daughter called Bobby.

The city had an office of the British Council near to the Realgymnasium. The appointed officer was a Mr Roach. He invited me and other English assistants to attend meetings there. It was here that I met Wolfram Brunner, whose sister Ingrid was in a senior class at the Realgymnasium. Wolfram was an accomplished pianist and artist. I struck up a very firm friendship with him and we used to make music and attend musical events together. I have a few of his sketches which still hang on our walls. He was deeply introverted and even though it lasted till his death in 2010, our relationship became very strained. He lived in his parents' flat in Ostendstrasse for many years and ended up in another flat in Mögeldorf, which was very alien to him. I never succeeded in discovering the circumstances of his death. I think the origin of his breakdown was the death of his mother.

On Sundays I looked for a place of worship. Various churches called themselves *freikirchlich* (Free Church), but I found one which was called a *Baptistengemeinde* (Baptist Congregation). I started going there and was very quickly integrated into their fellowship. I became part of their family and this played a vital role in the success of my year in

Germany. I was frequently invited out to a meal or coffee by members, including the Secretary, Ludwig Berges, and his wife, who were extremely generous towards me. Their minister was Prediger Johannes Schoof. I joined the choir and sang under the direction of Walter Pretzsch, whose mother also attended the church. He had a strong faith and was more than a choirmaster to me. He gave me opportunities to sing solo. I was known by all as *Bruder* (Brother) Hall. The minister's son Armin was an organist and was studying at the Nürnberger Konservatorium (Conservatory of Music). He suggested that I join the Conservatory and study *Gesang* (Singing) part-time. So I enrolled and was accepted. My teacher was Hilde Scheppan, formerly of the Berlin State Opera and the Bayreuth Festival. I got on extremely well with her, and soon she was recommending that I was *konzertreif* (ready to appear in a concert). With the vocal studies came Music Theory and other classes.

I was very happy in Nürnberg. I appreciated my teaching at both schools, despite the early start of classes. I made good friends and enjoyed the company of my compatriot colleagues, notably Chris and Betty. I had a job at the MAN factory teaching Berlitz English[3] and earning some extra cash. My German was making great strides. I was singing in a large chorus, the *Lehrergesangverein* (Teachers' Choir), conducted by the musical director of the Opernhaus, Max Loy. I was accepted into the family of an active church. I went to the Baptistengemeinde, in the Siebenkeesstrasse, for the first time on Sunday 19 October. The church building had real atmosphere, with the focus on one corner, encouraging a communal arrangement of the pews on three sides, and a gallery where the choir was placed. On Saturday 15 November I wrote in my diary: 'I am very happy here in Nürnberg.' I felt at home.

In February I accompanied a skiing trip into the Alps, south of Garmisch-Partenkirchen. This was an opportunity to get to know some of the boys. We were led by Karl, a small, agile, older military man. As far as the skiing was concerned I was the dunce of the party! I did not have the physique or the balance to succeed. However, we did have one long excursion on skis which were soled with material in order to obtain a better grip. We climbed to the top of the Blaicher Horn and from there we had a magnificent view towards the Zugspitze and, in the distance, the Bodensee (otherwise known as Lake Constance). I had not learned to ski properly, but this *Tagesausflug* (day outing), where my lack of ability was less important, validated the whole trip – and, maybe, helped to rescue my reputation. The following day I climbed up the Tennenmoorskopf, which was an even more successful climb than the day before. So, all was not lost!

Later on I visited this area again. I went to stay with a family linked with Malcolm Gale – he had an exchange arrangement with a girl called Christl Betz. Herr Betz was a builder by trade: they lived at Kempten in Bavaria, but to reach it by train you had to pass through part of Austria. This was my first visit to that country. When I was asked what I wanted to do the next day I suggested skiing! Even though I kept to the beginners' slopes, I fared a lot better than on the school trip: I felt much more confident. As my short, but most engaging, stay with the Betz family came to an end, Christl, who had borrowed a car, was driving north to Hamburg, to rejoin her university, and offered me a lift for part of my journey. She drove at great speed and talked about 'polishing off the kilometres' quickly! She dropped me at Frankfurt Airport, from where I took the bus to the station and the train to Nürnberg. These two encounters with Alpine Germany and

Austria added another dimension to the joy of my time as an *Englischer Assistent.*

My singing came on with leaps and bounds. I wrote in my diary on Monday 27 April: 'I suddenly felt I really could sing!' I had an excellent 2-hour practice in the morning at the *Kons* (Conservatory) and a most successful lesson in the afternoon, when I worked through most of 'The Creation' (Haydn's *Die Schöpfung*).

Another most interesting journey was to the Baptist Student Conference in Berlin. I went by car with a young couple and their baby. We drove via Bayreuth and Hof on the Autobahn. Berlin, divided into 4 zones (Soviet, American, British and French) could only be reached by crossing the *Deutsche Demokratische Republik*, or so-called German Democratic Republic. There were motorways, rail connections and air corridors, and the border had to be crossed twice. At the first border post there was an unpleasant atmosphere. On the continuation of the motorway there were huge potholes. We went through a poor-looking village. In the GDR there were posters and slogans everywhere, lambasting the 'American imperialists' and exhorting citizens to 'carry out the five-year plan'. At the Berlin border there were loudspeakers playing patriotic music. However, despite all the hype and the depression of the East, especially the Stalinallee, there was an encouraging side to this era: freedom of movement between the zones. I took great pleasure in walking under the *Brandenburger Tor* (Brandenburg Gate) from the American zone (which I was informed I was leaving) into the Soviet zone, where there was an ostentatious military memorial guarded by strutting Red Army soldiers. Crossing the zones on the *S-Bahn* (Overground Railway) and the *U-Bahn* (Underground) was also then possible. The infamous wall had not yet been built and Checkpoint Charlie not yet installed.

What I failed to grasp was that the most beautiful part of Berlin (apart from the kitsch of the *Stalinallee)* was in the Soviet zone: the *Staatsoper* (State Opera House), the Classical museums and the *Französischer Dom* (French Cathedral) - we discovered the latter on a later visit. The conference itself was most morale-boosting, in that Baptists were thin on the ground in Germany and the GDR was an atheist state. I stayed in a *Jugendherberge* (Youth Hostel). I returned to Nürnberg by coach.

One of the features of my post as *Englischer Assistent* was to meet the *Referendare* (trainee teachers) regularly. I enjoyed my contact with them. German teachers are often not exclusively language teachers: they combined English with other subjects, e.g. history, and were known as *Germanisten*. We had a Baptist conference in Nürnberg, based on the *Messehaus* (exhibition hall). At the service on the Sunday there were an estimated 1,500 present. I was in the choir on the platform. It was an inspiring occasion.

On 18 June I received a letter from London saying that I had been granted a post as *Assistant d'Anglais* at the Lycée Kléber in Strasbourg. This was very good news as it was the nearest possible place to Germany. I did not know at this stage how my relationship with Dorle would work out, but from that point of view it proved to be the best arrangement that I could have had (see below). And, in fact, because of the history of Alsace it was a mixture, culturally, of France, and Germany and even shared the two languages: it was now part of France but it had people who talked a form of German, with their own newspaper. The other great advantage was that I would have the option of continuing my musical studies at the Conservatoire de Musique.

Kenneth singing in a performance of Handel's Messias, *in German, in a church in the Vosges, Alsace, 1958 (?)*

1. Durey, Honnegger, Milhaud, Tailleferre, Auric, Poulenc
2. I met up with Geoff again when we lived in Kenton. He was a Church Warden of Cofton St Mary's, Cockwood, Dawlish, Devon, of which we were members. We visited him and his wife Gill once for a meal and he realised that we had met before. He was an English Assistant at Lyon and a member of this choir.
3. A particular method of teaching languages (a commercial language course)

KENNETH HALL

Wie schön leuchtet der Morgenstern

Voll Gnad und Wahrheit von dem Herrn

Die süsse Wurzel Jesse!

Du Sohn Davids aus Jakobs Stamm,

Mein König und mein Bräutigam,

Hast mir mein Herz besessen.

Lieblich, freundlich,

Schön und herrlich,

Gross und ehrlich, Reich an Gaben,

Hoch und sehr prächtig erhaben.

.

How brightly beams the morning star!
What sudden radiance from afar
doth glad us with its shining!
Brightness of God that breaks our night
and fills the darkened souls with light
who long for truth were pining!
Thy Word, Jesus, inly feeds us,
rightly leads us, life bestowing.
Praise, O praise such love o'er flowing!

Translation C. Winkworth

CHAPTER 8

Epiphany

The word 'epiphany' indicates a moment of enlightenment and also has the connotation of 'gift', because it is used for the Festival of Epiphany when we remember the Wise Men, who brought gifts to the baby Jesus. Both the ideas were manifested on Saturday evening 13 June 1959. It happened at the home of Dr Wolfgang and Frau Antje Becker. Wolfgang Becker was a colleague at the Dürer-Oberreaslschule. He was interested in drama, and with pupils we did some theatre texts together. His wife Antje was a teacher at the Lutheran Wilhelm Löhe Schule attended by a certain Dorle Büttner. The couple decided to invite both of us to a musical evening using their harpsichord. I both sang and accompanied and Dorle played the recorder, which she was studying part-time (like myself) at the *Kons* (as we called it). When the evening came to a late end, Dr Becker remarked that Dorle would be able to sleep on as the following day was Sunday. She replied that she would be going to church, as usual. I realised that she was a Christian and recognised that this was a significant meeting. However, I learnt later that we had 'encountered' each other on another occasion. Dorle had booked a practice room in the *Kons* but on approaching the double door had heard a tenor singing. She went to the office and they said that it must be 'our English student'. She was annoyed, but the incident passed and there was no mention of it on the evening of our official meeting.

Looking back at my diary of the time, my entry for that day was extremely bland. I wrote 'Went to Beckers for some music. Met Dorle Büttner for the first time.' Subsequent entries indicate a much more turbulent frame of mind. On the night after our meeting I could not sleep at all. There is no doubt that I had fallen head-over-heels in love with her, and that I wondered whether the Lord had provided her as a gift. The name Dorothea means 'gift of God' and that is what she seemed to me to be. It was the *Orgelwoche* (Organ Week) in Nürnberg. I met her, by coincidence, at the end of the first concert a week later in the Sebalduskirche[1] and accompanied her home. The contribution to the Festival of the *Lehrergesangverein* (Teachers' Choir), to which I belonged, conducted by Max Loy, was the *Missa Gladolitica* by Janáček. The performance was praised by the press. On the following evening there was an organ recital in the Lorenzkirche[2] and I got there early. Again, Dorle and I met by chance and I was able to sit next to her. I took her home and we arranged to meet for Sunday. The following Wednesday we were back at the Beckers making music. We ran into each other at the bus station. Amongst other items I sang Handel's wonderful setting of *Meine Seele rühmt und preist* with Dorle doing the recorder obligato (written for violin), which was a great joy. I have no recorded comment on the Sunday concert, but I do know that we agreed to keep meeting. She joined the Lehrergesangverein party going to Stuttgart on 14 July to perform Beethoven's *Missa Solemnis* at the Liederhalle, as my guest. Neither of us is very fond of this work but it was a wonderful day which included a trip to the hilltop park, the Killersberg. Her absence from school that day required the cooperation of her mother, whom we all called Mutti. In fact, I believe that Mutti encouraged our liaison. Her background was in the *Brüdergemeine* (Moravian Church). Her parents were missionaries in South Africa, and at one stage she was even interned by the British! Her husband Siegfried, Dorle's father, was pastor of the village of Ursheim – a Lutheran enclave, like Nürnberg, in the Catholic state of Bavaria – where Dorle was born. He was anti-Nazi and this had tragic consequences (*cf* Appendix *Wallace and Siegfried*).

My meeting with Dorle completely turned my life around. Our characters complement each other: she is ebullient and charming - I am retiring and shy. She is tidy and well-organised - I am scatty and somewhat chaotic. She is at home with technical matters - I am usually at sea. She had no interest in foreign languages at school but her command of English is better than mine and she has no trace of a German accent. We both enjoy public performance and share a love of Baroque music, having a great respect for J S Bach. We both love art, particularly modern art. We both enjoy study and are both teachers, she of adults, I of youngsters. We have both done research: we have both studied Management and are interested in leading and motivating others. Our love is passionate and physical, but never 'overstepped the mark' before our wedding night, when we were both virgins. We believe firmly in public marriage and in remaining faithful through good times and bad, sickness and health. This does not mean that we are unsympathetic to couples who have relationship problems, although the loose associations which are now paramount everywhere are not a feature we admire. The anchor, in our case, is our Christian faith and this is the most important factor that we share.

There was little time left to develop our relationship as my departure from Nürnberg was on 24 July. However, I had already applied for another year in France, mentioning that I would like to be as close to Germany as possible. The Ministry could not have been more obliging. They found me a job as an

Pfarrhaus (Manse), Ursheim, Bayern (Bavaria), birthplace of Dorle Büttner

Assistant d'Anglais at the Lycée Kléber in Strasbourg, very close to the Rhein border with Germany! By train it was about six hours away from Nürnberg. We corresponded during the summer holiday, when I was in Bedford, and there were moments of worry during this time as to whether Dorle would remain faithful, particularly after such a whirlwind romance, but fortunately she did not dither, at least in her correspondence.

When the day came to take up my new job in France I made my way there from Bedford to Strasbourg by train and ferry. I remember carrying a huge case and then taking it upstairs, with great difficulty, to my room in the Lycée Kléber, situated in the Place de Bordeaux. As in Valence, I was boarded at the school, with a group of *pions*. I had written to the *Conservatoire de Musique* and they had given me a date for my audition. They gave me a place. The school was a series of large blocks near the centre of the city and close to military barracks. One of my enduring memories is hearing soldiers parading through the streets singing, which appears to be the custom in the military in France. Strasbourg was a key city in the struggle for power between France and Germany. After World War Two it became, with Alsace, part of France but between the wars it belonged to Germany. The very high Gothic cathedral, with its single spire, dominated the city but there was, inevitably, a strong Lutheran presence. There was a network of canals and very picturesque timbered houses in the quarter called *La Petite France*. It was thus a mixture of intimate charm and military grandeur. At the Conservatoire there was a link with Albert Schweizer, who used to take classes there, and the Principal was the brother of the famous conductor Charles Münch.

I visited Dorle on various occasions and she came to Strasbourg twice. I loved being in Nürnberg in the summer.

Dorfkirche, Ursheim (Village Church – Lutheran)

We would go for cycle rides and go swimming at different pools – there was a very good open-air pool at Erlenstegen. On one occasion we went on a coach tour to Egloffstein, where there was a very fine castle. It was here, on the path leading to the castle, that I mentioned marriage to her for the first time and she agreed that we should get engaged. I was very happy.

I was given Germaine Hoerner as my singing teacher at the Conservatoire. She was a former star of the Paris Opéra.

Dorle, Killersberg, Stuttgart, summer 1959

She became a friend and even gave accommodation to Dorle when she visited me. I explored the French repertoire and continued my study of Fauré and Duparc songs. I did *solfège* (basic music theory) as well and I also attended harmony classes. I decided to gain a qualification and so I took an exam before leaving: I was awarded a *Deuxième Prix* (Second Class Diploma) at the end of the course. At my audition for this I was at some disadvantage as I was suffering from the after-effects, which included a sore throat, of glandular fever. I succumbed to this in the winter of 1960 and I was really quite ill. I had a swollen neck and underarms. I visited Dorle in Nürnberg when I still had the virus (which was not contagious), and she and Mutti were somewhat alarmed at my condition. In Strasbourg I sought medical help and ended up being tended by nuns in a Catholic hospital. I was eventually allowed to go home to seek advice from my own doctor. There is little doubt that my condition weakened my performance at the exam for the diploma.

Earlier I did quite a lot of solo singing, including a Christmas broadcast on local radio and a *Messias* ('Messiah') in German somewhere in the Vosges Hills, the beautiful equivalent of the Black Forest, in Alsace. I remember also taking part in a performance of J S Bach's *Magnificat* at the Conservatoire: an attractive lesser-known work with short movements and a duet for alto and tenor. I sang in the main Conservatoire choir and with the Principal we did the *Matthäuspassion* (Matthew Passion). The musical culture of the area was very much influenced by the German repertoire.

Vine came to visit me in the summer vacation and we went to the *Schwarzwald* (Black Forest). We stayed at a bed-and-breakfast establishment and did a lot of walking. I was not feeling fully fit yet but I enjoyed our holiday together. Part of Vine's reason for coming was so that she could attend our engagement party in Nürnberg. The day included a walk, as was the custom in Dorle's family. My mother had sent material for a dress for Dorle. She wore this again at the second party which was at 60 Bushmead Avenue in Bedford later, when my parents were present.

I had to think about the next stage, which was full-time employment. I looked towards a job in an independent school. I had an interview at Kent College, in Canterbury, which was then a Direct Grant state school. The headmaster said he wanted me, but for me the conditions were not quite right. I had also applied to Glasgow Academy, an independent boys' school in the west of the city. In order to claim my travel expenses to Glasgow (from France) legitimately, the Kent College head agreed not to offer me the job. The Academy on the other hand did offer me the post, and I accepted it, even though I had grave reservations about the city of Glasgow, which in those days was black and smoke-ridden. I liked the Head of Department, Moreton Black, very much and it proved to be a very sound foundation on which to build my career. I started in September 1960. I taught French and German, with the possibility of also doing some Russian. As part of the 'package' I agreed to join the school's contingent of the Combined Cadet Force.

Being separated from Dorle for so long, i.e. until our marriage on 28 December 1961, was not at all easy. We had to rely on lengthy letters to communicate. Telephone connection was difficult and rare. I lived in 'digs' in Hyndland and Hillhead in the West End of Glasgow near the Botanical Gardens and Kelvin Park. I attended Hillhead Baptist Church and eventually became Superintendent of the Sunday School. These were the days of great preaching and we were fortunate in having a master of the art as our minister, Rev. Dr. Guy Ramsay. The Secretary, James Jackson, and his wife were very

Dorle, Egloffstein Castle approach, where Kenneth proposed and was accepted, 1959

good to me, inviting me back to lunch on many Sundays. The membership was huge, divided into over twenty districts, and there was a church-planting project in Drumchapel, a satellite new town, as well as another branch in the nearby borough of Partick. I used to help with the project in Drumchapel on a Sunday afternoon.

I enjoyed most of my teaching but I had trouble with a fifth form, who were unruly. Moreton Black would sometimes swap with me so that he took the more difficult group and I taught his class I took rugby at the Anniesland sports field – the Academy was hemmed in with Kelvin Park on one side and residential flats on the other - not very successfully, and I accompanied one or two away matches. I got used to parading as an army officer once a week and spending the day in uniform. The CO, a single man, was very keen on drama and he would organise pantomimes in which staff and boys took

The Nürnberger Konservatorium

Kaffeetrinken im Garten (Coffee in the Garden) at Virchowstr.34c, Dorle's home: (left to right) Mutti, Siegfried, Dorle, Renate, 1959

part. I started by playing piano duets with the Head of Music, William Coulthard, as accompanist, but later had roles on stage. I was the Good Fairy in one, and in *Cinderella* I played one of the Ugly Sisters, with the CO as the other – he was short and fat, I was tall and slim! – and I had a 'whale of a time'. We did the duet from Lerner and Loewe's *Gigi, I remember it well* (with adapted words) which I am still performing today in Care Homes with a lady from our Clef Club concert party.

One of the advantages of belonging to the CCF was going off to camp. We were released early at the end of the summer term and we received extra pay for our efforts. Money was in short supply in those days: my first salary was only about £1,000 for a whole year! My first camp took me to Loch Ewe on the north-west Highland coast. It was immensely remote. Fortunately it was not in the part of the summer when midges are rife. We took the train from Glasgow Central to Achnasheen, which is a deserted station in the middle of a moor, and were ferried from there to our camp, which took us along the very beautiful Loch Maree.

I survived the camp quite well but found it very tiring. I was given the chance to drive an Austin Champ, the British equivalent of the American Jeep, and in fact I drove it back to Glasgow. Later on I was also allowed to drive, after taking a test, a 3-ton army lorry.

The autumn term, with the prospect of marriage ahead, dragged on, and I thought it would never end. Finally the term was ended. I spent Christmas at home, then took the train and ferry to Nürnberg. Vine and Neil came too, but my parents were absent, lacking the confidence to travel abroad. Vine and I stayed in a bed-and-breakfast house in Virchowstrasse, just around the corner from Dorle's home. We had to go to the *Rathaus* (the City Hall) for the first part

The Dürerhaus, Nürnberg

of the marriage, which was civil, according to German law. Neil came as a witness. Obviously they were used to GIs marrying local girls, as *Bayern* (Bavaria) was part of the American zone. When the registrar said, in English, 'You vill be faithful to your 'vife' Neil and I had to exercise great restraint to avoid bursting out with laughter! The church wedding followed in the *Reformations-Gedächtnis-Kirche Maxfeld* (Maxfeld Reformation Memorial Church) opposite the *Stadtpark* (City Park) and near the former *Messehalle* (Exhibition Hall). The minister who conducted it was 'Onkel' Hermann (not a real uncle), Pfarrer Kleinknecht, who was a fellow student at Erlangen University with Dorle's father Siegfried. Neil, gowned and hooded, also took part. Dorle, in a white dress with a veil swept back and bearing fresias, looked radiant. The service was in German and English. We had the reception in the Park Café opposite. We had lunch (neither of us had much of an appetite!). I made a speech, in both languages, and Dorle's brother Siegfried stood in for the bride's father. In the afternoon we had *Kaffeetrinken* (coffee and cake) in a church hall, which was an opportunity to invite a wider circle of friends. True to custom, there was singing, in rounds and parts.

We were keen to get away, in the British fashion, rather than stay in Nürnberg that night. Our first stop was in Würzburg. We then made our way down the Rhein to Bonn for a couple of nights. We caught the prestigious TE Express, which I had booked back in the UK as a surprise. We made our way to Ostend and over the Channel to Dover. Our honeymoon *per se* was spent at Eastbourne at the York House Hotel, at the suggestion of Dudley Chalk (Neil's father-in-law), who had used it on occasions. It was a fine hotel, but the problem was we were a young couple on honeymoon and the other residents, of whom there were just a handful, were old.

Honeymoon, January 1962. Visit to Brighton from Eastbourne

Marriage, Nürnberg, 1961

It was the coldest January imaginable and outside we were utterly frozen. Anyone who ventured out was considered brave! We did go out, as far as Beachy Head, but we found it very unpleasant. The only sensible thing to do seemed to be to go to bed. At least there we were happy to oblige! The week passed quickly, and soon we were on our way to Bedford to call on my parents, before striking north.

1. The Sebalduskirche (St Theobald's Church) and the Lorenzkirche (St Lawrence's Church), both Lutheran, are examples of Hallenkirchen (hall churches), where the nave, built in an earlier period, is lower than the choir, or chancel, which is higher and was added later in a different style. They lie on either side, north and south, of the river Pegnitz, and are very significant churches of their period. They were carefully restored after severe damage to the city centre from the RAF raid of 2 January 1945.
2. See reference to Sebalduskirche above

O Kelvin banks are fair, bonnie lassie,

O

When the summer we are there, bonnie lassie,

O

Then the May-pink's crimson plume

Throws a soft but sweet perfume

Round the yellow banks of broom, bonnie lassie,

O

Kelvin Grove – Scottish folksong, verse 3

CHAPTER 9

Scotland: Our First Home

Our first married home was a garret in Crown Circus, above
Byres Road, off the Great Western Road in Glasgow, with a
view, through the smoke, of the University. It was extremely
primitive, with little furniture and a split dormer window
which served as the kitchen on one side and the bathroom on
the other. You had to put a coin in the meter above the bath to
get hot water. The entrance to the block was a long way down,
and we had to go downstairs to use the telephone. The house
shared a phone number with another party and we had to ring
Exchange to get through. For Dorle it was worse: she had to
go to the Post Office to ring her mother in Germany. We
survived, and in fact had warm relations with Glaswegians.
Dorle spoke little English at first but she integrated well into
Glaswegian speech. She became pregnant, and on 29
December 1962 our first son, Martin, was born in the
Redlands Nursing Home along the Great Western Road. He
was about a week late, so we celebrated Christmas before the
birth. Our minister Ralph Martin and his wife gave us a
traditional lunch on the day.

Having a child made a big difference to our life, but Dorle
adapted to it very well. It meant regular walks with the pram
and engaging in baby care in an unsuitable flat several stair-
flights up. When the wind blew, black spots of soot would
seep through the gaps in the window frames and settle. We
would often put a nappy over Martin's cot and it would be

Glasgow University from Kelvingrove Park

Nellie Grant with Martin, 1963

spotted with black dots very quickly. The opportunities for pram walks, especially in the nearby parks, were welcome. We had visits from Mutti with Dorle's sister Renate, and my parents. We even had a summer holiday before the birth, with Dorle heavily pregnant, on the Mull of Kintyre, where we discovered that the seawater off the Scottish coast was ice-cold.

I was troubled with throat problems as my teaching career took off, and I had a very bad bout of tonsillitis. I saw a consultant at the Western Infirmary and he decided I should have my tonsils removed. I was admitted for surgery. The operation was a most unpleasant experience. I had to walk to the operating theatre and was given no pre-med treatment beforehand. I was in a ward with other men. The aftermath was horrendous. I had never experienced such searing pain. My throat was on fire: eating and speaking were traumatic exercises. At the time, at the top of the charts was the song *Don't throw your love away. No, no, no. Don't throw your love away, 'cos you will need it one day!* Everybody was singing it, staff and patients. So that song is forever associated in my mind with the circumstances of that operation and my subsequent, very slow, excruciating recovery. The staff at the Academy were very compassionate over the leave I was forced

Glasgow Academy Pantomime, Cinderella: *Kenneth as an Ugly Sister with colleague Gordon Carruthers, 1965*

to take, and I even received a visit from the Rector, Basil Holden. My throat eventually healed, but afterwards I suffered from what must have been a form of PTSD (post-traumatic stress disorder) for a couple of years. Fortunately a consultant from our church Managers' Court, Dr Charles Anderson,(with whom I had worked at Drumchapel, the Hillhead outreach project - see above - on a new housing estate, on a Sunday afternoon) helped me with medication, and I gradually recovered.

Eventually we decided we wanted to buy a flat instead of renting one. We organised a deposit, which we had to borrow, and a mortgage from the Abbey National Building Society, and we moved to a brand new ground-floor flat in Highfield Drive, with a view over railway sidings and beyond, to Maryhill. We were very happy there: we were comfortable; there was electric wall-heating, and there was a proper kitchen and a full-sized bathroom. The sitting-room merged with the dining-room and we had two bedrooms. Compared to the garret flat in Hyndland it was luxury. It was in Kelvindale, not quite as salubrious as Kelvinside, but quite acceptable.

Whilst in Glasgow we got to know the Professor of Music at the university, Kenneth Elliot, and also the chorus master of Scottish Opera and director of the Festival Chorus, John Curry, who played in a recorder group with Dorle. Alexander Gibson, formerly Musical Director of Sadler's Wells Opera, was a founder of Scottish Opera and also conductor of the Scottish National Orchestra. Dorle had no job, but her skill as a recorder player was recognised and she took part in a McEwan Concert, featuring Scottish composers, which the BBC recorded and transmitted. I was asked by John Curry to sing in a performance of the Brahms *Liebesliederwaltzer* and this was another exciting venture. I had singing lessons at the

Mutti and Renate

Royal Scottish Academy of Music, as it then was, in its old location next to St George's Tron Church[1]. The conductor of the Cambridge production of *Sir John in Love,* Leon Lovett, was appointed Assistant Conductor of the Scottish National Orchestra, and Scottish Opera and he invited me to join a semi-chorus of monks participating in their production of *Boris Godunov*; so I appeared on-stage in Glasgow and Edinburgh. All we had to do was wander on and off the stage singing praises to the Tsar!

We visited the Edinburgh Festival on several occasions, the most memorable of which was an early recital by Janet Baker, before she was well-known. She sang Schumann's *Frauenliebeundleben* ('A Woman's Love and Life') in Leith Town Hall and revealed her enormous potential[2]: she electrified us with her singing: it was a truly great sound from a woman of great spirit. One of the problems of the Edinburgh Festival was that it was not co-ordinated with public transport. On one occasion we had to leave before the end of a performance, because we had to catch a train home.

Before we left Glasgow, having previously bought an Austin Somerset which had severe defects, we acquired a Mini van: it had a seat at the back but no seat belts. It was, in the tradition of Minis, wonderfully primitive, with wire door handles. To me it was a dream to drive: very low on the ground,, and very stable and lively. We had a real car, even though it was only a van. Subsequently we had other Minis, including a Traveller, and they were all a joy to drive.

We had many outings in our spare time. We felt close to the western, highland part of Scotland and we explored The Trossachs, the Campsies, Loch Lomond and the Isle of Arran. A colleague at Glasgow Academy, Wallace Orr, an artist and an architect, who was Head of Art, built his own house at Kippen, near Stirling, with a view towards the Trossachs. He

My parents, by the lower river, Bedford

Drawing of my father in his 70s

was an amazing character. As a committed Christian he was hesitant about joining the armed forces at the beginning of World War Two, and so he enrolled in the London Fire Brigade. Feeling that he should join in the fight against the Nazis, he later joined RAF Bomber Command and became a rear gunner in a Lancaster bomber. He took part in the raid which destroyed the old city of Nürnberg. As an artist he would have objected to the destruction of one of the greatest architectural jewels of Europe, but he did what he felt he had to do. It was a brave act, as being at the rear end of a Lancaster was not only very uncomfortable but also very dangerous. He formed a strong friendship with Dorle and Mutti. Ironically Mutti saw the distant glow in the sky above Nürnberg from Ursheim as the bombing was taking place, and she would have seen the bombers, one of them crewed by Wallace, returning as they flew southwards from Nürnberg before veering westwards for home[3].

One of Wallace's paintings hung in Mutti's room when she died in 2008, and three hang in our present home.

1. Church of Scotland, in Nelson Mandela Place, next to Buchanan Street, in the centre of Glasgow. The Royal Scottish Academy of Music, now called The Conservatoire of Scotland, is situated in Renfrew Street, central Glasgow

2. Janet Baker was the greatest mezzo of the twentieth century - greater in my opinion than Kathleen Ferrier (who could be classed as a contralto). She had the most glorious, rich tone, placed beautifully forward, and a very warm personality which coloured all her singing. I would put her in the same category as Maria Callas.

3. I have written this as an article, published originally in 1995, called *Wallace and Siegfried,* which is in the Appendix

PROMOTION SHOULD NOT BE MORE IMPORTANT

THAN ACCOMPLISHMENT,

OR AVOIDING INSTABILITY

MORE IMPORTANT THAN

TAKING THE RIGHT RISKS.

Peter Drucker

CHAPTER 10

Onward and Upward

After five years at Glasgow Academy I felt I needed to move on. I had one or two interviews, one of them at Bishop's Stortford College, an independent school with a Congregational background which took some pupils from the public sector. This is where I accepted a post on the Modern Language staff. The school was probably the school nearest to my heart in its culture, size and atmosphere, and the one at which I met my great mentor, Walter Strachan. Walter was Head of Modern Languages and Deputy Headmaster. He had a keen interest in modern art and sculpture, as well as architecture of all eras. He was a personal friend of Henry Moore, who lived nearby. He was an editor of modern language texts and a translator, from French, Spanish and Italian. His chief and most original interest was in the *Livre d'Artiste*, a combination of illustration and text, of which he had a vast collection. At the school there were modern paintings everywhere, evidence of Walter's strong influence on the Headmaster. The school had a recreation afternoon on Wednesdays, and Walter ran an Architectural Society. He was delighted when I asked if I could assist. Our main activity was to visit and sketch historic buildings in the area. He was a great cyclist and he expected the boys to follow him on bicycles. I, however, stuck to the van. We saw churches, mansions, country houses and barns, and we discussed with

Dorle at the Guildhall, Thaxted, Essex, circa 1966

him their style, building texture and construction. My sketches were primitive but that did not matter.

The staff were quite remarkable. Two of them became heads of well-known public schools, one of them, Kim Jones, of Bedford School. The Head of Music, an albino with very poor eyesight, was Ernest Warburton. He eventually became Head of Music on BBC Radio 3, and Administrator of the BBC Philharmonic Orchestra. Ernest recognised my musical talents, and not only gave me some music class teaching but also used me as soloist on various occasions. The high point of this for me was a production of Mozart's *The Magic Flute* in which I played the part of Tamino. My voice had moved up to tenor by then and I revelled in the part. All the music is superb, and I loved both the arias and the ensembles. I found no difficulty in the range.

When I was interviewed, the Headmaster, Peter Rowe, made it quite clear that I would be offered the job of Head of Department upon Walter's retirement in two years. This may have been a misunderstanding on my part but, when Walter retired, the job was not available. I decided I had to move on, after only two years in this School, which was the sort of establishment I would have been happy for our son to attend. I bear no ill will towards Peter: he had been so good to Dorle, making her in effect a German Assistant and encouraging her. She was offered adult German teaching at Bishop's Stortford Boys' High School by the local authority and this was the start of her career. Undoubtedly the work at the College helped her get the other job. One very big difference for me was that, being a boarding-school and allowing for an activities afternoon on Wednesdays, it had Saturday school. Terms were shorter, but our weekend freedom was limited. As I did not have sport to offer, I started a sailing group. There were a few boys interested, and boat building was part of their interest.

We lived in Elsenham, quite close to the station on the line to Bishop's Stortford and London Liverpool Street. Formerly this was the junction of the line which went to Thaxted. There was a level crossing, and we had to be careful to wait if the gates were closed, before crossing the line. We bought a new semi-detached house, which had an unusual structure: it had a steel frame. We were in a close with other types of such houses, but at the cheaper end. The fact we were no. 13 did not worry us at all, but it may have been why it was still on the market. We now had three bedrooms, although one was no more than a box room. Before moving we were staying at my parents' home because there was a delay in gaining entry, since the builders did not yet have access to the sewage treatment facility down the road. The builders carried out the decoration of the walls and allowed us to leave our furniture in the middle of the floor in each room. We protested about our lack of access, and the foreman very kindly gave us the key and posted a power line through the letter box. We were prepared to risk being sued! In the end the matter was solved quite quickly.

We joined Saffron Walden Baptist Church and drove there on Sundays. I also had a job as organist there just for evening services. This meant that I had to practise, which I did usually on a Saturday afternoon. Our association with this church continued later in the 80s. It was very interesting to notice the difference in the sort of people living in Saffron Walden – and hence the congregation – as it became more of a commuter town for Cambridge and the City. The other transforming feature was the decision to go ahead with the development of Stansted Airport, with its rail connection.

My next job, in 1967, was Head of Modern Languages at Solihull School. Career-wise this was a good move for me. It was another independent school with strong local authority support, but in this case with a link with the Anglican Church, sporting two chaplains and a large chapel. Saturday school was out, and this felt as if every weekend was a half-term holiday! I was given a lot of freedom by the Headmaster, Basil McGowan, and I took over a new building for the Department, which included a language laboratory. I had my own office. We decided to install a cassette system, with the boys very much in control. This had enormous difficulties, and we would have done better to use more conventional machinery. What we discovered later was that language labs were limited in use. They were not the panacea expected. I introduced the Nuffield Course for both French and German, and this was very exciting. Each lesson started with a filmstrip accompanied by an aural tape using simple but fairly natural language. The language was further simplified and analysed to reinforce the grammatical structure which was the hub of the lesson. Each course was based on a real place and this enabled a connection to be made between theory and practice and also gave it authenticity. I tried to make language learning alive and exciting and used many aids to do this. We were trying to abandon the grammar/translation approach, and start with the language as it was spoken and expressed and the psychology of the people who used it. I am not sure the method totally succeeded but it was certainly worth trying.

Musically, I was not given the opportunities I had at Bishop's Stortford, but nevertheless Michael Wild was appointed Head of German in my department and he was an excellent pianist. We had some good sessions together and on one occasion we performed in front of the pupils. I sang *Dichterlieder* (by Schumann) with him and songs from Benjamin Britten's *Les Illuminations*. I also tackled ABRSM Grade 8 Singing, with some tutoring from a very kind Music Department colleague. He was a horn player, so we did the

Dorle, wearing a traditional Dirndle on the Untersberg, near Salzburg, Austria, 1971

Our last meeting with my mother at Hastings, Sussex, 1980. She died in 1981. At back, Martin and Kenneth; in front; Mother and Robert

Schubert song *Auf dem Strom* with horn obligato together. I attended the Birmingham School of Music[2] for singing lessons and my teacher was René Soames, who was the tenor singer from my school days at Bedford. I was drafted into the CCF Army Section and did a second five years in the force. One of my duties was to take boys on a police course. We used to go to a local police HQ where the lectures were delivered. I much enjoyed this and was so glad it could be worked into a CCF afternoon. Eventually I became CO and was known as Captain Hall! There was an alternative to CCF which was Social Service. I found that certain boys liked the discipline of the CCF and its orderly structure.

My sailing took off from this point. There was a group of very keen sailors, and we went on Games afternoons to Oulton Reservoir which was north of Solihull, nearer to Birmingham. With Dorle I went with our best sailor to the Public School Championships in Chichester Harbour. They were conducted in one class of boat, a Firefly, a wooden boat with buoyancy bags. Our representative did well but I cannot remember the result. On several occasions I went with a team to a match against another school. One was on Aldenham Reservoir in Hertfordshire. It was preceded by a match between two top public schools, Harrow and Eton. We had to wait a very long time before getting started whilst the referee heard a protest between these two. To these arch-rivals, arguing a point of the racing rules seemed more important than sailing!

We bought a house in Dorridge. It was detached and at the end of a road in a superior development. Dorridge was a pleasant village with a few shops, close to Knowle, where there was a station. We had difficulty in selling our Elsenham property, probably because of the uncertainty of Stansted Airport, about which there were three planning enquiries.

However, in the end we were able to sell it without using an estate agent. The new property was late in completion and there was thick mud all round the house, but we coped and were glad of the extra space. Martin went to the primary school in the village. Robert was born in Solihull Hospital on 26 January 1967. There was a gap of six years between the two boys.

My father died in June 1967. He had a stroke: he was eighty. Although thin, he had been fairly healthy, despite poor circulation. This was probably because he walked everywhere and never possessed a bicycle or a car. In those days eighty was a grand old age. He had retired early as a solicitor's clerk, because of a nasty bout of pleurisy. It was then that my parents decided to use the considerable size of the house (thirteen bedrooms and five garages!) to form an alternative boarding-house for pupils at Bedford School and the Girls' High School, and from other schools in the holidays where the boys and girls had parents serving overseas. Peter Renouf, from Jersey, was one of the term-time boarders. In the holidays we had a strange international mixture! My parents would take us all off on holiday together, using a school or a hotel. I recall visits to St Mary's Bay in Kent, where my Uncle Stanley lived with his eccentric wife Kitty, and Dawlish in Devon, where the main attraction was the railway running along the coast, dipping in and out of coves.

Eventually I needed to think about moving up the promotion ladder. I applied for the deputy headship of Ashford Grammar School, which I had earlier visited, and rejected when looking for a headship of department. It was a step into the state sector, which I never regretted. It was selective and therefore the pupils had ability: some no doubt chose it in preference to an independent school. The headmaster was Philip Cox, a Cambridge graduate (St John's).

The interview panel was headed on this occasion by the Deputy Chairman of Governors, Canon Sharpe, Vicar of Ashford. The Chairman was Lord Brabourne whose family had a link with the School. I did well at the interview and was offered the job.

1. We re-joined Saffron Walden Baptist Church when moved to Newport FGS and we lived in Widdington. We would drive there on Sundays and always sat upstairs. Dorle took over direction of the Sunday School and became a Deacon: there was no problem about her membership of the church. Robert joined the Boys' Brigade company there.

2. Now re-named The Royal Birmingham Conservatoire

Never in the Field of Human Conflict

Was So Much Owed

By So Many to So Few

Winston Churchill, 16 August 1940, in the House of Commons, as the Battle of Britain was being fought in the skies over Kent

CHAPTER 11

The Garden of England

This appointment ushered in what was probably the happiest period of our family life. We looked for a house in Kent in the Ashford area. We did an evaluation exercise, listing the criteria and grading their importance. This led us to a house in Ashford. However, we did not want to move there! We looked elsewhere and this brought us to the delightful, small village of Brook, near Wye, tucked under the North Downs. It was a rainy day and the bungalow we visited was architecturally an English cliché: it was in the worst taste imaginable, the sort of design repeated by small builders all over England, especially at the seaside. It even had false outer shutters! We rejected it out-of-hand. It had an enormous garden, three-quarters of an acre, and when we were asked if we wanted to inspect the garden, in the rain, we politely refused. It was called Red Tiles – another cliché! But this is what we decided to buy, and this was very much the house and the village that the Lord had chosen for us. We paid a very reasonable £12,000 for it. It was up a very narrow lane, without street lighting, and was positioned, behind a hedge, along the brook which gave its name to the village. In front of it was a large willow. The garage was a temporary one. The houses, some of which resembled Russian *dachas*, were strung almost exclusively along the main street. There was a pub, The Honest Miller, a small Norman church and a rather decrepit Baptist Chapel. To the west stretched cultivated land belonging to Wye Agricultural College, London University.

The prospect of living in this beautiful, remote part of the Garden of England was wildly exciting. Inevitably Dorle and the boys had to move there on their own and we were temporarily separated. I managed to sell our property in Dorridge, again without an agent.

At Solihull School, I had interviewed a single man, Martin Lake, as my possible successor but did not appoint him. I kept him in mind for the same post at Ashford Grammar School and he was interviewed and accepted. He also bought a house in Brook, and thus began a long and firm friendship between him and our family. He became a regular guest at our Sunday lunch table. He did not share our faith, sadly, but he was a great community supporter and was responsible for the building of a new village hall.

Our first reaction to the Baptist Chapel was one of reserve. It was run by two maiden ladies, one of whom played the harmonium, who were not resident in the village and, to us, seemed like traditional missionaries depicted in etchings arriving by canoe to evangelise the natives. We went to the mother church in Ashford and were greeted by the minister Richard Soar with 'So, you have arrived!' He said that they had been praying for two years for a Christian family to settle in Brook! So, this was an indication that our decision to buy Red Tiles was right, and that we could do no other than support the Chapel. We enquired about membership of the mother church, which was essential if we were running the Chapel. Dorle was not eligible because the membership was 'closed', i.e. restricted to those who had been baptised as believers by total immersion, and she had been baptised as an infant by her father. However, they changed their constitution to accommodate her. Our association with the Chapel was

Brook Baptist Chapel interior, after renovation

enormously fruitful and lasted throughout our nine years in the village.

We had a great supporter in Harold Wickings, a retired Congregational minister. We ran a Holiday Club together, and then formed a joint Sunday Club with the Anglican Church, with the full cooperation of the Vicar of Wye and Brook, David Marriott. Sunday Club was held on Sunday mornings and included activities as well as Christian teaching. There were plenty of children in the village and most of them enrolled. We followed Sunday Club with a prayer meeting and then had a service in the evening. We were joined by another couple, Hugh and Liz Nunn. Hugh was working at Wye College and later ran a garden centre in Ashford. They had a different background (Brethren) but in due course they gave the Chapel their full support. Hugh was a lay preacher. We relied on preachers like him to take our services and we formed strong links with certain of them. Later on we were joined by another couple who were more local to Kent, Clem and Jenny Oliver. They bought a gardener's wooden cottage up the road. We were given responsibility for the Chapel by the Ashford church. Our activities were by no means confined to Sundays: we went camping, and we had excursions, which included a seaside trip to Dymchurch, with the use of the Methodist Church there as a base. For our two boys and the children of our friends this was a great time.

I enjoyed my job. As deputy head, my door, next to the staffroom, was always open so that my colleagues could drop in when they wanted a chat. I got on well with the head, Philip Cox, even though we were very different characters. He was a strong Christian, of Nonconformist persuasion (although he went into the Anglican clergy after his retirement), and our assemblies, complete with a choir-led daily hymn, reflected this. I enjoyed my teaching, which included O Level Russian as a Sixth Form subsidiary subject, and I had some gifted pupils who took up this language. I was fully involved in extra-curricular activities. My sport was sailing, and here I was most fortunate in being able to go weekly to Dover Harbour with the Head of PE. With his encouragement I joined a training course for Day Boat Instructors, and eventually was given the qualification of RYA (Royal Yachting Association) Instructor. There was a dinghy sailing centre run by Kent County Council at the harbour, and the warden was coxswain of the Dover lifeboat – a very colourful character as one might expect! Later, we moved to a small lake, formed from a gravel pit, near Hythe, attached to a private sailing club. I went on a series of courses, at various centres in Kent, one of which was at Lydd, and I owe a great deal to these.

James Fehr was appointed Head of Music and this was one of the elements of our happy existence in Ashford and Brook. James was a very generous person as well as a very skilful musician. I founded a Madrigal Choir: typical of James was to sing as a member of the choir rather than direct it himself. Much of the singing was, as expected, *a capella* (unaccompanied). We appeared at various concerts in the area, including some in Brook Church. James used me as a soloist on various occasions, and also Dorle. The height of James' and my collaboration was probably the world première of *The Eatanswill Election* by Adrian Cruft, who was not in the first rank of contemporary composers but was reasonably well-known by those in the trade. The libretto was based on a story from Charles Dickens' *Pickwick Papers*. This came about through Johanna Platt, wife of Norman, who founded and ran Kent Opera. I went to an Amnesty International event in Wye, where Johanna, as a member, was helping. She knew about my musical activities at the School and she asked if we were interested. I consulted Philip Cox, whose son Malcolm was a talented singer, and he agreed. James was due to conduct: I was the producer and would have played the piano accompaniment, but James realised it was beyond my capability. So he invited me to conduct the work while he played the piano. It was a necessary but very magnanimous gesture, and for me it was an enormous privilege to be totally in charge.

Martin Lake and I, in collaboration with James Fehr, produced a series of musicals. We started with Gilbert and Sullivan: we did *HMS Pinafore, The Pirates of Penzance* and *Gondoliers*. We used girls from the Girls' High School. However, when it came to the 350th anniversary year we chose *My Fair Lady* by Lerner and Loewe. We were most fortunate in having an enormously talented young man, Daryl Brown, to play Higgins[1]. He was gifted both in acting and singing: he had a natural baritone voice which was rare in boys of that age. So he was able to do better justice to the Higgins' songs than Rex Harrison in the film version. The Chairman of Governors, Lord Brabourne (or John Brabourne as he was professionally known as a film producer) saw us rehearse and gave his approval. He specialised in Agatha Christie and used Peter Ustinov to play Hercule Poirot. Through him we managed to get Ustinov to present the prizes at a Speech Day.

James Fehr, who had married the daughter of the Principal of Wye College, split from his wife and moved to Sandgate, near Folkestone. He had moved from Norton Knatchbull School (the former Ashford Grammar School) to be Head of Music at Ashford School, a prestigious independent school for girls, when the post became available. Sadly he died of cancer in a hospice. At his funeral in

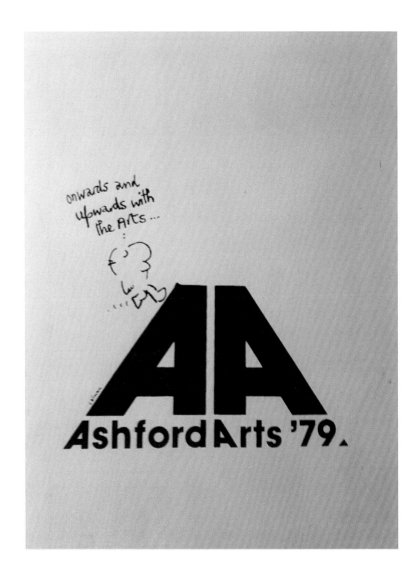

Poster commissioned for the Ashford Arts Festival by Calman

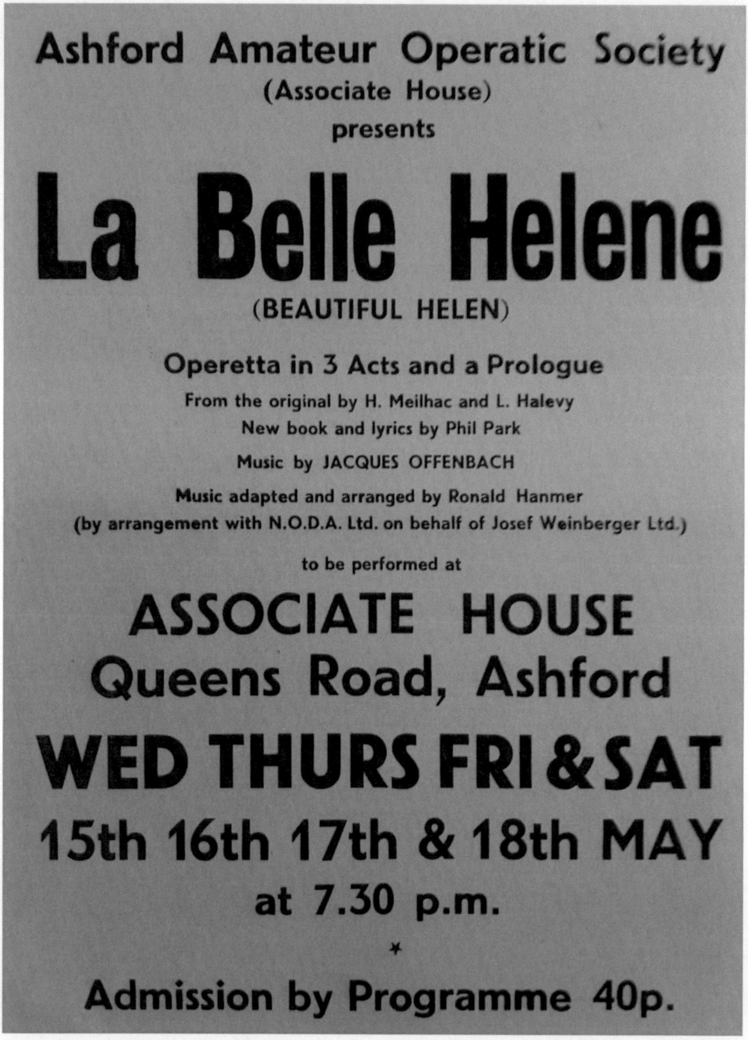

Poster for the production of La Belle Helene *(Offenbach)*

Sandgate Parish Church the man who gave the eulogy made no mention of James' time at Norton Knatchbull. Philip Cox and I were in the congregation and sat there absolutely flabbergasted that this most formative period in his career should be completely ignored. I can only surmise that the speaker was completely contemptuous of state education. In fact, it was ironic that when I took a mixed party to the Soviet Union in 1981 half of them were girls from Ashford School!

I joined the Ashford Operatic Society, based on the adult education centre, Associate House, and became the lead male singer. I played Baldassaré in *The Maid of the Mountains* (Harold Fraser-Simpson), Paris in *La Belle Hélène* (Jacques Offenbach), Danilo in *The Merry Widow* (Franz Lehar) and Barinkay in *The Gypsy Baron* (Johann Strauss II). At Wye College, by special invitation, I played Nanki Poo in their production of *Mikado*. I was asked to sing annually in Kennington Parish Church at their Easter performances, which included singing the Evangelist in their *John Passion* by J S Bach. Through the organist of that church, I was elected Chairman of the Ashford Federation of the Arts when the position became vacant. I had little experience of committee procedure at that stage and none at all of working with local authorities. I was even vague about the difference between elected councillors and salaried officers. So, it was for me a very useful step. The Federation was a bringing-together of existing societies, some of them professional (like the Stour Festival and Kent Opera), but most were amateur, and all dedicated to serving the local community. The Stour Festival was based around Alfred Deller and the Deller Consort, and consisted mainly of performances of Renaissance music. Kent Opera was making a name for itself, frequently using Jonathan Miller as producer and Roger Norrington as musical director. Alfred Deller was undoubtedly the greatest

Kenneth (centre) in the role of Paris in a production of La Belle Hélène (Offenbach) by the Ashford (Kent) Amateur Operatic Society, circa 1975

counter-tenor of the twentieth century, both for the unique quality of his voice and his equally unique manner of singing which went to the heart of the music. I instigated a biennial Arts Festival in Ashford and ran three in all, in each of which pieces of music and art were commissioned. For the first Festival in 1975 the distinguished graphic artist John Ward, who lived in the area, was commissioned to do a sketch of Ashford Market. He produced a racy pen-and-ink drawing which summed up perfectly the bustle of this lively hub of commercial activity. We had a limited number of prints made and sold them. There were some distinguished contributors to the Festival. One of the orchestral groups was the Academy of St Martin-in-the-Fields, and one of the individuals was Jonathan Miller who delivered a talk at The Norton Knatchbull School which had the audience in stitches of laughter, in what was for me the wittiest piece of 'raconteurie' (no doubt *ad lib*) I had ever heard. We also had an exhibition of the famous cartoonist Mel Calman 1931-1996), who used his comic skill to embellish our Ashford Arts logo on our printed programme.

In this sphere I came up against the district and county councils. Ashford built the Stour Centre, but it did not include a decent space for performances. There was a large sports hall which was used for orchestral concerts, and a smaller hall without a proper stage. The Federation received some funds but without enthusiastic commitment to the arts. On the other hand South East Arts, based at Tunbridge Wells had an arts officer who was sympathetic and gave us funds for Festivals. When we proposed that Ashford Mill, which was redundant, should be acquired and turned into an arts centre we applied to the Arts Council in London, with the assistance and presence of Lord Brabourne himself, but we got nowhere.

Kent changed the system of selective education to one of

Guided Parental Choice at the age of thirteen. This meant the first 2 years were taken away from the Norton Knatchbull School and they all had to go to the North Boys' High School first. The school's name was also changed to that of Norton Knatchbull School. Robert had to go through the system, too, and this meant that he never reached the more senior, selective school of this name. Martin, six years older, attended the primary school in Wye and then gained a place at Kent College, Canterbury, which was then a Direct Grant school, with a Methodist background. It later went independent, but Martin retained his place and no fees were ever involved. So, neither of our boys passed through Ashford Grammar/ Norton Knatchbull School. Kent reverted eventually to the old system of transfer at eleven. The county council was Conservative-led.

I was encouraged by Philip Cox to enrol on a Management course at the Mid-Kent College of Technology. I was given time off on Monday afternoons and all my fees were paid. I found the course immensely interesting, and I was fascinated with the theories and history of management and the process of motivating people, both clients and staff. I was with other professions outside teaching, e.g. nursing, which made it even more interesting. It helped me to decide I would try for a headship, so that I could 'run my own show'. I got on very well with Philip Cox – we shared a love of music and a dedication to the Christian faith – but I still wanted to try for the top job in a school. At the same time Dorle's career was developing and she also studied at the same college as me (the Mid-Kent College of Technology). She was much encouraged by the principal of Associate House, Pat Dawkins (as she then was), and got the job of directing the English teaching of Vietnamese Boat People which was based at a redundant hospital, Hothfield, near Ashford. She later became fully trained as an adult education teacher, and she did an in-service management course, too.

1. Professor Henry Higgins, a phonetics expert who fulfilled a bet to transform a common flower seller into an elegant lady. The musical was based on the play of *Pygmalio*n by George Bernard Shaw (1913).

.

WHERE THERE IS NO VISION

THE PEOPLE PERISH

CHAPTER 12

Top of the Ladder

One of my interviews was at Newport Free Grammar School, near Saffron Walden in Essex, an ancient boys' school founded by a woman, Dame Joyce Frankland, in 1588, initially for the sons of the poor, but eventually becoming the selective state school for Bishop's Stortford and Saffron Walden, thus having connections with both Herts and Essex. It had gone comprehensive, but not yet co-educational, when I was interviewed. There were doubts about its continued viability, with a falling intake, and quite naturally with a number of parents and staff who regretted the change of status. I was offered the job and, despite the fear that I might be joining a sinking ship, I accepted it. I believed that my experience at Bishop's Stortford College was in my favour. Dorle was not keen on the move, but I was unhappy at the prospect of remaining 'number two' for the rest of my career, even though I valued the support and friendship of Philip Cox.

Almost immediately after my appointment I received a letter from a future colleague suggesting a radical scheme of an integrated curriculum which I knew would not go down well with existing and potential parents, who desired a more traditional establishment. There was a controversy in the seventies about a London primary school, the William Tyndale School, where the head had misjudged the mood of his clients. This story was used in a speech to Ruskin College,

Etching of Newport Free Grammar school, circa 1900

Oxford, by James Callaghan, the Prime Minster who succeeded Harold Wilson, to show that in educational matters, as in other spheres, we had to be pragmatic. For a Labour MP it was surprisingly un-doctrinaire. This was after the oil crisis which followed the Yom Kippur War in 1973, when the price of oil soared. Callaghan made the important point that education had to be paid for and we ignored this at our peril. I had the same sentiments: it was all very well having marvellous theories, but it was useless if they could not be realised. I ignored the advice of this future colleague. When I was in post he ploughed his left-wing furrow regardless of my opinions. Nevertheless he became a loyal member of staff and a Governor, and in the end we got on fine. His main contribution to educational theory was to encourage, quite rightly, group work in his teaching method.

We bought a modern, architect-designed bungalow in Widdington, three miles from Newport in a country lane called Bishop's End. It was very well appointed: for the first time we had an en-suite bathroom. We had open country behind us, and the lane petered out eventually past a random row of houses into a pebbled path. We shared a drive with the next property of the same design as our own. The village was definitely up-market and housed commuters who worked in the City. We rented an allotment and in this way came into contact with more ordinary village folk. There was a delightful small Anglican Church, linked with St Mary's Newport, and a Congregational chapel which related to the Congregational church in Newport which was later demolished. After our experience of Brook we tried to support the chapel, but discovered it was utterly dead spiritually. We re-joined Saffron Walden Baptist Church. Robert joined the Boys' Brigade Company there, and Dorle and I became heavily involved: she ran the Sunday School –

in those days eighty-strong – and I took on the nominal job
of Director of Music. Our Minister was originally Dennis
Horwood, whom I had met at Luton when I was on the
student mission there, and he was succeeded by Brian Tucker.
We had very good relations with both.

Occasionally I played the organ at the Widdington
Anglican church. Coping with the Anglican style of Psalm
singing, i.e. knowing when to change the chord in a non-
metrical setting, was difficult, but I enjoyed it. What really
delighted me and brought me into contact with village people
was my appointment as Christmas carol choir director. We
had an ad hoc collection of singers, of varying ability who
came together once a week. I was able to choose the repertoire
and we sang some ambitious carols. We even managed the
Pearsall setting of *In Dulci Jubilo* using a quartet as the semi-
chorus. Our neighbour opposite, Alison Cinque[1],a primary
teacher and very able musician, with whom we formed a close
friendship, was indispensable to the group. The Vicar of
Newport was Scott Sanderson, a down-to-earth, outgoing
evangelical who was once a pig farmer. He was a breath of
fresh air at Newport and Widdington. He took our Friday
assemblies at the school and was unafraid to deliver an honest
Christian message. He related very well to the pupils: he was
an ordinary bloke with a frank, open style. He was also an
enthusiastic sailor.

One of the great joys which I experienced throughout my
headship at Newport and our residence at Widdington was
that of walking. I covered the three miles into Newport every
day, in every season at all times of the year, on foot. I would
set off very early, about six-thirty, in the morning and return,
often in the dark, at night. If people in cars stopped to offer
me a lift, I refused. The aim was mainly to keep fit, but it also
opened up for me the great pleasure of enjoying the solitary

atmosphere of the countryside and the routine of putting one foot in front of another, never quite knowing what was round the corner. There were hazards: at one stage I fell down; at another I was chased by angry geese, and at another I threw myself onto the grass bank to avoid being knocked over by a car. These twice-daily walks were my private space, of which I was familiar with every step, every feature and every garden gate. I loved it. Latterly, when we had a rather idle young caretaker with a Rottweiler dog, who would not open up the school early enough for my arrival, I had to de-set the alarm, which was linked to a police station, myself. One morning I forgot to do this. The alarm went off and a policeman arrived. The caretaker was making his rounds at this stage with the dog off the leash. The dog bit the policeman, savagely. Quite naturally he complained bitterly. He was, in fact, the father of a former pupil. I decided the dog must go. The caretaker's father was a strong union man: he supported his son when he objected to my decision. The story reached the local press and I was interviewed on television. It became a *cause célèbre*. I stuck to my guns, however, and the Rottweiler departed. The caretaker maintained that the dog was gentle, but I was having none of it: its presence was too big a hazard for the pupils. Because of the media–generated controversy, I was interviewed by the local ITV channel. I even had to do the customary walk before the interview to prove that I was actually a living person!

One of the extra-curricular activities I started soon after I was appointed was a Sailing Club. There was a solid core of boys who were keen on the sport. Fortunately Essex County Council was very well organised for this sport. They had sailing centres in various parts of the county where there were boats and a warden to supervise. I used to take a group on Fridays after school to the centre at Nazeing, based on a former gravel pit. I would drive the school's old 43-seater coach, on which I had passed a county test. I just revelled in the role of bus-driver. I did not have a seat belt, nor did the boys. The steering wheel was almost flat. There was a special technique of taking corners: you had to do it with a wide swing, realising that one false move could easily destroy a row of houses. Every movement and speed was monitored by a disc tachometer which had to be completed for each trip. On the way home I would drop off boys at various points. Robert would come with us and he became a very competent sailor himself. This after-school activity meant that I had a late return home, but I always felt it was worth it.

I also ran sailing courses on the Norfolk Broads, usually in the summer half-term. We would take our own dinghies and hire a cruiser and usually also a large sailing boat from a yard, the most famous of which was at Potter Heigham. I always had other adults present and sometimes our son Martin would come, too. Michael and Pam Craner regularly came, with their son Jonathan, one of the most loyal members of the Sailing Club. I formed a very good relationship with them, which lasts till today[2]. We had some adventures, one of which was on Horsey Broad where there are stakes. I misjudged an approach to one of these on a broad reach, with the boom well out and the 'main'[3] dangling dangerously. The latter caught on a stake and the mast was very nearly dragged down. The yard was magnanimous about the damage: they were probably used to incompetent amateur sailors having such accidents! I was on the Essex Schools Sailing Committee and helped to organise two national school regattas at Brightlingsea. These were based on Colne High School, the local comprehensive. The high-profile head teacher of the school, who was a keen sailor himself, was found dead one morning; this made me realise how stressful the job of headship was, and how seeming success in the role can be very deceptive.

I appointed a very popular Head of Music, Nigel Partridge, and we together hit on the idea of performing musicals, with me as producer and Nigel as musical director. Nigel brought a fresh approach to music, using more relaxed styles, e.g. big band and jazz items, which were popular with the boys. He ran a very active choir. Our first attempt at a musical production was down a more traditional route: *The Pirates of Penzance* by Gilbert and Sullivan. We always used a mixture of staff and pupils in the cast. It was at a time of unrest in the teaching profession and our lead tenor, a member of staff, withdrew. He was probably instructed by his union (the National Union of Teachers), but I do not blame him at all. We found a replacement and the show went on, very successfully. Nigel managed to recruit members of the First Rugby Fifteen as Policemen, and they distinguished themselves in this role. We went on to do *The Boyfriend* (Sandy Wilson), *My Fair Lady* (Lerner & Loewe) and *Godspell* (Stephen Schwartz).

Rehearsals had to be conducted after school and in the lunch hours, so it was a labour of love, but it was all very worthwhile. Each time we formed expert teams, e.g. we found a very gifted choreographer for *The Boyfriend* (essential for twenties-style dancing), and a distinguished graphic designer for *Godspell* who invented a set based on boxes. This was Val Ailes, a parent, with whom I still exchange Christmas cards. Working in teams like this, with pupils (mostly boys but also including girls, who formed a very important part of our Sixth Form), staff, parents and outsiders, was enormously satisfying. At the final concert before my retirement in December 1990, Nigel very generously put on extracts from the musicals I had produced.

Part of the fun was planning the lighting with the stage crew, who were experts in such matters and then collecting it from an agency which supplied amateur productions. We had quite sophisticated sets, sometimes with a gauze, onto which images were projected. My 'signature' gimmick was to use a single girl dancer to illustrate a song, so that there was a visual element to the performance during the actual singing.

I often used to think that I was paid to enjoy myself. Of course the enjoyment came with a price. In schools generally there was much unrest during the eighties. But out of this came a proper contract which laid down the duties of teachers, that included compulsory in-service training, which were called 'Baker Days', as the Secretary for Education during these changes was Kenneth Baker. We had strikes, sometimes called at the last moment. My job was to 'keep the show on the road' and to avoid too much criticism from parents. The tactics often depended on the political stance of the union. I hold no grudge against these staff members whatsoever: they were doing what their unions told them. However, it was reassuring to have some staff who soldiered on loyally, whatever the provocation or expectation. I worked very much on a collaborative basis. I formed a Management Team, based on status (two deputy heads, and heads of Lower, Middle and Upper schools). We discussed everything together, and we did it regularly. For most of my headship I had two wonderful deputies, Richard Priestley and Gordon Scott. I also had a regular Heads of Department meeting and a Pastoral Committee, consisting of Heads of House.

I instituted a weekly staff information sheet and regular letters to parents. The old style of headship was different: the head made the decisions and the staff followed. The deputies were usually long-serving very loyal older staff. For some this was the easier way: it was his responsibility, not theirs. I believed in working from the grassroots upwards where possible. That was consistent with the management course I attended. I completed this in my first year as head and received a Diploma in Management Studies from Anglia Polytechnic University, Cambridge (currently Anglia Ruskin University). One of my most loyal members of staff was Keith Huddlestone, Head of Science, who was also Secretary of the Old Newportonian Society, a post which he still holds. He has remained a firm friend, with his wife Jo, and is my main contact with the school, of which, at the time of writing, he is a Foundation Governor.

We celebrated our twentieth Wedding Anniversary in Budapest. We took Martin and Robert with us, and left them

Silver Wedding 1986: Martin, Kenneth, Dorle, Robert

with Siegfried and Lotte (and Mutti who was visiting) in
Koblenz on the way. We drove to Harwich and left the car
there in a car park before boarding the ferry to The Hook,
from where the rest of the journey was by rail. Our stay in
Budapest was on the Margaret Island on the Donau.

1. Now Alison Knight, after the death, from cancer, of her former
husband, Carmine. They lived opposite us in Bishop's End.
2. We have exchanged Christmas cards since my headship. Sadly
Michael died in 2021 from a brain tumour.
3. These are sailing terms: a 'broad reach' is sailing with the mainsail at a
wide angle, but without the wind directly behind; the 'main' or
'mainsheet' is the rope which extends to the end of the boom and
controls the mainsail. If the 'mainsheet' is dangling, then it is particularly
vulnerable to snagging against a post.

Gonville and Caius College, Cambridge, Newport Quartercentenary Dinner 1988, under the portrait of Dame Joyce Frankland, foundress of Newport Free Grammar School

ES HAT NOCH NIEMAND ETWAS
ORDENTLICHES GELEISTET,
DER NICHT ETWAS AUSSERORDENTLICHES
LEISTEN WOLLTE

No one has ever achieved anything ordinary, who did not
want to achieve something extraordinary.

Marie von Ebner-Eschenbach:

EIN GUTER WITZ REIST INCOGNITO:
Aphorismen und Sentenzen

CHAPTER 13

Accompanying Pleasures

Although my style was different, I had a great respect for my predecessor, Geoffrey Elcoat. He was a Cambridge linguist, like myself, and he had a French wife. One of his regular Saturday-morning activities was to watch sport. I emulated him and every Saturday would stand on the touchline of various inter-school matches on the wide expanse of sportsfield (which eventually grew to vast proportions). It was here, at a rugby match where his son was playing, that I met a parent who became a great friend, Jim Williams. His son, Justin, was one of my sailors, and Jim himself possessed a sloop which he kept at the Suffolk Marina, at Levington, on the River Orwell near Ipswich. He invited me to crew for him. I spent many happy hours cruising the Essex and Suffolk coasts with Jim, probing even as far as Woodbridge over a very tricky sandbar on the River Deben. I loved this flat coast, with its many creeks, and above all the clang of the starboard buoy bell opposite Devonport on the Orwell. Jim was an architect and he designed the house which we constructed at Ness, Cheshire, in the nineties.

One of the greatest pleasures of my nine years at Newport was to become founder and chairman of the Saffron Walden Twinning Association. I was on the standing committee looking for a partner in Germany. We originally selected Rüdesheim, on the Rhein, a very popular wine-growing town. The Saffron Walden County High School, however, was already linked with a secondary school in Bad Wildungen, a spa town near Kassel in Hessen. We decided it was better to go along with the local school and link with this town, which was unknown to myself, and I was heartily glad we made this decision. It proved to be a felicitous and very suitable match. Both towns were historic and highly picturesque: architecturally both were of great interest. But more than that, the personnel of both became great friends. The fact that I was reasonably fluent in the language and had a German wife was an enormous advantage. We were billeted with Wolfgang and Rosemarie Fischer. He was a teacher at the Gymnasium, with whom Newport formed a loose partnership. We got to know the *Bürgermeister* (Mayor), Albrecht Lückhoff, and his wife Margarete, extremely well and later stayed with them. We

Twinning: carriage transport through Bad Wildungen, Hessen, at the founding of the partnership, Germany, 1986

formed a liaison with the Lutheran *Stadtkirche* (Parish Church) there and also had a strong musical connection. The Uttlesford Orchestra, conducted by George Barker MBE, performed there, and one of the concerts featured Robert playing a Weber Clarinet Concerto.

In its Quartercentenary year Newport commissioned an opera, *The Two Lockets*, from a libretto by Fred Thompson (retired staff and school historian) covering a century of history from the Armada (1588 – the year of Newport's foundation) to William of Orange (1689 – 1702). The composer was Christopher Brown. This became another musical offering to Bad Wildungen. It was a remarkable undertaking, both in its conception by Fred Thompson, weaving a fictional story across one hundred years, spanning the Civil War and ending on a note of optimism with the arrival of William of Orange. Because of the funding, and because part of the Civil War took place in Northamptonshire, we combined with that Authority and the second production was in the theatre of one of their schools: such an ambitious enterprise required wider support. Christopher Brown, a former choral scholar of King's College, Cambridge, had a lyrical, tonal style which was ideal for amateurs. The cast at Newport included staff and pupils.

There was also a very strong Fire Brigade link with Bad Wildungen which, in the German tradition, had a Fire Brigade band. One extraordinary event was the transportation on a low-loader lorry of a steam engine by Stephen Neville, who was Mayor of Saffron Walden at the time. It was a bold idea, typical of the owner, which caused a storm of delight when he drove it round the German town. There were two other special points of interest: Kassel was right on the border with East Germany, and a visit to the border post and a view of 'no-man's-land' was part of the interest of going there; it was also close to the Ederdamm, which was one of the targets of the famous Dambuster raid.

From Widdington we had enjoyable and adventurous holidays. In the summer this included camping in our VW van, by this time a T3, yellow in colour and very different from the previous van, but still with the engine at the back. We also had a free-standing tent. Travelling to the Continent of Europe gave me great pleasure. I loved the process of driving to the port, latterly Dover, on the Norfolk Line (now DFDS) sailing to Dunkerque, but also on the Olau Line (the Isle of Sheppey to Vlissingen, Holland) and the Sally Line from Ramsgate. I relished the act of boarding the ferry and the euphoric feeling of freedom on the other side as we set off to unfamiliar parts and adventures. We also from time to time used the hovercraft, which was an extraordinary, noisy and spray-filled experience. Driving on the right-hand side of the road on the Continent, with Dorle watching the left when we overtook, gave me no problems. The only real hazard was when turning left at a junction and remembering to drive to the far side. We camped in Belgium, several times at Niewpoort on the coast, and at various locations in Germany, both in the *Bundesrepublik* (Federal Germany) and in the GDR (German Democratic Republic), and also at Prague in Czechoslovakia. With my knowledge of Russian, we had a predilection for Soviet Europe, which we visited on various occasions. Perhaps we were drawn by the whiff of danger that the other side of the Curtain embodied.

We also travelled to North Africa for the first time. One year in the eighties we flew to Marrakech in Morocco, landing first at Tangiers. This provided a most refreshing trip as it took place at the February half-term and was an instant change of climate. To hear the birds chirruping joyfully at this time of year, recalling that they could have been the same birds who had been in Britain the previous summer and autumn, and to see so many flowers in bloom, was balm to the soul. We were based in a hotel with a swimming-pool. In the old, walled city the buzzing souks were quite amazing, full of competitive traders enticing wary Westerners to buy what they neither wanted nor needed. We avoided buying a carpet, but nevertheless succumbed to the offer of a *gandoura* – a flowing white garment - to which we added a fez. We had a day trip by coach to the Atlas Mountains. We were besieged with local people on the way trying to sell goods to us, the wealthy visitors from the West. Some of the sellers were children. When we reached the upland parts of the range, it was interesting to note that the ancient buildings of the city settlements seemed actually to grow out of the desert, in an amazing, sandy unity which was quite magical. It was a different world, inhabited by very different and, it seemed, exotic people. It was, in fact, straight out of *The Arabian Nights*.

Robert did some touring on the Continent with the Essex Youth Orchestras, latterly as first clarinet of the senior orchestra. The first tour was in Poland in 1985. We went to Nürnberg in our Austin Metro, as Dorle had crashed our VW van in London, which was a write-off as a result. We drove to Bad Wildungen from there and camped on the edge of the Edersee in a tent. This was prior to the formation of the Twinning partnership between the German town and Saffron Walden. From there I took the train to Warsaw with Robert, so that he could join his orchestra. We stayed in a hotel in the city. We had to cross the border between the *Bundesrepublik* and the Czech Republic at Hof. At the last station before the border, local people brought us refreshments, as there were none on the other side of the border, and the whole train was rigorously searched, using dogs, as we entered the Soviet world. It was, as expected, a completely different world – a world of suspicion and hatred, like a prison.

The following year we had a holiday in a less traditional spot, in fact in a town which was created for the tourist industry, near Sousse, Tunisia. It was called Port el Kantaoui. This was during the Easter break. The highlight of this second venture into North Africa was a minibus trip with a guide to parts of this very historical country, which included travel in a train on a line which was created to serve mines. We saw Roman remains (an arena, a colosseum and temples) and an ancient Christian baptistry, which indicated that the early Church dipped their converts fully in water. We drove South as far as the edge of the Sahara Desert. We stayed overnight in a genuine desert hotel and had a camel ride early the next morning, which demonstrated to us how extremely uncomfortable camel-riding is! We also visited a primary school on this trip. Our guide was charming, teasing and jovial and had an idiosyncratic way of pronouncing 'Tunisssia'. Another experience which was both mysterious and exciting was our attendance at a Christian service on Easter Day at Sousse. We had asked our hotel waitress about Christian churches in Sousse the night before at dinner. She was uncertain but suggested we take a taxi and ask to be taken to a church. There was a certain risk in our request in this very Muslim country. However, the taxi driver took us to the centre of the town and left us there. There was a man in a brown suit standing there when we emerged from the taxi. He said simply, without our saying what we were looking for, 'Follow me!' We did so obediently. He led us up a flight of stairs to an upper room, where there were about thirty people, many of them sitting on the floor. We enjoyed a glorious, inspiring Easter service there, with a warm welcome. For us, this was the 'underground church' meeting in secret and worshipping counter-culturally on this most important and triumphant day in the Christian calendar. We were delighted to be there. What the authorities did not know, or refused to recognise, was that there was a longer history of Christianity in Tunisia, than of Islam.

In the summer of my retirement in 1990, Dorle and I decided to tackle the very demanding walk of 168 miles along Offa's Dyke, which was constructed in the eighth century by King Offa of Mercia. It started (on the North to South route) at Prestatyn on the North Wales coast and ended at Chepstow on the River Severn estuary. We decided to do it with our motor caravan and our car, by sections. We were walking from North to South but discovered that the most economical way to do it was to drive to the Southern-most point of each section and walk South to North. On the first night we stayed at a bed-and-breakfast guesthouse recommended in our guidebook, but after this we camped in our van. We had a fortnight free and resolved to do just half the walk in the first year, as far as Knighton, in Powys, Wales, and the rest in 1991. The first section (North-South) was tough, as the route climbed sharply towards the Clwyd Hills from Prestatyn. It led via Moel Fammau.[1] However, the views were spectacular, particularly looking back. Our guidebook, in two volumes, was very detailed and contained Ordnance Survey maps. As a whole the route was very varied and had some interesting and beautiful features. What was constant were the stiles, over which we had to climb, and the sheep, who invariably shied away when we tried to get friendly. The Dyke was usually quite well defined, but at times rather vague: nevertheless, our guide kept us on the right path. We soon came to Llangollen, famous for its international Festival, and we walked along the dizzily-high aqueduct. We were very much on the border between England and Wales, called The Marches, and a lot of the Dyke went through Shropshire, a most picturesque county, which includes the Long Mynd. Many of its place names appear in the collection of bitter-sweet poems called *A Shropshire Lad*, e.g. Wenlock Edge, Bredon and Clun, by A E Houseman (1859-1936). Knighton was the highest point of the walk.

In 1991 we did the Southern half of Offa's Dyke. This again took about a fortnight. We used the same system as the year before, with our motorhome and a car, walking from South to North in each section, except towards the end. We crossed the Black Mountains, from Pandy, where we stayed the night and left the car. At one stage here we were going in the wrong direction and we had to double-back. This was the longest stretch on our Offa's Dyke walk (in both years): as these were mountains we just had to keep going till we reached Hay Bluff and took the long downward path, with some relief, to Hay-on-Wye. We followed the River Wye, where we experienced our first spell of rain. We passed Tintern Abbey, a Cistercian skeletal ruin (founded in 1131) shrouded in eerie, misty mystery on the winding river. This led us to the town of Monmouth, with its remarkable, distinctive gatehouse bridge over the River Monnow, dating back to the thirteenth century, which had served as a guardhouse, a watchtower and a prison. The walk led through the town, without a waymarked route. We continued to follow the Wye for another fifteen or so miles as it flowed Southwards towards the Severn and the town of Chepstow, beyond which there were the limestone Sedbury Cliffs which marked the end of the Offa's Dyke Path. Here we parked the car and continued walking Southwards. There was a great temptation not to do the last few steps, but I insisted that we complete the whole of the walk. It was a great moment when we finally reached the mudflats of the Severn and could see the famous bridge designed by Sir Gilbert Roberts and opened in 1966. We might have taken two years and done it in short sections, but we had covered all one hundred and sixty-eight miles. What an achievement!

Other pleasures, connected with the schools where I served, were the organised trips to France and Germany. My appetite was whetted by the tours which Moreton Black ran from Glasgow Academy. I remember a memorable one - with Marion, Moreton's wife - to Königsberg, on the Rhein, when we stayed at a hotel near the *Drachenfels* (Dragon Rock). Such trips were a beneficial way of getting to know the countries and also using the language. It was also a good opportunity of interacting with the pupils outside the classroom. In the case of the Soviet Union it was also, for me at least, the only way of visiting Russia (as recorded elsewhere in this book).

On several occasions I combined a visit to the Loire Valley with a trip to Paris. I was fascinated with the history and architecture of the châteaux along the Loire. I prepared notes on architectural features of these remarkable buildings along this meandering, sauntering river which was so different from the Rhein and so eloquent of the civilisation of the time they were built: Renaissance, Baroque, Rococo, and Classical. My favourite was the 16th-century Azay-le-Rideau, 'floating' elegantly and delicately on a moat, and my most interesting, Blois, blending - successfully - several styles. The most exotic, with a whole 'wedding cake' settlement on its roof terrace, was undoubtedly Chambord. What an extravagance! These magnificent castles are unique. They are immensely elegant, rather than defensive. They speak of culture rather than military might – although the two may have been synonymous at the time they were built. We normally stayed in Tours in this part of our two-resort journeys. Usually at this time of year, Spring, the weather was warm in the Loire Valley, whereas in Paris it was misty and cool: we had moved from early Summer to late Winter. We were mostly allocated to a two-star hotel. The boys could sometimes be boisterous. In one room in Paris they were throwing pillows at each other with the window open: the potential target of one pillow ducked and the 'missile' flew out of the window into the street below. The hotel staff were, understandably, 'unamused'! The pillow was retrieved and returned to its right 'home' and the incident was not repeated. Perhaps dealing with such miscreant behaviour was the price accompanying staff had to pay for getting a free ticket to such places!

Sometimes Mutti, Dorle's mother, would accompany us, and on another occasion Dorle and I took an infant Robert with us. There were other amusing moments, too. One young lad wanted to express his reaction to something by saying the equivalent of 'Never mind', using his dictionary. He looked up 'never' and 'mind', and came out with 'Jamais esprit', which is, of course, complete nonsense! On one of our trips to Paris we were staying at a hotel in Montmartre. As I was feeling unwell one evening, Dorle was delegated to take the boys for a walk. Being in the 'red light district' she had to shepherd them very skilfully past the tempting attentions of prostitutes, male and female, plying their trade! She returned without losing a single pupil!

I much enjoyed organising such trips and did not consider them a burden. We used a school travel company, who would do all the booking of transport and accommodation, but I had the responsibility of gathering the participants, collecting the fees, and making all the preparations. We took more risks in those days than would be allowed today, and the term 'risk assessment' was not part of our overt vocabulary, even though it may have been in the back of our minds. Each trip was an adventure and perhaps this was part of its fascination.

Other pleasures were our own holidays both in the UK and abroad. We bought a VW T2 van when we lived in Kent and made many camping journeys. With an engine at the back, air-cooled, and an enigmatic gear change, it was difficult to control. It was converted by the Reading company of Holdsworth. In the UK we did a lot of camping, using a frame tent to accommodate Martin and Robert. One of these trips was to Cofton Country Park in Devon, which in those days was a farm extension. This was next to Cofton St Mary's Church. Little did we realise then that one day we would be members of this church and Dorle would be Church Warden. With the boys safely housed in the tent, near the hedge, Dorle and I spent the night parked on a more open stretch of the site, but by the morning we were firmly stuck in the mud and could not move. The farmer, George Jeffrey, hauled us out of the mud with his tractor. This was a foretaste of what was to come, both in our relationship with the Jeffreys but also in our use of Cofton Country Park in later years. On this occasion we used this site as a staging-post to visit my aunt Enid in Torquay.

In the mid-eighties I took our T3 van to Ramsgate and caught the Sally Line ferry to Dunkerque - Dorle was not with me as she was working, having only recently taken up the job, and could not get away. I spent the rest of the night there and then drove to Boulogne. Here I met up with Robert who had arrived by coach with the Essex Youth Orchestra: they had been performing in Venice. I had my Topper sailing boat on the roof rack, and Robert and I planned to drive South to the Côte d'Azur and to sail as and when the opportunity arose. The aim also was to immerse Robert in the French language before his French A Level year at Newport. He was also doing

Exmouth Dock with Chaika (Seagull) at our mooring

German and Music A Levels. We drove to Paris, where we encountered bridges on the Boulevard Périphérique. It was essential to remember that we had a boat on the roof rack!

We drove south to La Chapelle-d'Angillon, the birthplace village of Henri Alain-Fournier, author of *Le Grand Meaulnes*. Alain-Fournier died, as a lieutenant in the French Army in 1914. His novel, describing a fantasy, is an important work in French literature and is often chosen as a set book for students of the language. His parents were primary schoolteachers and we visited the classroom where he studied. As we drove South it became warmer, until the heat was palpable, as if it were straight from the Sahara. We stopped at the Ètang de Berre, a seawater lagoon about 25 km from Marseille on the edge of the Camargue. We lowered the Topper, and Robert had a sail here. We went as far as Cassis, which I had discovered in 1958 with my German colleague Jost, when we were at the Èmile Loubet Lycée in Valance, and Robert had another sail there in a *calanque* (deep narrow inlet, equivalent to a Norwegian fjord). We eventually made our way north again via the Camargue and returned to the UK.

1. The ruins of Jubilee Tower, built originally in 1810 to commemorate the Golden Jubilee of George III, but blown down by the wind in 1882, at The top of the highest hill in the Clwyd range on the Offa's Dyke route.

LEARNING IS THE ONLY THING THE MIND

· NEVER EXHAUSTS,

NEVER FEARS

AND NEVER REGRETS.

Leonardo da Vinci

CHAPTER 14

Twilight Career

As my career drew to a close, Dorle, who had risen to the position of Education and Development Officer of the Women's Institute, with an office in Victoria, London, felt the need to move on. Her specialism was voluntary adult education. She was offered the job of District Secretary (i.e. Chief Executive Officer) of the Workers' Educational Association (WEA) in the District of Merseyside, based on Liverpool. This included parts of Cheshire, Lancashire and Cumbria. I encouraged her to take it, even though it meant living apart while I finished at Newport. I retired at the end of the Christmas term 1990. I was 58. I pleaded disability: I had osteoarthritis affecting most of my joints. I had bought in an extra three years on my pension, as my full-time teaching career had got off to a late start. Essex gave me another two years. I was given a lump sum. And so, although I was a few years short of a full pension, I welcomed retirement. I felt it was right for someone else to be at the helm at the school, and in this case it was my first deputy, Richard Priestley, who took over. For me, it was the opening of a door to some exciting adventures and, in fact, to a 'twilight career'.

The first thing Dorle and I did together was to fly to Australia to visit Vine and Stuart, and, on the way home, Martin in Hong Kong. This was our first experience of a long-haul flight. It was a Boeing 340 'jumbo' jet. For the first time we could watch our progress eastwards across Europe, over

Middle Asia to the Far East. We stopped for a couple of hours at Singapore Airport and then flew on to Sydney; from there we caught a connecting flight to Melbourne, where we were met by Vine and Stuart, who lived in North Caulfield, south of the city, with their adopted daughter Rachel. They also had a holiday property at McCrae on the coast. Martin joined us from Hong Kong for Christmas. It was incredibly hot, up to 41 degrees celsius. We could hardly venture out. We had a most interesting time, meeting up with their friends, of which there were many. We visited a vineyard, spent a night or two in a lodge at Wilson's Prom, the most southerly tip of mainland Australia, and visited Melbourne and Sydney, where we stayed with the parents of an exchange teacher who spent a year at Newport under my headship, Howard Grant.

When we left Australia we flew to Hong Kong, gliding through the high-rise blocks before landing, as was done in the days before the new airport was built. By now it was January, and Hong Kong was misty and cold. We stayed at Martin's flat in the New Territories and visited his school in that area. We found Hong Kong frenetic, in the sheer number of people moving around and living in very high residential blocks. We also took the ferry out to Lantau island, which was a lot calmer than the centre of the colony. We were given better seats, on the upper deck, for the flight home to Manchester. It was a long haul, and therefore the improved legroom was welcome.

And so, for me a new life opened up in a place which was totally unknown. Dorle had a first-floor flat in Liverpool's old docklands area, in Wapping Dock, a former warehouse. The Albert Dock, at the centre, had been renovated, and enclosed a branch of the Tate Gallery, as well as shops, cafés, restaurants, and the HQ of Grenada Television News: in fact, it had become a tourist centre. Dorle's office was at the old

Bluecoat Hospital, nearer the city centre, which earlier became a school and was currently an arts centre. It was a historic building of great beauty and reputation. She could walk there from Wapping Dock. She bought a semi-detached house in Little Neston, on the Wirral, and that became our next home, right on the edge of a huge estuary which was marsh for most of the time. It was built over coal mines which stretched under the estuary. The house was very cramped but it was a second home, because the Widdington property remained unsold. From Little Neston we could drive via the Mersey Tunnel to Liverpool, or take the ferry. With a change, we could even take the train.

I had a great deal of free time ahead of me, and I thought the best way of filling it was to study again. However, before that, I wanted to fulfil another ambition and that was the ownership of a sailing boat. I bought a part-completed four-berth glass-fibre sloop from a manufacturer in Essex, a Hunter 23. The next problem was to find a boatyard where I could complete it. There was such a yard at Heswell, further up the Wirral, very dependent on the tide: the Dee estuary dries out almost completely, and launching a boat from the yard was extremely hazardous. The owner of the yard was very welcoming, and he gave me a 'berth' where I could place the boat and work on it. I had to complete interior wooden panels and generally install fittings. Very fortunately there was a man at the yard who was willing to stick the inner lining, a sort of carpeting, onto the inside of the cabin. I gave him a fee. A sink had to be fitted, and a cooker, fuelled by a canister. There was a well in front of the transom into which an outboard motor could be inserted. I bought a second-hand Mariner outboard, which proved to be very unreliable.

When it was completed, the boat was launched into a channel, which was severely starved of water and I invited a

few friends along to share the occasion. I named the boat
Chaika (the Russian for 'Seagull') which is the title of one of
Chekhov's plays. The next problem was getting the vessel to
the main river, the Dee, and then to a mooring point. I
decided to join the same Club as John, the yard owner, at Red
Wharf Bay, Anglesey. I gathered a crew together: my friend
Alan Leach, a trained mariner, Pat Banfill, an experienced
dinghy sailor, and her daughter Jenny. To use the best of the
tide we had to set out very early - it was still dark. Under
Alan's wise guidance we found our way to the Irish Sea, past
Colwyn Bay and the Great Orme headland at Llandudno, to
deeper water and to the choppy seas of the Menai Straits. We
tried to start the motor, but it just would not fire. Taking up a
mooring in tidal waters is extremely difficult, so the only
thing to do was to use our sailing skills and tack into Red
Wharf Bay and take up any mooring we could find. In the end
we attached ourselves to a free buoy which was not ours. The
owner, who was not present, later expressed his anger and
dumped our boat on a beach. Fortunately with twin keels it
remained upright, and Robert and I were able to rescue it and
attach it to another buoy, this time with the knowledge and
agreement of the Club.

At such a long distance from home it was difficult to have
much sailing. However, I came up with the idea of sharing
ownership with Alan Leach, whose parents lived in Exmouth,
Devon, and we transferred it to a creek just behind their
home. At a high spring tide[1] we took it out of its winter
quarters and moored it in Exmouth Dock. At first, getting
onto the boat down a sheer iron ladder, and then hauling it in
on a rope to get onboard, was hazardous but later pontoons
and walkways were floated and the approach was much easier.
In fact the whole Dock was redeveloped with flats, a chandler,
a restaurant and other facilities, making it a highly desirable

place to live or have a holiday apartment. The buildings attached to the original commercial purpose of the Dock disappeared. Even the entrance bridge was transformed. One thing, however, did not change: the sailors' and fishermen's café remained the same, just like its clientèle. This is where Alan and I would sometimes have a 'full English breakfast'! I was never very adventurous on my sailing trips and would confine myself, often with Martin and Robert onboard, to coastal waters, usually no further than Torbay. The channel was narrow and very shallow in places, and making one's way through the starboard (green) and port (red) buoys was a delicate business. If you went aground you had to wait four hours for the tide to float you again. The channel up the Exe Estuary was a lot worse. Despite these and potential hazards, we had some very enjoyable sailing on *Chaika*, but I have to admit I always felt safest when Alan was on board.

Having achieved my first retirement ambition I went on to my second: study. I enrolled at Liverpool University, originally to do an MPhil. A member of the education staff, Ray Derricott, was on Dorle's management committee, so there was a connection with the Continuing Education aspect of the University. I already had a personal link, in that my Uncle Leslie and his wife Ethel (my Aunt Ethel) were graduates of this University. I was delighted to be accepted, and I also felt youthfully liberated at being a student again. I chose as my topic (for the MPhil) *Corporate Identity in State Secondary Schools in England and Wales.* It was a topic which incorporated several of my interests: management, marketing, design, history, psychology, and colour. It was original: there was very little literature on the specific topic. There was, however, some literature which related to universities, as they were in more direct competition with each other. The competition in the state sector of school education came about overtly because the Thatcher government had abolished strict catchment areas, thereby encouraging parents to 'shop around' and compare. Selection had been abolished in many areas, and comprehensive schools, of equal status, been established. We at Newport had experienced the effects of competition: from being the school of first choice, as a selective school, we now had powerful rivals in our surrounding towns, Bishop's Stortford, Saffron Walden, Dunmow, Sawbridgeworth, Harlow, etc. We had to market ourselves more aggressively. A single descriptive sheet of information no longer sufficed. One of the first things I did when I took over was to change the font of the name of the School for official stationery. We had to upgrade our image and make sure that we projected it well. For the first time at Newport we devised a collage of photos depicting activities and aspects of the School, put these together in a folder, with the help of a graphic designer parent, and inserted sheets giving details. It was an overt marketing tool which raised the eyebrows of some of my headteacher colleagues in the area.

Early in 1989, when I was still at Newport, I received in my postbag a publication from BP, with which the School had an industrial link through their office in Harlow, entitled *An Image for the 90s*. It was here that I first became properly aware of the process of corporate identity creation[2]. It was at this time, too, that I learnt the name of Wally Olins, the chairman and co-founder of the design agency Wolff Olins, and the author of the book which became the starting-point of my University study, *Corporate Identity* (Thames and Hudson, 1989). In that year, also, I completed a Diploma in Management Studies. The BP publication prompted me to write an assignment on the subject of image. When I came to choose the subject of my Diploma project (short dissertation), I decided on the marketing of my school, in which, as already stated, the question of image also arose. Apart from price, petrol and diesel fuel sell themselves almost entirely on image, in this case the letters **BP** in a green colour. The company paid a huge sum to have this logo revised. Examples of other iconic logos are McDonalds, Shell, BT and the London Underground (signs, trains and the famous network map). I was fascinated by the whole process of creating an image, based on the culture and/or product of an institution, and seeing what difference it made. This was the basis of my MPhil dissertation.

I was enormously fortunate in having Ray Derricot as my supervisor. He was not an expert in my field, but he was an experienced, inspirational tutor. Every tutorial opened up new areas for me to investigate and provided me with fresh food for thought. They were a dialogue more than a monologue: he was never prescriptive, but merely suggested the direction I should take, and was ready to listen to what I had to contribute. Each session was a delight, both socially and intellectually. As expected, I started with secondary research, examining literature associated with the topic. I spent many hours in the University Library (there was no internet in those days), and bought many books. A visit to a University bookshop was an enormous temptation, to which I succumbed on multiple occasions.

Taking my cue from Wally Olins, who mentioned the strong identity-creation of the NSDAP (*Nationalsozialistische Deutsche Arbeiterpartei*) in Nazi Germany, I included a historical account of German identity in my introduction to the topic. Germany as a complete, federated country existed only from 1871. It was a grouping of German-speaking peoples. There was an attempt to create an identity in the Weimar Republic between the World Wars, but the forces behind it, both to the right and the left, made this very difficult. Under the dictatorship of Hitler and the complete dominance of the NSDAP propaganda department, they were much more successful. My brother-in-law Siegfried Büttner was Vice-President of the *Bundesarchiv* (West German Archives) in Koblenz. I was able to access archives which reinforced the ruthless imposition of an identity, which was symbolised by the highly ritualised party rallies in Nürnberg. This was corporate identity creation on a massive scale, affecting every aspect of community life, sinister though it was. It was reflected in another state system, just as sinister, further East in the Soviet Union.

I then proceeded to primary research, but I started with commercial organisations, whose very existence depended on sales, and graduated towards organisations which relied on public support but did not sell products, i.e. those that bridged the gap. I visited and conducted recorded interviews with product industries (Cabot Carbon, Shell UK and Vauxhall), service industries (Liverpool Airport, Stansted Airport, British Telecom and Air UK), public administration (Liverpool City Council and Warrington-Runcorn Development Corporation), charities (Christian Aid and Church of England), political parties (Liberal Democrats and Labour Party), higher/adult education institutions (LIHE, Liverpool Polytechnic, University College London and Burton Manor College). The choice of institutions was eclectic and depended on distance or personal connection. The interviews were structured and had a previously despatched agenda. The interviewees were remarkably cooperative and seemed to enjoy talking about the issues they encountered every day. They were all dependent on having clients, and they all shared roughly the same problems. They all had to go through a process of marketing: they were all up against competition of some sort. Some were more seasonal;

others survived on day-to-day sales. Every aspect of their image-creation mattered, from waiting-rooms to reception telephone manner. They proved to be a very sound base for my investigation of state schools.

The nub of my project was a survey of Secondary Schools in England and Wales. I had to decide first what size of response would give a valid sample. I also had to decide how to categorise the recipients of the questionnaire. I consulted the relevant literature, and notably Cohen and Manion's *Research Methods in Education* (3rd Edition, Routledge 1989). I decided to limit the survey to State Secondary Schools and to exclude Sixth Form Colleges. I also decided that a third of the category chosen would give me valid statistics. The total Secondary Schools (in England and Wales) were 3,574 units, of which a third would give 1,191. I had to make sure that the recipients would be distributed evenly geographically and that they would be reasonably heterogeneous. The response was encouraging: I got 46.3% returned. I had a few rude replies, which was only to be expected. The questionnaire was in three parts: (a) the identity and profile of the School, (b) its culture or ethos, and (c) its deliberate corporate identity creation. Responses were given in YES/NO boxes. There was space given for comment, and the final question asked whether they would favour a visit from me. The next step was slow and painstaking: I had to 'number-crunch' the data I had received. I used the University's analysis scheme SSPS/PC, and was assisted very generously by a colleague who had done a doctorate previously at the University, Sabah Toma, who came originally from Iraq. He was remunerated but he also gave me great encouragement and confidence. The usefulness of the resulting data was however more in the follow-up. Analysing the responses I chose, which included a willingness to receive a follow-up visit, I went to 41 schools. Just as with my earlier investigation into non-School institutions, the reception I received was invariably warm. The staff I interviewed (and recorded with their permission) seemed only too happy to talk about their schools, including their problems of recruitment.

As the academic year drew to a close, my supervisor suggested that my work was good enough to change to a PhD. I agreed willingly: I was enjoying study as never before. I was given seven years to complete it, but I did it in four, part-time – the first year was full-time. I was given an Honorary Fellowship of the University Education Department and a desk in a shared room. I financed my study by teaching Management courses in the Continuing Education Department. We had a group of researchers like me and we had special training days. I was elected Chairman of the group. We had a most sympathetic Secretary of the Department, Joanna Millward, who was always onhand to help and advise. The careful and economical management of my time was at the centre of my study. Although the ideas were important as well as the actual write-up (which I did without much editing: I let it flow and produced a section for each visit to my supervisor), it was the collection and organisation of the material (both primary and secondary research) which really mattered. Getting the questionnaires out – I was assisted here by the two children, Jenny and George, of our friends Phil and Pat Banfill – the analysis of the responses, the organisation of school visits, and the collation of my historical and theoretical research, were all crucial to the success of the project. I read that most PhD students thought of abandoning the whole project in a fit of suicidal despair at some stage. Such a task is long-term and requires vision, patience and tenacity to reach completion. But the joy of completion is overwhelming, only surpassed by passing the final stage, the *viva voce* (oral test), and the formal graduation, which took place at the Philharmonic Hall, in the presence of Dorle and Mutti. To celebrate my success I climbed up to Moel Fammau in North Wales, which was an invigorating but simple trek, rewarded with superb views at the top. (*cf Appendix Abstract of PhD Thesis*)

I have mentioned our friends Philip and Pat Banfill. Philip was a lecturer in the Liverpool University's Architecture Department, just round the corner from my department, and we formed a friendship which lasts till this day. Pat was a social worker in Liverpool, and as such formed a bond with Dorle. They lived in Ness and attended St Michael's Church, Little Neston, and were members of my choir, when I was organist there. Like me, Phil had thespian tendencies, and we took part in the entertainment at the Harvest Supper organised for the whole Benefice (Neston, Little Neston and Parkgate). Phil and I were part of a dance group and we also did Flanders and Swann songs together.

My other big activity in Liverpool was in the Merseyside branch of the British Institute of Management (of which I am a Fellow under its revised name, the Chartered Management Institute), which with a thousand or so members was the largest in the North West. My involvement was due to the evangelistic enthusiasm of Max Block, who was the Recruitment Secretary. He became a great friend: his other job was as a Financial Advisor, which he pursued with equal zeal. I joined the committee and became Education Secretary. I organised School management days, which were very popular and successful. Eventually I was elected Chairman, a post which was tenable for two years. I started a branch news-sheet and also one for the area. Through the latter I was contacted by an old friend from Russell Park Baptist Church, Bedford, Stephen Crow. He had a very successful career with

KENNETH HALL

Graduation at Liverpool University, 1995

Metal Box and lived in Bury, near Bolton. He noticed my name and recognised my photo as editor and got in touch. A lay preacher, he attended a very lively Anglican church in Bolton, St Peter's, Halliwell. Dorle and I used to go to their evening service from time to time, when we needed a spiritual uplift.

When we settled in Little Neston we decided to support the local church, which called itself a 'community church'. It was located in a new building and had excellent facilities. It was a sister church of St Helen's, Neston and there was a third in the benefice at Parkgate. Dorle had already joined a house group in Neston. The style was definitely High Anglican, putting a strong emphasis on the Eucharist. However, there was an evening praise service which was much more relaxed. Dorle's background was Lutheran, centred on the preaching of the Word rather than the Communion. This caused a certain amount of tension with the clergy, who felt that the worship was incomplete without Communion, which Dorle took rarely. I was invited to become organist at Little Neston, playing an electronic instrument and leading the choir. We were all robed, which for me was a novelty. Suddenly I was told that the Curate would take over the choir. I objected, and was sacked as organist by the Vicar! I stayed with the choir and continued as an ordinary member, under the direction of a friend. Dorle left the church and joined the URC Church in Parkgate, where I was also acting as choirmaster, and where I in fact played as temporary organist for a few weeks. There, I was given a very warm reception. Ironically enough, eventually I was appointed organist and choirmaster of St Helen's, the parent church.

One compensation for the dysfunctional relationship with the Anglicans was the annual Harvest Supper (as mentioned above). This was a chance for thespians like me to

Neston St. Helen's Harvest Supper Entertainment: Andrews Sisters Mime Don't sit under the apple tree with anyone else but me. *Left to right: Jim Wilcock, Kenneth, John Thomson, circa 1992*

perform. It took place in the Parish Hall, which had a stage. Among the acts which I took part in was a mimed trio *Don't Sit Under the Apple Tree*, to the recording by the Andrews Sisters, by three men 'of a certain age' in drag – with suitable hip wobbles and 'feminine' swaggering. As expected, this went down very well! On such social occasions church folk were certainly encouraged to let their hair down. Another compensation was the very well-organised pastoral system, divided into small groups. Dorle had a group, which she served conscientiously, and she remained in touch with them for several years. In fact, one of them, Alan Leach, who became the co-owner of my boat, was encouraged by Dorle to go for ordination. He and his wife Ruth were in her group.

1. A spring tide occurs at a full moon, but there are certain times in the year when the tide is unusually high.

2. Corporate identity arises out of the corporate culture, sometimes referred to as corporate personality, which includes the product, the values, and the rituals of the organisation. At the opposite end of the spectrum is the corporate image which is the view of the organisation from the outside. The aim of marketing is to match the identity (consciously created) with the image.

'I AM THE ALPHA AND THE OMEGA',

SAYS THE LORD GOD,

'WHO IS AND WHO WAS, AND WHO IS TO COME,

THE ALMIGHTY.'

Revelation 1: 8 NIV

CHAPTER 15

Alpha

It was in the mid-nineties that I first heard about the Alpha Course. We visited Bromham Baptist Church, near Bedford, where my father had been Lay Pastor for ten years, and they were doing it there. By this time the church was a substantial building, far removed from the wooden hut we used to visit as children and teenagers. It was, in fact, the second re-build: formerly they had extended the accommodation from the hut, which was well set back, towards the road, but now it was a completely new building, of substantial size. They had a leaflet, which we took away with us, which invited people to take part. Their course started in the January, but they were already advertising the next one, which would follow in May. They used the words: *This might be just what you are looking for!* In terms of evangelism, we echoed these words, particularly as our home church in the Wirral was not inclined towards spreading the Gospel. The course emanated from Holy Trinity Church Brompton, London, and the driving force behind it was Nicky Gumbel, who is now the Vicar there. We tried a pilot initially, in the summer of 1996, involving Anglican churches in Neston, Willaston and Burton and the Neston/Parkgate URC Church. There were four of us doing it. The first official Anglican course was in the autumn of the same year, when fourteen were involved. In the spring of 1997, the URC adopted it, too. Neston Methodist Church also ran their own courses.

When we moved to Kenton, in Devon, we took Alpha

with us. We led eleven courses. We were members of Kenton All Saints and Cofton St Mary's churches. We did a daytime course in the upper room of a pub in Dawlish Warren (which was part of the Cofton Parish) when there were over twenty involved, and later used the church hall at Dawlish Warren for a Senior Alpha (for older people) The smallest number on any course was two. We usually had a launch event, with a speaker and refreshments, and we also made special arrangements for the Holy Spirit Weekend, sometimes at a Christian guesthouse in Teignmouth. We saw lives changed. Some people who were regular churchgoers were unaware of what the Christian faith was about before they did the course. Others were changed by the work of the Holy Spirit. One such was Douglas Brown, a former RAF engineer who was very interested in motor cars: he had a large garage with an Armstrong-Siddeley limousine, on which he was regularly working. He had a Nonconformist church background but he was not a regular churchgoer. He had lost his wife and felt this loss deeply. Opposite him lived a former RAF comrade, Peter Stapleford, who invited him to come to a social event, and this led to an invitation, by Dorle, to join our Alpha. He joined, and his life was completely transformed. He became involved in the running and maintenance of our St Mary's Hall at Dawlish Warren, and was baptised and confirmed into the Anglican church. As a practical member of Cofton St Mary's he became a tremendous asset. Dorle and I personally also benefited enormously from the Alpha sessions. We witnessed the transformation of several others, too. Douglas invited a friend from Exmouth, a dentist, who was initially quite cynical about the faith, but he was transformed by the Holy Spirit and ended up running an Alpha course himself in Exmouth. Before leaving Devon we did Senior Alpha at St Mary's Hall.

Since moving back to Scotland we have done further Alpha courses, one of which was in a café in central Galashiels. We are now (in 2021) on our twenty-eighth course, in all, and are doing it online. The advantage of the online revision of Alpha, that has taken place for this new method of presentation, is that visually and in participation it is more varied.

Alpha is really about answers to questions. The course book written by Nicky Gumbel is called *Questions of Life*. It deals with the ultimate question: 'Why are we here?' It starts with the historical Jesus – not with the existence of God – and poses the question: 'Why did he die?' The course is very practical and deals with Prayer, Bible Reading, Guidance, Healing, Evil, and Telling Others, but its main focus is the Holy Spirit, an aspect of the faith which has traditionally been neglected – probably because it used to be called the Holy Ghost. There are three talks on the Holy Spirit and, as already mentioned, a weekend or, for us, usually a longer session on a Saturday. Essential to the process is a shared meal. This does not have to be anything elaborate. There is, in fact, an Alpha cookbook with simple recipes in it. In our case, when we have done a daytime course we have lunch, with soup and a sweet. Hospitality and fellowship are essential elements in the process of Alpha. The meal is followed by a talk, which for us has nearly always been one given by Nicky Gumbel on video. He is a brilliant speaker, with a charming manner. Personally, even though I know his talks almost by heart, I find them thrilling each time I hear them. He has a keen sense of humour and a joke is normally a feature of every Alpha meeting. However, amusing stories also punctuate his talks. After the talk there is a discussion in small groups, usually prompted by specific questions. The whole session is relaxed and focused on the participants.

Currently we are doing an online course, through Zoom. This enables people to join from their homes, which can be in any part of the UK - or the world, provided the technology allows it. At the moment we have not only local people but also a guest from Grangemouth (Scotland) and a couple from Dawlish, Devon. The online facility has also enabled really excellent training to be delivered from Holy Trinity Brompton. With this new style has come a different method of presentation. People are interviewed in the street, the material is delivered by different speakers, in a variety of locations, and there is usually a testimony from someone whose life has been changed by Alpha. Initially there was scepticism about the online method, but this has been replaced by enthusiasm. Even ministry via Zoom is possible. Formerly Alpha relied very much on long talks – lasting about

Alpha Holy Spirit Day at Thornley House, Teignmouth, 2001

forty minutes – by Nicky Gumbel. We have always enjoyed his presentations and ideas, and we have almost always avoided having a visiting speaker (except on the Holy Spirit Saturday), but the greater variety, particularly the testimonies of people whose lives have been transformed, is better.

What I find so helpful about Alpha are its clarity, its scriptural basis, its relaxed delivery and its humour. In no way is it stuffy or boring. Its honesty, too, is refreshing: there is not a hint of self-righteousness in it. It is about lives being transformed and people being healed, but it recognises our vulnerability. Another great advantage is that it is spread over fifteen sessions and is thus unhurried. There is time for friendships to develop in the process and these friendships are very important. Its target audience is outsiders who have nothing to do with the Church, but it is equally suited to existing Christians who are unsure about their faith and less sure about the need to pass it on to others. In these uncertain days, when there is no generally accepted view of the truth of the Christian faith (as there used to be in the UK), it is more than ever relevant to our society. We shall continue to do Alpha, as long as we are physically able to do so. It is the best method of passing on the Good News we know.

A HOUSE IS MADE OF WALLS AND BEAMS;

A HOME IS BUILT OF LOVE AND DREAMS.

William Arthur Ward, 1921- 1994,
. *author of* Thoughts of a Christian Optimist *(1968)*

CHAPTER 16

The Dream Studio

It was about this time, i.e. when we were living on the Wirral, that we set about creating our own purpose-built home. I was ill in bed one day when I noticed in the local press that there was a plot of land for sale in Ness. It was, in fact, the paddock of a house, with some outbuildings, on the road to Chester. The boundary of the paddock was defined by a stone wall on Well Lane. The attraction was the panoramic view from this towards North Wales, over the very tidal estuary of the River Dee, with a glimpse of the Clywd Hills and Moel Fammau, a peak which lies on Offa's Dyke to which we often trekked when we felt energetic (see Chapter 14). We approached our friend Jim Williams and he agreed to be the architect. Our brief was to create a working space with a large window framing the view and a bungalow section adjoining. What emerged was a highly original house, with a Swiss-style overhanging roof, a sitting/dining- room, small kitchen, two bedrooms and two bathrooms, one en-suite.

Dorle was still working and we could just about afford the very large mortgage. First, we had to open up the entrance to the plot via Well Lane. This involved rebuilding the stone wall and splaying it, for ease of access. The front door to the house was at a lower level, and the stairway leading into the working area was slightly splayed making it wider at the top. There was a raised area just behind the large window, giving an interior viewing spot, and a balcony outside. Inside there was a mezzanine balcony up a spiral staircase. This area could also be used for sleeping if necessary. The back of this balcony looked down into the corridor in the living section, which was broad, encouraging the display of pictures - almost like a picture gallery. We found a builder who was willing to undertake the construction at a reasonable price. However, he built the studio area one brick course too high, so that the design had to be adapted. This was fortunately not disastrous. Dorle and I love modern design and found this an enormously exciting project. We discovered a branch of IKEA at Warrington and were able to purchase suitable furniture to add to our existing sixties-style items which we had bought at Elders' in Glasgow. Jim produced a strong colour scheme which brought out the best in the spaces provided. The outbuildings proved very useful but we could not afford a garage. The garden had to be designed from scratch, and here we were most fortunate in using the services of a student at Ness Gardens, the botanical garden of Liverpool University, nearby. We had a vegetable patch and soft fruit bushes.

We had a garden water supply but no mains water. The owners of the property above us, from whom we bought the plot, would not allow us to take a pipe through their garden, even though the garden supply already existed, and we had no access to water in the lane. This threatened the very existence of the project. However, a friend who owned a nearby access lane allowed us to take a pipe down his lane, and finally the former owners of the paddock agreed to allow a pipe to pass through their land close by their boundary fence – but only after I had threatened to put a telephone line across their sight line. For the front door, at the lower level, Jim designed a small circular window. We commissioned a stained glass window for this space, using a local glass artist. We also commissioned a circular ceramic sign for the front wall with the name of the house on it. We called it, predictably, 'The Studio'.

We were in our dream house, but it was not to last. When Dorle retired after seven years in the job we realised we would have to sell up. With only two bedrooms the accommodation was limited, so we decided to build another bedroom. Jim came up with a beautiful design, on brick stilts, accessible from the mezzanine. It was lit from a delightful oriel window looking forwards, towards the view, and from ceiling lights. It included storage, which was most useful. We put it on the market and found buyers who were Chester opticians.

A small part of their payment was in kind: a month's stay in their holiday apartment in the Algarve, Portugal, and a hefty sum (more than we would normally pay) towards glasses prescribed by the optician. The backlash was the amount of time we had left: we had to move out in three weeks! Very fortunately the URC Manse was empty. We asked if we could rent it and the church agreed. It was a very roomy house, with six bedrooms. This provided plenty of space for storage. We moved within the time limit and settled, happily, in this URC environment. The parish church was just up the road, which suited me fine as I could continue there as organist.

Dorle trained as a counsellor in the last year of her appointment at the WEA and the first year of her retirement. Her job had been enormously stressful, and I was happy to act as a good listener to her frequent recitals of her problems. Liverpool really did live up to its reputation of Trotskyism. I was told by my supervisor that what was depicted in the television drama GBH[1] really happened. There was bullying and political manoeuvring of the worst kind going on. The professional teaching staff were the problem for Dorle - she got on very well with the administrative staff. The teaching

The Studio, Well Lane, Ness, South Wirral, 1995

staff did all they could to make life difficult for 'management'. They had to, for it was part of their credo to create mayhem, so that they could take over themselves. They did it on behalf of the people, but they had no intention of letting the people take over in the form of democracy. Dorle and I would often meet after she left the office and chew over her day, sometimes during a meal out. One of our favourite restaurants was a self-service vegetarian establishment underneath the Everyman Theatre. Her retirement was a thankful release, and for her the best employment, albeit only part-time, was yet to come, in Exeter. For me, the same was true, but I do not regret her appointment to a Liverpool office because I was able to study at Liverpool University, and I also had the exhilarating experience of fulfilling the role of Chairman of the Management Institute branch. For some, life has some strange twists and presents some strong challenges! But such challenges are good character-moulders!

1. This referred to *Gross Bodily Harm*, a serial on BBC TV based on stories around Derek Hatton, a Trotskyite Liverpool politician. Leon Trotsky (1879 – 1940) was a Russian politician who believed that socialism should be established right around the world through continuing revolution. He was assassinated in Mexico City on 20 August 1940.

GO WEST. GO WEST. GO WEST.

LIFE IS PEACEFUL THERE.

LOTS OF OPEN AIR.

The Village People, from their album
Go West 1979

CHAPTER 17

Going West

When Dorle officially retired in 1999 we discussed where we wanted to live next. We decided that Exeter was the right place. This made sense because my boat was at Exmouth and I was sailing down there on occasions. We looked at properties in the city but could find nothing that suited us. One day, when I was in Devon to sail my boat, I was in Paris Street in Exeter, near the centre, and I noticed a property in an estate agent's window which was situated in Kenton, a village we had passed through on holiday but with which we were not acquainted. It was a split-level house on a slope with the sitting-room, dining-room and kitchen downstairs and the bedrooms upstairs. The garden sloped away, and beyond a beech hedge at the bottom was a stream. It was quite close, via steps and a footpath, to the centre of the village, which was linked to Powderham Castle, the home of the Earl of Devon. I thought it looked ideal and fortunately Dorle agreed with me. We viewed it and put in an offer and it was accepted.

Quite soon after our arrival in Kenton I joined the group performing a pantomime in the village hall (the Victory Hall) every other year, always during the October half term. Initially I thought I might assist with direction. However, the organiser and director, after an audition, drafted me into the cast of *Cinderella* as Baron Hardup for the 1999 show. I was truly delighted to be on stage, and I made sure that I was available in subsequent alternating years, so that I could take part if asked. When it was decided to do *Snow White and the Seven Dwarfs* I was asked if I would be the Musical Director. I was less happy in this role: my knowledge of the pop repertoire was almost nil and I had virtually no choice in the songs chosen. However, I trained the principals in their songs and also rehearsed the whole company, which was for me familiar ground. Most of the cast playing the dwarfs had to walk on their knees to reach the right height: this was not an elegant sight! In *The Sleeping Beauty* I played the King, and in *Puss In Boots* I played King Rat. In *Jack and the Beanstalk* I was the Giant. With plenty of padding I had to perform a Michael Jackson Song called *Bad* with an accompanying dance. I was accompanied by two teenage girls, whose dancing agility and skill were far in advance of mine and far closer to that of Michael Jackson. This number required a lot of rehearsal, some of which I did at St Mary's Hall, with a recording of the music. However, the role which I relished most was that of the Demon in *Jack and the Beanstalk*. I was the earthly agent of the real villain, the Giant, who was, of course, up the beanstalk. I was dressed and all made up in red, and I had horns. I used an ear-splitting, menacing, screaming laugh to evoke the hisses of the audience – which is part of the pantomime routine, of course. I was utterly evil but was given the opportunity to reveal a tender, compassionate side to my character before the end of the story: there was, it seemed, a reason for my wickedness. If I were asked which I prefer to act, a saint or a sinner, I would definitely say the latter. I think most thespians would agree!

And so a new life opened up which had many positive aspects. We liked Exeter as a city very much. It had a glorious cathedral and a series of small, pretty Anglican churches in the centre. It had a city wall. It had a university. Shopping facilities were good and became even more so when the

Princeshay Centre was rebuilt. Both Dorle and I landed part-time, paid jobs. I joined Exeter University and had an Honorary Fellowship at the Education Department, situated at St Luke's College. When they heard that I was a linguist I was roped into the Modern Language Department and appointed as a University Visiting Tutor. This meant that I was assigned to a group of teacher trainees and visited them in their teaching practice schools. I did mostly German, but my main task was to inspect methodology and to make sure that the system was working properly. My brief was pretty wide and I even once observed an Arabic lesson. I was given a series of criteria to check. Each trainee had a Mentor and a Tutor. The Mentor would look after general welfare and the Tutor would be a linguist. I really enjoyed this work: it took me to a wide variety of places, in Somerset, Dorset, Cornwall and Devon, and included such cities and towns as Exeter, Crediton, Plymouth, Poole, Bournemouth, Bideford and Barnstaple. I would often stay overnight. I was provided with a hired car from St Luke's. One of my favourite places was Weymouth, where I visited three schools and was able to link up with Dorle's friends Judith and Colin Kennedy. Most of the schools were comprehensive but there were a few selective schools. I also took part in a scheme whereby a trainee teacher could be appointed direct to a school, without attending the necessary course at St Luke's. The monitoring of this scheme had to be done meticulously as the training was carried out solely by the school itself. On a couple of occasions I visited an independent school and I realised how much better off the pupils were there, in terms of facilities and class sizes, although there was one small school near Bournemouth where it was quite clear that the pupils were academically weak and had been 'dumped ' there by wealthy parents to avoid a state school. I saw different levels of teaching and empathised with the trainees who struggled. I even had one who burst into tears after a difficult lesson. Dorle had a job with the Council for Voluntary Service in central Exeter. She ran workshops for people in the voluntary sector (e.g. running meetings, listening skills). She wrote, with two others, modules for a management course, and she conducted City & Guilds 7307[1] teacher training for adults. She also worked with a mental health group.

Kenton is a village in a dip, with a small green at its centre and a huge parish church, All Saints, close by, perpendicular in style. The church tower dominates the village. We started to worship there but found it too formulaic and dull. We preferred to associate with a very small Anglican church at Cofton, where we had once camped in our Volkswagen T2 motor home at the farm next door. These two churches were part of a benefice of four parishes, which also included Powderham and Starcross. In due course I was appointed organist at All Saints. The organ had two manuals, the lower one, the Grand, having a tracker action. The swell pedal (to set the volume level) was on a spring mechanism, which did not allow the player to maintain a constant volume as it always sprang back to soft. Fortunately we were able to get this replaced with a balanced pedal. The tracker action meant that playing the lower manual was laborious. We had a small choir, with adults and a couple of girl singers. I introduced a book of arrangements of worship songs, *Sing With All My Soul* from which we would sing during the distribution of communion. We also sang special settings of the Psalms, which were different from the traditional Anglican chants. During my tenure of the post I planned the music, and played, for the weddings of two of the Earl of Devon's daughters: although they had their own church at Powderham, All Saints was larger and could accommodate the high number of guests. I was a member of the PCC (Parochial Church Council). Eventually I transferred to Cofton Church and became organist there when the post became available. Dorle was elected Church Warden and we were both on the PCC. We started Alpha courses, as described above.

Cofton Church had a mission Hall at Dawlish Warren. This was a millstone around the neck of the PCC and there were calls to sell it. However, when Dorle proposed that this should happen (even though she wished the Hall to be retained) they rejected her proposal. The local community were consulted and we proceeded to refurbish it, doing a lot of the work ourselves. Eventually Sure Start were looking for a venue for their branch and we offered our Hall. In this way a large grant was obtained from them which completely transformed the hall: a new roof and floor, a boiler and central heating, tarmac for the car park, a small office and a room divider were all provided. The kitchen was updated, too. Through Dorle's stewardship, £120,000 was raised for the refurbishment. It was used by beach missions[2] as a dormitory for the young ladies and for feeding the whole team; Sunday evening services and other meetings were held there; it was an excellent space for social events and it was the venue for a Senior Alpha course. So, because the people running it really cared, a millstone became a distinct asset!

Another important aspect of our life at Kenton was my involvement as a school governor. I joined the governing body of Kenton Primary School, which was housed in an old building near to the church. In order to do this I had to attend a Devon County Council governor training day. When the leader of the Devon Governor Training Unit heard of my experience as a secondary head, and hence governor, she invited me to join her unit. I agreed and took part in many sessions for new governors in different locations. The training

St Mary's Hall, Dawlish Warren, Devon, after renovation

*Kenneth, Vine and Neil at Neil and Rosalie's Golden Wedding,
Hereford, 2007*

menu was already in place and my chief job was to lead a group in further development and discussion. I enjoyed this work immensely and I was paid for it. It included a free lunch and travelling expenses. From this work I was invited to become a governor of a local secondary school and also of a local primary school with a large proportion of Special Needs children in Newton Abbot. I was also appointed Chairman of Governors at Kenton Primary School, which gave me frequent access to the work of the school. I was involved in the appointment of a new Headteacher. The composition of the governing body was according to a national formula, but basically the governors' responsibility was to represent the interests of the clients, i.e. the pupils, their parents and the community. I had some forthright, strong-minded governors and this gave us at times lively debates! However, I do not regret the crucible nature of this situation. It was all worthwhile and in a noble cause, which was the best possible education of the children. I was very happy, too, to serve the local authority, Devon C.C.

1. Certificate in Further Education (Part 1) by City & Guilds based in London
2. We invited UBM (United Beach Missions) to come to Dawlish Warren and obtained official permission from the Council Beach authorities. Their base where they had their meetings and meals was the Hall, and the women slept there using it as a dormitory. The men slept at Dawlish Baptist Church

HE WHO DWELLS

IN THE SHELTER OF THE MOST HIGH

WILL REST IN THE SHADOW OF THE ALMIGHTY.

I WILL SAY OF THE LORD:

'HE IS MY REFUGE AND MY FORTRESS,

MY GOD IN WHOM I TRUST.'

Psalm 91, vs. 1 – 2

CHAPTER 18

Chelsea Bypass

In my teens I had a heart rhythm problem. This came about after extreme exertion when I rowed in a four for my school house, Paulo-Pontine. I got over the problem and it did not impair my National Service. However, in my late midlife I suffered from angina. I could not walk uphill without having chest pains. I referred myself to my GP, and I had an assessment by a very glamorous female surgeon at a Liverpool hospital. She decided that I should not have any surgical intervention at that stage. However, when we lived in Devon my angina worsened. I had an angiogram at the Royal Devon and Exeter Hospital, which revealed that I had a hardening of my heart arteries. I saw another specialist and talked to my GP. We agreed that I would request a bypass operation. I was given a choice of hospital: either Derriford Hospital, Plymouth, or the Royal Brompton Hospital in Chelsea, London. I chose the latter because I knew that Holy Trinity Church, Brompton, provided the chaplaincy. This was the church which ran the Alpha Course. The disadvantage of this decision was the fact that Dorle would have to find accommodation in London while I was in hospital, but I felt the spiritual advantage was paramount. As it turned out, the Royal Brompton was able to offer a room in a nurses' home nearby. We attended a preview session during which we met some of the staff. They were very frank, but optimistic and cheerful. I spoke to the anaesthetist and expressed my fear of being put to sleep. We had a meal there during the day and were informed that the food generally was excellent.

I had the maximum wait for my operation, according to the rules at the time. It was due on 27 August which was just before the Bank Holiday weekend. We were taken to London by taxi, picking up another patient on the way. At the hospital I was installed in a bed next to the window in a six-bed ward. I realised that I was far better-off sharing a ward than being in a private cell. A man arrived who was looking for a bed. It turned out that he was a Christian who had been converted at Spring Harvest. He was also an Alpha leader. He took the bed next to mine and was a source of strength to me. There were other Christians in the ward and, with the permission of the other patients, and with Dorle present, and the wife of my neighbour, we had a prayer meeting in the ward. An older man from Cornwall in one corner had to wear a catheter. He called it 'This bloody cafetière'! We felt sorry for him: he had had a heart attack. On the due date of my operation, Friday 27 August, there was a danger that it might have to be postponed till the following Tuesday, because of the Bank Holiday Monday. The thought of having to spend the weekend at the hospital, with nothing to do, was regrettable. Very fortunately they took me on that afternoon. I had already received a chaplaincy visit from Jamie Haith from Holy Trinity Church. He was a young man who had only been ordained in the previous month. He promised to be on call at any time, day or night. He was a great support to me. He read a psalm and prayed with me. I was given a pre-med tablet and was quite calm when I bade farewell to Dorle on my way to the operating theatre. I mentioned the words of a favourite psalm (in fact, 91) but I was unsure of the number. Dorle went off to the chapel and read through all the psalms in order to find it.

My next memory was waking up in the Intensive Care

Unit. I was being looked after by a woman from the Far East (a Filipina?) who appeared to be under considerable stress. This did not worry me at all: in fact, it probably helped me as I was under stress myself. I was so heavily sedated that I appeared to be rising and falling in the ward, a sensation which continued until I got back to my bed in the original ward. The next few nights were horrendous. On one night I awoke completely drenched in sweat. The angelic night-nurse changed all of my bedding there and then, and this was an enormous relief. On the Sunday Dorle went to a service at Holy Trinity. Jamie Haith brought sermons on tape for me. When we mentioned that I had a player but had run out of batteries, Jamie produced batteries of his own: he was well prepared. One night, I was in grave distress and thought I might be dying. In these circumstances the sermons were a lifesaver. In fact, amidst all this anguish and pain I felt nearer to God than ever before. There is no doubt that Dorle's presence was crucial to my recovery. She gave me practical and spiritual support. She showered me and took me on exercise walks round the corridors of the hospital: she prayed with me. One particular cause for distress was the arrhythmia which I often experienced: the surgeon and I had decided that he would not try to correct this during the operation. One memory sticks indelibly: the noise of aircraft on their approach to Heathrow Airport. They would start early in the morning and continue all day, ceasing only in the late evening and the dead of night. I have the very highest regard for the Royal Brompton Hospital and for the staff, at all levels, who served me.

We were taken back to Kenton by ambulance. The most painful aftermath of the operation was the effect on my left leg, from which they had taken a vein. Rehabilitation was a very slow business. I joined an exercise class at the Westbank

Wemding, Schwaben, Germany: Wallfahrtsbasilika Maria Brünnlein

Health Centre at Exminster, and I enrolled at the leisure centre near St Thomas's Station, Exeter. I was given an exercise programme by a member of staff at the centre. This included a treadmill, rowing-machine, weights, etc. As it was close to the station I could often take the train from Starcross, leaving the car in the station car park. I have continued to exercise in this way, twice a week, and I am certain that this has helped to keep me alive.

I AM CONTENT WITH WHAT I HAVE,

LITTLE IT BE, OR MUCH.

AND, LORD, CONTENTMENT STILL I CRAVE,

BECAUSE THOU SAVEST SUCH.

John Bunyan 1628 - 1688
Pilgrim's Progress

CHAPTER **19**

A Taste of Heaven

Dorle and I decided that it was time for retirement from our professional work, even though it was only part-time. However, there was more to come. We had been members of a group called Senior Volunteer Network for several years. This had started when a woman called Ruth had mentioned the group in one of my management classes at Liverpool University, having ascertained that I was a Christian. She suggested I should join. We both joined, but nothing came of it for a few years. One day in 2008 I noticed there was a request for someone to fill a modern languages post at Hebron School in Ootacamund, Nilgiri Hills, Tamil Nadu, in India. I said to Dorle that I thought the call had come, even though it was not directly from SVN but from the principal, Alastair Reid, who was a friend of the SVN founder, John Hallett. We could share the post: Dorle could do the German, and I could do the French. So we applied and were accepted. We did a day's training in Cheltenham. There were a number of issues: the food and the possibility of 'Delhi belly,' and the height at which we would be living, over 7,000 feet. We would go out as volunteers but the hospitality at the school would be free, although we had to pay our own fare. Here, in Cheltenham, we met a married couple, Tom Pennant and Helen Hughes, for the first time. They were going out, too, as Senior Volunteers. We have remained friends and see one another a few times every year. We obtained visas from the Indian Consulate in London.

We took a British Airways direct flight from Heathrow to Bangalore. As we flew into darkness, I remember feeling very uncertain in the plane about what we had let ourselves in for. It was a comfortable flight, with adequate meals, and we arrived safely. From here we were due to take a taxi to Ootacamund (Ooty, as it was called for short). This would take us through 36 hairpin bends up to our destination. Ooty had a reputation as the summer residence for the state of Madras (now Chennai) government in British colonial days. It was the 'Queen of the Hill Stations', but it had lost much of its attraction and looked decidedly faded when we got there. However, when we reached Mysore, our Tata taxi (which was hired from Ooty and had met us at the airport) broke down. Nothing could restart the car, despite the efforts of the driver. As we sat there waiting, another car drew up and stopped in front of us, and what seemed like an angel appeared at the window and said 'Hello, I am James'. It was James Horlock, a young man who was also heading for Hebron School. He was in a larger car and he had with him his young wife, Alex, and their baby son, Nathaniel. Their driver had recognised our car as coming also from Ooty. He realised we were in trouble and that is why he stopped. Fortunately they had enough room, and a roof rack, to accommodate both of us and our luggage. So we proceeded, and finally arrived at Hebron School in twenty acres of wooded grounds above the Botanical Gardens. The estate was called Lushington Hall, and housed the administration and teaching blocks, the dining-hall and kitchen, boys' boarding houses and other departments, as well as sports facilities. The senior girls' boarding house was situated two kilometres away on another site. The girls were transported every day to Lushington Hall by bus. We were allocated a bedsit, with a small toilet and washbasin. This was by no means luxurious but it was adequate. There was an open fire on which we burned wood. It was constantly damp, and we were glad, later, to receive a heater. Apart from breakfast, all our meals were taken in the dining-hall.

The community was thoroughly Christian: there were regular assemblies, and there was a small chapel. Students (as they called them) were encouraged to attend local churches on Sundays. The principal, Alastair Reid, was the best head I had ever served under. He had a relaxed, open style and involved the staff as much as possible. Staff meetings were one-third worship, one-third prayer in small groups, and one-third discussion. In this way there was a strong atmosphere of unity, even though we had a wide spread of churchmanship amongst the staff, from Roman Catholic to Brethren. I have never belonged to a fellowship as closely bound-together in Christian love as this one. For me no church has come anywhere near this community. We were diverse, but united by the way we lived together, the way we prayed and worshipped together, and the way we related to one another.

Dorle and I were given a work-base a little way down the hill in a subsidiary staffroom. Here we regularly met staff from other departments. The main staffroom, where we had refreshment at breaks and where meetings were held, was in the older building which also housed the administration. On the way, there were small terraces with flowers which strangely outlived the seasons. With a more constant temperature the seasons were less defined. We had a young woman as our head of department, Elly Crofton, with whom we formed a very warm relationship. She stayed at Hebron for three years. Teaching, using dated textbooks, was challenging. My biggest problem was remembering names: I insisted that students sat in alphabetical order to assist my memory. I used an overhead projector frequently. I had Standard (year) 8 and Standard 9 French. I also took Lower Sixth French, which was a harder task, as my language at that level was distinctly rusty. The classes were small (about sixteen) and the students amenable. I had informed the school that I was a choirmaster and I was appointed to take the choir here. I also volunteered to take part in a Riding Lights[1] drama, and this led to my being joint leader of a Standard 7 group which participated in the annual drama competitive festival in October. I was also chosen as one of the judges for this festival at a more senior level.

One of the music staff wanted to give up training the choir at a local girls' school, St Hilda's, on the other side of town, and I agreed to do this. Every Monday a car would arrive to pick me up. After I had been vetted by the headmistress, two senior girls wearing saris would meet me and take me to the hall where the rehearsal took place. As Christmas was not too far away, I taught them a two-part carol by Patrick Hadley (professor of Music, Cambridge), *I sing of a maiden*, and also *From the squalor of a borrowed stable* by Stuart Townend. Their carol service took place in St Stephen's, Church of South India (an amalgamation of the Anglican and Methodist Churches in India), and I ended up conducting the music of the whole service in a crowded church, which was attended by all the girls and some of their parents, with the staff. This was a thrilling occasion. Later on a group from the choir called at our room at Hebron School and sang carols outside our door. This was a generous gesture. The Hebron staff put on an annual show in the main hall. Dorle and I were part of a song-and-dance group which performed *I will follow you* from *Sister Act*. In this case Tom Pennant and I had to dress as monks! In the same programme Mary Fairfield and I performed *I remember it well* from *Gigi*.

We belonged to a Bible study group and would go off in

the darkness of the evening to another flat on the campus. On Sundays we attended The Union Church in the town - a free, evangelical church, where Dorle served for a time on the AV/PA desk. Sometimes we would be asked to pray in small groups where we were sitting: we were amazed at the ease with which young people prayed, prompted by points displayed on the screen.

We made the best of our 5 months' stay in Ooty to explore the area. We were in the middle of tea-growing plantations. Nilgiri tea is mild with a very pleasant aroma. A tea factory was very close to the school campus. Just up the hill behind our estate was a Toda settlement. The Toda tribe were very skilled at embroidery: they would sell their cloths near the Botanical Gardens. We had a week's break at half-term in October. The local train, the Blue Line, from the mainline uphill, which was steam rack-and–pinion as far as Conoor and diesel thereafter, was a tourist attraction. We took this to the mainline railway in order to catch a train to Chennai (Madras). The steam train broke down, and we were stuck for two hours at a very remote station. However we did not miss our connection. We had booked seats in the 2AC (second class air-conditioned) section. It was a train of immense length. It cruised through the countryside at moderate speed. It was comfortable, and we were plied constantly with edible titbits and drinks by enthusiastic sellers. There were bunk-beds for the overnight part of our travel. When we reached Chennai Station we were shocked at the number of people lying on the platforms. Even worse were the multitudes lying on the beach as we proceeded to our holiday destination, a Scripture Union family centre at Mahabalipuram, which was famous for its temples, some of them carved from enormous lumps of natural rock. This tourist spot was about twenty-five miles south of Chennai. The warden was the father of a boy,

Jonty, whom I taught in one of my classes. It was extremely
hot. We took our meals mostly at a nearby vegetarian
restaurant. On the Sunday we had a service led by Jonty's
father who used to be in the Indian navy. Instead of a sermon
he set us a puzzle. Outside he had three podiums, and three
planks which were too short to stretch between the podiums.
The challenge was to cross from one podium to another using
the planks without touching the ground. The solution was
simple although we did not guess it. By interlocking the
planks you could form a bridge which was sturdy enough to
carry a person. He demonstrated the solution, and a girl
student from Hebron, who was one of the guests at the
Centre, stood on the construction, quite securely. The lesson
from this was that the planks represented God, man and
others. We are all interdependent. I have used this illustration
many times since then, often demonstrating it with knives
rather than planks.

After Dorle's birthday (for which I ordered a cake from a
baker in Ooty), we went to a holiday park for a couple of
nights. Here we dined on a very large terrace overlooking the
jungle. A woman sitting near the balustrade suddenly leapt
back and screamed. A monkey had jumped onto her table to
grab some of her food! On another occasion we went to
Jungle Retreat, a holiday park where the wildlife could be
viewed. We stayed in a lodge and had to go to a central
dining-hall for meals. We watched elephants being washed
and cared for, and we went out on a night safari looking for
other wild animals but without success.

As I was taking Warfarin tablets I needed to have blood
tests. These were carried out locally in what seemed to be very
primitive conditions, but I came to no harm. We had a
medical centre, which we called 'Hos' and they arranged for
me to go to a large clinic (in fact; a hospital) at Coimbatore,

south of Ooty and in a less temperate climate zone. We went there by taxi. Gaining an entry permit was a problem but the taxi driver was very helpful. We had to pay a small fee. I saw a heart specialist. He produced a very thorough report and I was most impressed with the attention he gave me. This was not the NHS, but nevertheless, provided you could get an appointment, it was a most efficient system. What was less impressive was the nursing care: the family of a patient admitted to hospital had to care for their feeding and other needs. Dorle also had a consultation, with a lung specialist.

Our contract was for only for a semester, i.e. till Christmas. As there was no obvious successor we were asked if we would stay for a second semester, till June. However, in those damp conditions Dorle was suffering badly with her asthma, and we had to decline. We stayed over Christmas, and we had a short holiday before leaving India. Our son Martin, Caroline, Oliver and Emma joined us for this period and stayed in an apartment on the campus. We celebrated Christmas at Selborne, the boarding-house for senior girls. We had traditional British and Indian Christmas fare. After this we had a short family holiday at Kovalum. Martin's firm had an office at Trivandrum nearby. However, Dorle and I stopped at Cochin for a few days on the way. We went for a day trip on the Backwaters (almost reminiscent of the Norfolk Broads) on a traditional boat. This was a very peaceful experience. At Kovalum, a fairly busy holiday resort, there was a woman selling fruit on the beach. We failed to respect the taboo that eating fruit, when you were unsure of the water which had been used to wash it, is fatal. That evening in our hotel we suffered the devastating effects of eating that fruit – at both ends! It was 'Delhi belly' with a vengeance! We were due to fly the following day, and we thought we might not get away at all. However, we flew from Trivandrum to Bangalore,

Dorothea and Kenneth at Selbourne, Hebron School, Ootacamund, Tamil Nadu, South India, Christmas 2008

where we had a night in the hotel we had used earlier, before returning to Heathrow. On the return journey we were offered an upgrade to Business Class, with food to match, which was sheer luxury.

Our time in India was an utterly amazing adventure in the twilight of our careers (*cf* Appendix *A Day in the life of Senior Volunteers*). At the farewell party for leavers at Hebron Elly Crofton produced a poem about us called *The Golden Pair*. It was unjustly flattering but sums up our experience wittily well. Here it is:

> This is the story of the Golden Pair,
> All the way from Devonshire,
> The story of two servant hearts,
> And this is how I think it starts.....
>
> It came upon a midnight clear
> The glorious but mad idea
> To Kenneth and to Dorothea
> To stick retirement and come out 'ere.
>
> The Golden Pair,
> The Golden Pair,
> Did we entertain angels unaware?
>
> So all the peace of England fine
> They left for BA flight 119
> And headed to the Nilg'ri Hills
> To serve the Lord with multiplc skills.
>
> They rescued one Department there,
> With experience and energy and lots of prayer,
> And when A2 marking at last was done,
> They'd look for ways of having fun.

KENNETH HALL

The Golden Pair,
The Golden Pair,
Did we entertain angels unaware?

Now Dr. Hall was quite an actor
And this is an important factor.
From day one he's been on stage –
Fur-clad, robed (without a wage).

He's also known for socks and ties,
And having his fingers in lots of pies –
Hebron choir, St Hilda's too,
Barber shop, Sister Act, to name but a few!

The Golden Pair,
The Golden Pair,
Did we entertain angels unaware?

And Dorothea's not outdone,
With easy worship and board game fun,
Assemblies and recorder teaching,
Her legacy is quite far-reaching!

A calm support through busy days,
No matter Mrs. Hall would faze:
With grace and kindness she would meet
All problems with a word quite sweet.

The Golden Pair,
The Golden Pair,
Did we entertain angels unaware?

Now Hebron life was not all easy,
At times these angels felt quite queasy!
But optimism saw them through
Damp flats, insomnia and prep time, too!

The tarmac-mixers[2] did appal,
But they had free History lessons through the wall!
And, for all the bits they found uncouth,
They surely have the secret of eternal youth!

The Golden Pair,
The Golden Pair,
Did we entertain angels unaware?

So, Dr. and Mrs. Hall from Devon,
We think, perhaps, you came from Heaven,
To develop the students' linguistic notions
And to cause us laughs in Staff Devotions.

We'll miss your faith, your breezy air,
Your readiness to share, share, share,
So we wish you well and all God's speed,
And THANK YOU for your great good deed.

The Golden Pair,
The Golden Pair,
We entertained angels unaware!

In 2009 we returned to India and did a project, this time
on behalf of SVN, in another Christian school. We went with
John Hallett, the founder of SVN, so we were a team of three.
Samaritan School was situated in the Yellagiri Hills near the
town of Vellore, which lies seventy miles west of Chennai. The

project lasted a fortnight, but we decided to spend a month in India. We first went back to Hebron School, offering our services wherever we could be used. We stayed in the town. We were given the task of teaching music for a week, which we thoroughly enjoyed. The night before our departure there was a terrible cyclone. There were landslides in the Nilgiris, and the railway and roads leading out of Ooty were closed. It was reported that forty people were killed in the storm. We thought we were trapped. I was due to take the assembly that morning, but we found a taxi that would take us through some back roads which were not blocked, provided we left very early. So I had to forego the assembly. We were due to catch a train on the main line to Chennai. When we alighted from the train, we were met by representatives from Samaritan School and taken to our living quarters in a modern block close to the Chapel. There were pleasant views from the flat roof. Food was brought to us by a member of staff, a lovely Indian Christian, who lived with his family in another block close by.

Our brief was to help the staff with their English, which was the language used in class, and with their teaching methodology. We observed classes and we ran seminars. It was a failing school which had been visited by SVN before. There was much discontent amongst the teaching staff, because of the conditions under which they served and the poor salaries they received. Rote learning was very much the system used, particularly at the junior end, and structuring a lesson, with some more relaxing elements (e.g. a game) to reinforce a teaching objective, was alien to most of the staff. The campus housed elements (such as an aviary) which were ambitious but unrealistic or incomplete, and indicated that the School was full of ideas but lacking in their execution. We had a delicate task as we did not want to seem too negative.

On Sundays there was a service in the Chapel. I was due to speak on the second Sunday, but my talk depended on carefully prepared visuals on an overhead projector. Unfortunately there was a power cut, so the technology was unavailable, and I had to manage without my visual aids. Funnily enough, the power came back on towards the end of the service!

We were given a lift to Bangalore at the end of our stay, so we did not have to take the train. We stayed a few nights at the same hotel as before (with a rooftop garden terrace restaurant), and used the opportunity to explore the city. I ordered a shirt from a tailor. On Advent Sunday we went to St Mark's Cathedral for their morning service. It was so packed we had to sit outside – fortunately the weather was warm. John Hallett was with us for part of the time: he left for home earlier than ourselves.

Our third overseas project (our second for SVN) was in Bangladesh in 2012. We were seconded to a school in Dhaka, to assist them with the English language and teaching methodology, as at Samaritan School. We went as Christians, but it was a school of Muslim culture, like Bangladesh itself. The school was vast, with over 13,000 pupils spread out in diverse buildings all over Dhaka. The Principal, Colonel Nabi, and senior staff had a military background. It was called Milestone College: it was fee-paying and very successful. It had two sections, Bangla-speaking and English-speaking. We were housed in a new flat, with staff to feed us and care for us. Every night a mosquito net was installed over our bed by the staff. An amusing feature was that, despite the recent construction, the showers didn't work and we had to use 'bucket showers' instead. We were joined by a colleague, Jane Hunt, who had previously been staying with the Principal. We joined in with the life of the school and celebrated their festivals. I laid a wreath on Independence Day: they were very proud of their history and their breakaway from Pakistan (when they were East Pakistan), which was mostly over the Pakistani decision to force the Bangladeshis to use Urdu and not their own language of Bengali (or Bangla, as they called it). They had student martyrs who were honoured every year. I even spoke at an assembly, using material I had prepared for Hebron School but without mentioning the name of Jesus. I quizzed the pupils afterwards and was most impressed with their answers and the level of their attention.

We believe that part of the motivation for Col. Nabi calling on SVN was to promote the tourism of Bangladesh. They were very keen that we should go on a short cruise in the Sunderbans, which is the estuary area of Bangladesh, where the Ganges and the Brahmaputra emerge into the Bay of Bengal. This is the home of the Bengal Tiger. We took a coach to Khulna: this was the most uncomfortable coach journey I have ever experienced. The vehicle was badly sprung and the roads were full of potholes. Added to this, there was no toilet on the coach. We reached the Ganges, which was very wide at that point, and took a ferry across. Fortunately there was a toilet on board! Just getting the coach onto the ferry was a tremendous fight, with vehicles careering all over the place to maintain their place in the queue. When we reached the other side, the coach took us to Khulna, a fishing port with a strong shrimp industry. Here we boarded a river-cruising ship with about twenty-four cabins on two levels. To get over to the ship you had to take your luggage onto an open boat with no seats and then climb aboard. It was an extremely hazardous operation! We were given a two-berth cabin on the upper deck. It was very basic and did not have en-suite facilities. Washing had to be done at a basin publicly, and if you needed a shower you had to collect the hot water from the engine-room and take it to a shower cubicle, which was fortunately private! Meals were taken corporately in the dining-hall. At one stage we took a smaller boat and went ashore. We walked through the jungle looking for tigers. Our supervisor carried a gun, which was reassuring! We saw only paw prints of tigers but we knew they were not far away. From our cabin we saw a very large crocodile floating on the edge of the river bank, reminding us of another danger. The return journey was more comfortable, although the potholes remained, as we were able to sit at the front of the coach. However, when we approached Dhaka the road was so packed with vehicles, some bearing passengers just hanging onto the outside, that our progress was extremely slow. Some people were merely walking, which added to the chaos. Evidently this was the early morning rush into the city to get to work. As a rule, the centre of the city was bad enough – the worst traffic we had seen anywhere in the world – but this early-morning rush was even more frenetic.

Apart from arranging this most interesting trip to an important aspect of Bangladesh, the management of the school were very generous to us. They took us to a Fairtrade shop in the centre of Dhaka called Aarong, which was the smartest shop we encountered anywhere in the capital, and bought us delightful clothes and other objects. Two other visits were of particular significance in this poverty-stricken city. At the 'Sisters of Charity' orphanage in the old city, we felt we were in the presence of Mother Theresa herself as we encountered the familiar, characteristic dress and the same supremely compassionate care of mothers and children by the nuns. A visit to the centre for the Rehabilitation of the Paralysed was equally moving: here the patients were receiving expert medical care, and also training in the use of their very limited faculties. It was the inspiration of the physiotherapist Valerie Taylor, forty-three years earlier. The beauty of the lovingly-cultivated campus contrasted strongly with the polluted chaos of the city outside. As a bonus we had the great privilege of meeting Valerie Taylor herself – a true modern saint.

It was on this latter trip to the old city that we met the Vice Chancellor of Jarhangirnagar University, Professor Shariff Enamul Kabir. Our guide for the day, who generally managed our stay in Dhaka (he was on the staff of Milestone College), was an alumnus of this university and was keen to show it to us, as we passed it on the outskirts of Dhaka. We were taken to see the Professor of English. He insisted that we should be presented to the Vice Chancellor, who broke away from a meeting in his office to meet us. One unscheduled, unexpected visit led to another. Such was the warmth of Bangladeshi hospitality which we encountered everywhere. In this predominantly Muslim, but nevertheless open (in those days, at least), country we were keen to meet up with other Christians. We attended services at a Pentecostal and a Nazarene (Baptist in style) church, where the men were separated from the women and where we were asked to identify ourselves publicly.

We took a five-day holiday, in order to explore the Delhi Golden Triangle (Delhi – Jaipur – Agra) before returning home. We stayed first at a hotel in New Delhi, and from there hired a car and driver to do the tour. The driver, who was a devoted Hindu and came from Himachal Pradesh, in the Himalayan foothills, was really first-class and most accommodating. He gave us a running commentary on the places we passed through. We went first to the Red Fort, commissioned by Shah Jahan in 1639. On the same campus was India's biggest mosque, the Jami Masjid, built of sandstone and marble. This huge fort was immensely impressive: it got its name from its red sandstone walls. We then drove to Jaipur, the most uniform and most tourist-friendly city, all painted pink. A distinctive feature was the observatory behind the City Palace, set up by Jai Singh II, which consisted of huge constructions, which were instruments of cosmic measurements. We also visited the old part which was more like a fortress, the Amber Fort, on a hill overlooking a valley. We moved on to Agra, not nearly as beautiful as Jaipur and, in fact, a disappointingly mundane city. We spent the night in a hotel there and set out early for the Taj Mahal. This gave us the best, cooler, part of the day to see this awe-inspiring, breathtakingly beautiful building, by which India is identified by travel companies in their promotional literature. It is ironical that India is a fiercely Hindu country, and yet it is remembered by a Mogul (Muslim) image. It was built in 1630-48 by Shah Jehan, as a mausoleum to commemorate his wife Mumtaz-i-Mahal. It certainly lived up to its reputation, yet was much more detailed in its intricate, coloured decoration than the distant eye saw: the overall impression was dazzlingly white. Inevitably we posed on the famous 'Princess Diana' marble bench for a photograph.

1. Riding Lights was a troupe of Christian actors based in York; this particular sketch was based on the Parable of the Talents (Matthew 25).
2. The road leading up to the school and our bedsit was resurfaced, with much noise and activity.

IT IS ONE OF THE MOST HAUNTINGLY

BEAUTIFUL PLACES

IN THE WORLD.

J K Rowling

CHAPTER 20

Back in Scotland

We decided we needed to be closer to Rob and his family in Scotland, so we looked for a house not too far away. Our initial search was in Peebles, but we could find nothing we liked. We had details of a property in Clovenfords, which had been built by Fjordhus, an agent of a Norwegian firm. They had built a group of 'prepack' houses in the upper part of Valley View, which branched off from Bowland Road and led to the A7 road to Edinburgh. The property, which had a large garden of two-fifths of an acre, was on the upper edge of the village, and had a stream flowing through it. The views from here were spectacular. Behind it was Mains Hill, rising to a couple of a thousand feet. The property had woodland of about thirty trees. The house was very well insulated. It had an open staircase leading to an upper floor where each room was under a sloping roof. It had a double garage. Our Kenton property sold at a good price so we had money to develop the new house and the adjoining land. We called in Fjordhus, and they put in a dormer window in our spare room, increasing the size considerably, and they also built a room in the roof of the garage, which we called the Studio. Downstairs they installed a toilet and shower, making the accommodation self-sufficient. We commissioned our friend John Blyth, who was a forestry academic, to re-plan our woodland. He, with a small team, removed about ten trees. At the same time we refashioned the rest of the garden. We made a winding path

Our 5 grandchildren standing on 'Woodhenge' at 15 Valley View, Clovenfords. Left to right: Jacob, Jemimah, Oliver, Ethan, Emma, 2015

through the trees and installed a series of podiums in a circle, forming what we called 'Woodhenge'. We also tidied up the grass areas. The wild garden and woodland was thus given shape and significance. Finally we had a bench made, from the wood felled, by our gardener, Kenny, who was a skilled woodworker. An inscribed brass plate was screwed onto the back of the bench dedicating it to John, who passed away in 2013, and mentioning Kenny. We dedicated the bench with some people from our House Group in the presence of Margaret Blyth.

Our removal to Clovenfords was made in two phases, in October and November 2011. We moved our furniture first, then returned to Devon and hired a holiday home at Cofton Country Park, as we had two obligations to fulfil: to finish a Senior Alpha Course based at St Mary's Hall and to perform a commissioned cantata, composed by our son Robert, at All Saints' Kenton, on 11 November (11-11-11). The unusual latter date prompted the Exe Singers, which I directed, to arrange a special programme commemorating the First World War, and from this grew the idea that an original work would be commissioned. It was called *The Vine and the Fig Tree*. The text of the work, which was in three parts, progressed from a short poem written by Sarah Parfitt, a sixth form student at Richard Huish College Taunton, proclaiming the futility of war, to a combination of *Strange Meeting* by Wilfred Owen, representing World War 1, and *Counter-Battery Fire* by J Bevan, set in Italy in World War 2. The text of the final part came from Micah 4 (verses 1-4) and is full of optimism for the future, when people will *beat their swords into ploughshares.....Nation shall not lift up sword against nation, neither shall they learn war any more. But they shall sit every man under his vine and his fig tree, and none shall make them afraid.....* The performance of this most moving and

Camping: motorhome at Glen Nevis, 2021

effective work went extremely well, and it was a fitting end to my time as musical director of this chamber choir.

Camping: Kenneth's sketch of beach at New England Bay, The Rhins, Galloway, July 2019

KENNETH HALL

From Stettin in the Baltic

to Trieste in the Adriatic

AN IRON CURTAIN HAS DESCENDED

ACROSS THE CONTINENT.

Winston Churchill 1874 - 1965
Westminster College, Fulton, Missouri
5 March 1946

CHAPTER 21

Behind the Curtain

Having studied Russian and served in the Intelligence Corps, I was keen to see what life was like beyond the Iron Curtain. In the seventies and the eighties I ran two school trips to Soviet Russia. But as a family we travelled to Eastern Europe on various occasions. Such forays into the dark totalitarian world were full of adventure and danger, and each trip had its moments of potential and real peril. The first school trip was from Solihull School. We flew on the Aeroflot Russian state airline to Kiev (the Ukraine was part of Russia in those days). Our booking was with a school travel company which specialised in Eastern Europe, so in a sense we were not without expert advice and guidance. We also travelled with other schools (which had both positive and negative aspects). Kiev was very much the cradle of Christian Russia, and was therefore a suitable introduction to what was to follow. It was incredibly hot there, in the forties celsius, and pupils from another school caught dysentery. Some of these pupils ended up in hospital: there was the danger that we might be stuck in Kiev and unable to complete the tour. However, all turned out well and we took the scheduled overnight train to Moscow. We were never told by the Russian travel agency which hotel we would occupy, so there was always an element of mystery about these trips. We were met by our allotted guide and taken to the hotel. One thing we discovered straight away was that Soviet commercial enterprises were not geared towards the customer. At the check-in desk we had our first experience of a female 'dragon' who regarded the customer as a nuisance: without any competition, why bother?! We also encountered the phenomenon of full employment which meant that certain employees stood around doing nothing. It was a highly centralised, government-oriented society which had no regard for the market or what their citizens needed or wanted. Typical of this was a national shortage of toilet paper, which would have been settled in the Western World by the system of supply and demand. But even worse was what Russians did with toilet paper after use: they put it in a basket and did not flush it away! The ordinary shops were utterly miserable, with very little stock on display. There were on the other hand hard currency shops for foreigners, i.e. for the privileged few, who were, officially, the enemy. The range of goods on sale in these islands of privilege was impressive. The ruling party wanted to show that the Soviet system was better than the West, a form of paradise, champions of the people. The problem was, with no alternative to the Communist Party, the people had no choice. One of the most trenchant manifestations of this were the slogans exhibited everywhere – a feature of the whole of the Soviet bloc, in fact. Citizens were enjoined to 'Fulfil the Five-Year Plan', and were reminded that the real villains of the world were the 'American Imperialists', forgetting that the Soviet bloc was itself an empire. Nevertheless, we had a sympathetic young female guide, and we were shown the most important sights of Kiev and of Moscow. We visited the eerie Catacombs of Kiev and the magnificent Kremlin in Moscow. It was strange that the latter and other most impressive monuments were Christian Orthodox in origin and, still, in use. We managed to attend an Orthodox mass, which was dominated by men in beards singing with very low bass voices, and we rejoiced that this was still possible in an officially atheist state. We visited Red Square and photographed the colourful, iconic St Basil's Cathedral. We queued to see the embalmed corpse of Lenin. We entered the famous superstore GUM, where abacuses were still in use.

We took another overnight train to Leningrad, dubbed the Venice of the North (and now known by its old name of St Petersburg). Again, we were in the dark as to the designation of our hotel. Here the climate was very different: it was cool, cloudy and misty. We made the best of our time there and visited the Hermitage Art Gallery and the Tretyarchov National Museum. The most awe-inspiring visit was by ferry to the Peter and Paul Island, the heart of the city. This is a fortress on the River Neva, with a cathedral, designed by Domenio Trezzini. In fact many of the important buildings in St Petersburg/Leningrad were designed by Italians, in a Neo-classical Baroque style. It was a city created by the tsar Peter the Great (1672-1725). It was also the cradle of the Russian October Revolution in 1917 (actually in November). We flew home from Leningrad Airport, which was amazingly primitive in its passenger facilities, again by Aeroflot.

The second school trip to the Soviet Union was from the Norton Knatchbull School, Ashford, Kent, in 1981. I had continued teaching Russian there, and I even prepared a boy for Oxford University entrance – successfully - who was dyslexic in his own language but could cope with a language like Russian using a different orthography. For this trip we combined with a prestigious local independent girls' school, which had a link with the Royal family, Ashford School. We took with us staff from both schools, and both of our sons came with us. It turned out to be the most adventurous trip I ever organised and led. We used the same school travel agency as before. I was the overall leader of the group, but the

Head of Music at Ashford School was responsible for the girls. The outward journey was by ferry and train. The first problem occurred early, at Ostend: a Nigerian girl from Ashford School did not have a visa for Belgium. The border authorities would not let her through. So she had to leave the party, and we had to send a member of staff with her, i.e. the Head of Music. They made their way to London and obtained the necessary visa, but we had no communication with them – there were no mobile phones in those days. We had no idea whether they would be able to rejoin the party. Our next stop was West Berlin: they flew there and joined us at our hotel (which, being in the West, was known). Berlin was split in those days, and we had to transfer to East Berlin to continue: this was done by a connecting train. We travelled on, eastwards, our next stop being Brest, on the Polish border with the Soviet Union. When we reached the East German border we were visited by guards and our documentation checked: we had a joint visa for most of the party, who also had their own passports. The Norton Knatchbull Head Boy discovered that his passport was missing. He said he had left it on the connecting train in East Berlin. The guards went berserk! There was only one course of action possible: the boy was arrested and had to return to East Berlin to look for it. He also needed someone to go with him. As a German national, it had to be Dorle! They got off the train, into the darkness, and we did not know when we would see them again. They knew we were continuing on to Brest, but they did not know the name of the hotel, nor did they know to which hotel we were heading in Moscow either. It was a worrying moment. Without hearing a word from the missing pair, we moved on by train to Moscow. We settled into a new hotel. We were told later that the boy's passport had been found in the train by an official. Dorle later reported that they had been escorted back to East Berlin by train, under guard. The passport was returned to the boy and they were given tickets as far as Warsaw. The next train to Warsaw was a sleeper and there were no berths available, they were told. However, Dorle had some West German currency and she bribed a steward who gave them a compartment with two berths. There they were not able to join a train going to Brest till the evening, so they had to spend the day in Warsaw and to avoid being seen by the police. When they reached Brest they were told by the station staff that the rest of the party had moved on. They managed to scrape enough money together to pay for tickets to Moscow. Apparently the KGB were fully aware of what was going on and they met them at Moscow and said, 'Come with us'. Whether these men were genuine or not Dorle and her companion did not know, but there was no alternative so they complied. They were taken by car to our hotel. I breathed a huge sigh of relief when they arrived.

However, this was not the end of our problems. That evening I took a group to Gorky Park, and Dorle and another member of staff stayed at the hotel. I had given strict instructions that the boys and girls should abstain completely from alcoholic drink, and that they should not visit other school parties (because their rules might be more relaxed than ours). A seventeen-year-old girl said she had a headache and would not accompany us to Gorky Park. This was a cover-up: she wanted to visit a party put on in another part of the hotel by another school. They were drinking vodka and the drink ran out. She went to the bar to get some more. There she met a young Russian man who invited her to his flat to 'listen to some records'. She spent the night with him. We had no knowledge of what was going on, obviously; as far as we were concerned, when the count was made there was one girl missing. We spent a terrible night wondering where she was:

she could have been at the bottom of the Moscow River for all we knew. She returned in the morning, with a cock-and-bull story that she had been visiting friends in Moscow. However, eventually the truth did emerge. The problem now was whether she was pregnant as a result of her night out: she needed a pregnancy test. Dorle accompanied her to the hospital: very fortunately the test was negative. The incident was reported to the police. The following night KGB men arrived and said they had caught the young man responsible and were intending to set up an identity parade. The girl appeared in her nightdress and several men were paraded. She said she could not identify the culprit. At this point one of the KGB men whispered to me, 'On ooje prisznalcya' ('He has already confessed'). I told her this and she agreed she had lied. However, the KGB men told me they were unable to charge him because she had gone to his flat and slept with him willingly, i.e. that it was consensual. There was nothing further we could do, except to keep a very sharp eye on the girl for the rest of the trip.

We moved on by train to Leningrad. At the hotel there the young man tried to contact the girl: somehow he must have found out where we were staying. At this point I decided that the girl must be sent home. I had already consulted our designated staff contact at Ashford School, the Bursar, but at this stage I contacted the parents and told them they must pay for the flight back to the UK. They agreed. The rest of our stay in Leningrad went very well. We made all the usual visits, as on our previous stay in the city. Some of us were able to get to the opera or ballet on each of the evenings we were there. The final stage of our journey was a cruise on a former World War 2 troop ship. Boys were put in one dormitory, girls in another, with strict instructions to stay apart. However, all the staff, men and women, were lumped together in one cabin which was below the water line – like being on the inside of a washing-machine! Dressing and undressing had to be 'by arrangement', in turns! The cruise took us to Tilbury Dock, on the Thames, via Copenhagen, Helsinki and Stockholm. We disembarked at Helsinki and visited the Sibelius Memorial, and wandered around Stockholm, a beautiful, well-ordered and clean city. The crew were very friendly and they formed a dance band in the evenings. The food was excellent and the menu had comic names for some items. There were 'fellow travellers' on board, with decidedly 'rosy spectacles' when considering the Soviet Union. One of these we were told was a member of the PLO (Palestinian Liberation Organisation). The Head of Music informed us early one morning that she had met him on deck and he had proposed to her! No doubt this would have been a ruse to gain UK citizenship! She refused him! There was just one more irritation on this 'trip to end all trips'. Boys in one of the cabins were accused of wrecking the steel mesh of a bunk. I was sure there was no truth in this whatsoever, but as the person in charge I was responsible.

However, this was not quite the end of the story. One of the parents had, apparently, spilt the beans regarding the errant girl's night out in Moscow. The local press were very interested – probably because the reputation of Ashford School was vulnerable. They indicated that they knew the details but asked if I would tell my side of the story. I was very reluctant to do this and refused. Nevertheless, I agreed to do so provided they limited their account in their report. I wanted them not to write that the girl had slept with the man. They kept to their word, I am glad to say. Although I had taken the right precautions on that night and what the girl did was entirely her fault, my own future was at stake: I had been appointed head of Newport Free Grammar School, and the incident took place in the summer holiday before I was due to take up my post. Fortunately there was no negative backlash.

Our other trips to the Soviet empire were private, family ones. We had a VW T2 camper van and once we drove it to Czechoslovakia via the Bayerischer Wald. We camped near Prague and from the campsite visited the city. We crossed the Charles Bridge, which was for pedestrians only, over the Vltava River and walked up the hill to the impressive Royal Castle and the beautiful St Vitas Cathedral. We had our two sons with us: Robert was only four years old. We visited the following day, also, and crossed the Charles Bridge again, on which there were a number of traders. We suddenly became aware that Robert was no longer with us. This was a terrifying moment: the parapet of the bridge was very low and he could have fallen into the river. I found a couple of policemen and tried my German (which was understood by many Czechs). They did not respond – or just did not want to know – so I tried Russian. They agreed to look but found no one. I returned to the bridge. I spotted Robert at the far end and ran towards him like the father in the Prodigal Son story. It was a moment of intense relief and unmitigated joy, such as happens only once in a lifetime: whereas our son was lost, he was now found, dead, but now alive! He told us he had walked up to the castle, as we had done the day before and then, very sensibly, turned round and come back again. He had sat at the end of the bridge and prayed!

On another occasion we visited Jugoslavia, when it was a united country. We drove in our T2 van, as before, and went via Venice, bypassing Bologna. We camped near Venice and found the mosquitoes a real problem. Venice itself was both impressive, in its mixture of superb architecture and canals, but also disappointing, in its dilapidation. It was a place to be visited rather than inhabited. We drove on eastwards to

Trieste and from there towards Jugoslavia. We went through a long tunnel under the Dolomites and emerged in Jugoslavia near Ljubljana. We tried a site on the way to Rijeka, but the state of the sea water there was so disgusting that we moved on to another site at Icici. The washing facilities were primitive: you had to wash yourself down with a hosepipe. Inflation was soaring out of control, so buying food and supplies was a real problem. It was a beautiful country, but the socialist paradise was flawed, even if less oppressive than other East European countries. Climate-wise, it was ideal: warm but not too hot. We returned via Austria, München (Munich) and Nürnberg.

Our second trip, to the area, in the eighties, was before the War of Independence (1991-97). It was very different, and it was after the dividing wall was lifted on the collapse of the Soviet Empire. Croatia (still part of Jugoslavia) was like any other tourist country, welcoming people who wanted to enjoy its history, its beauty and its wonderful coastline and islands. This time we were in our T3 van, with the engine still at the rear of the vehicle, but yellow in colour.

We took the ferry across to Cres from a harbour near Icici, and from there to the island of Losinj and a smaller narrow island called Mali Losinj, which had good sandy beaches on its western and eastern coasts. Driving along very narrow roads next to a steep drop was hair-raising. The campsite was crowded, but we managed to find a pitch right by the water next to some Hungarians. We really enjoyed this remote little island with its small harbour, and we made the best of its sea-bathing possibilities. We then took a ferry along the mainland coast past other Adriatic islands to Zadar, the former capital of Dalmatia. We drove north to the Plitvice Lakes National Park, which was highly recommended in our guidebook, although we did not camp there.

Crossing the Berlin Wall (the iron curtain) at Checkpoint Charlie, Berlin 1981

My first venture into the *DDR* (Democratic Republic of Germany) was much earlier when I was in Nürnberg. I was taken by car to the German Baptist Convention in Berlin. This was before the erection of the Wall in 1961 (12-13 August). To get to Berlin we had to drive along the 'no-man's land' corridor of an *Autobahn* (motorway). It was a very strange, rather frightening experience. However, upon arrival in Berlin there was no restriction at the Brandenburg Gate. You could just walk through, past the guards, with no hassle. You were reminded that you were leaving the British Zone and entering the Soviet Zone. Shortly beyond the Gate there was a memorial to Russian forces, guarded by strutting Russian soldiers, to be visited by anyone who wanted to do so. There were no restrictions on the *S-Bahn* (overground railway) passing from one zone to the next, either. After the building of the Wall, getting across and passing through Checkpoint Charlie was a long, nerve-wracking procedure.

Another amazing experience is also worth recording. Shortly after the Wall came down, Dorle and I accompanied the Mayor of Saffron Walden and his wife across the border at Kassel, from Bad Wildungen. East Germans were flooding across to the West, apparently full of glee that they could experience the joy of prosperity and the prospect of making purchases. Many of the vehicles were *Trabbies* (small cars made in the *DDR*) which were far inferior to Western cars. They have since become an icon for some people, but they were a symbol of the much poorer inhabitants of East Germany. I later learnt, after a visit to Leipzig for the *Kirchentag* (Lutheran church convention) that prayer played an important part in the collapse of the *DDR*. Regular prayer meetings were held on Mondays in the *Nikolaikirche* (St Nicholas' Church) in Leipzig at five o'clock in the afternoon, when prayers for peace were offered, led by *Pfarrer* (Pastor)

Christian Führer, with the lighting of forty candles to represent the forty years the Israelites spent in the wilderness on their way to the Promised Land. With soldiers and tanks outside the church, they came out bearing candles and saying *'Keine Gewalt!'* ('No violence!'). The soldiers did not resist and the political regime was overcome. Military power was conquered by prayer, hatred by love.

Whilst she was in Liverpool in the nineties, Dorle led a study tour to Grossmühlingen, near Magdeburg, on the River Elbe in what was the old *DDR*. The village looked as though it was still in the fifties and had missed out on the developments since the Second World War: it was in a time-warp. There was an enormous gap in the economies of the *Bundesrepublik* (German Federal Republic) and the *DDR* which took years and much heart-searching to heal. But on the other hand the ecclesiastical and cultural history of the *DDR* was of enormous significance, with a strong influence from the Lutheran Church. Near to Grossmühlingen was the boarding school run by the *Brüdergemeine* (Moravian Church) which Mutti (Dorle's mother) attended as a girl, in a community village where each member had a role (which was part of the philosophy of the Moravian Church). The wife of a Grossmühlingen farmer, Thea Becker, whom we later visited, also attended this school, in a later era. She and her husband Georg, a farmer, had suffered the privations of collectivisation under the regime of the *DDR*.

In the nineties I formed a relationship with Moldova, which was on the fringes of the USSR, but now an independent state. It was once prosperous, producing grapes, wine, soft fruit and cereals which supplied the USSR. It is now reputedly the poorest country in Europe and very much an inheritance of the Soviet system. My interest stemmed from a charity, which provided help to its impoverished citizens. I connected with an ethnic Russian lady who had a spastic daughter who was unable to speak or eat and was completely incontinent. Initially my intention was to pay for adult nappies, but she has since died and I have kept up the payments. She wrote to me in Russian and I did my best to reciprocate. Unfortunately the correspondence has since dried up, although I do have an English-speaking contact, Emil Nahaba, with whom I speak on the phone or exchange emails. Dorle and I have made two visits to the capital, *Kishnyov* (Chisinau), where my friend lives. On the first occasion we drove our motor home, by then a T4 with a forward engine, but still yellow, right through Romania and stayed at a hotel in the university city of Iasi. With the permission of the hotel we left our van there and took the night train to Kishnyov. This train originated in Bucharest. We were told we could obtain a visa for Moldova at the border. However, when we reached the Moldovan border station, we were told this was impossible. Instead, we were arrested! Significantly the woman steward on the train asked, '*Vee veroyashchiye?*' ('Are you believers?') Maybe she thought the arrest was a form of religious persecution. The female border guard, with whom I spoke Russian, was very polite but insisted we had to return to Romania: we might be able to get a visa at another border post. We had no alternative but to comply. When we reached the Romanian station, there was a taxi driver who offered to take us to another crossing point. He was very friendly and spoke English. We obtained our visas. At this border post there was no bus, as we had been told, and we were not allowed to cross into Moldova on foot. However, it turned out that there was a Moldovan man who was in transit in a large car from Ireland: in good English he offered to take us. As his car was stuffed full of his belongings, including some tyres, we had to wait a couple of hours while he was checked through, but he 'went the second mile' and took us all the way to our destination – the very address! Another example of an angel!

For our second trip to Moldova we flew by British Airways to Bucharest. This gave us an opportunity to sight-see the Romanian capital and, in particular, to visit the brainchild of the dictator Ceausescu, his infamous Parliament Palace, an ugly monster for which he destroyed a part of the city. It was luxurious and incorporated craftsmanship from every corner of Romania, we were told by the guide. A main staircase had small steps because the dictator was short and wanted to maintain his dignity. This was the palace from whose balcony the pop singer Michael Jackson said to the adoring crowd below: 'Welcome to Budapest'! We went to the station and boarded the night train to Kishnyov, as before. When we reached the Moldovan border the whole train was jacked up, with us still in it, and the bogies changed. Obviously the rail gauge in Moldova, being formerly a federated state of the Soviet Union, was different. This process took two hours and involved a large team of mechanics. We were met by my correspondent, Maria, and a young woman, Irina Rotaru, who was very proficient in English. We stayed with her family in Bachioi, a village near Kishinyov, on this occasion. Her father, Vasile, was a pastor. To our embarrassment we discovered that our case had gone missing, because the label had come off, and we had only a limited amount of clothing with us in our hand luggage.

While we were there we attended a service in a very run-down, incomplete block of flats, and I was asked to give a message, using an interpreter. We also called on some families. With Irina we visited my correspondent Maria in Kishnyov and had a meal with her. Her daughter and her former husband (they were separated but had continued to live together) had died and she was on her own. We claimed our case on the last day in Moldova and flew home. The poverty we had witnessed was truly shocking: the relief of poverty was the main focus of the charity, which was also active in Romania. The person who took responsibility for the Moldovan arm, Hugh Scudder, lived in Kenton, and that was how I came to be involved. I have since continued to support Maria financially, but I now send her money direct rather than via the charity. Emil Nahaba visits Maria every now and then.

KENNETH HALL

WHO WOULD TRUE VALOUR SEE,

LET HIM COME HITHER;

ONE HERE WILL CONSTANT BE,

COME WIND, COME WEATHER.

John Bunyan 1628 - 1688

CHAPTER 22

Battles Royal

Our second residence in Scotland came about because we wanted to be near Robert, Abi, our daughter-in-law, and their family, and where we had started our married life. There are three children: Jemimah (born 2000), Jacob (2003) and Ethan (2008). Being able to see them more frequently has been a real joy. We are about an hour away by car. However, we are not enamoured of Galashiels, which is a very run-down town that has outlived its *raison d'être* as a tweed-producing mill-town. There were once over forty mills here, strung along Gala Water, a tributary of the Tweed. Now, the main shopping area, Channel Street, is a sad sight, with many of its shops empty, as the retail focus has shifted further downstream, leaving the town centre pretty bare. There are two large supermarkets, Tesco and Asda, with M&S Food representing the slightly up-market food shops. There is no Sainsbury's, nor is there a Waitrose. In sharp contrast to Galashiels is the small very picturesque adjoining town of Melrose, famous for its annual Sevens Rugby Tournament and home of the area hospital, the Borders General, which is possibly the greatest local asset. Further up the Tweed is the delightful Royal Borough of Peebles, actually sited on the river. This is where we wanted to settle. However, we could find no property there which suited us and was available. It is a place, nonetheless, which we visit often, and where we belong to a music club which puts on a very rich programme of professional chamber concerts at the

Eastgate Theatre, a converted church which also has a café: this has become a favourite venue for morning coffee or afternoon tea. We have formed a strong friendship with a couple, Philip and Robina Hutton, with whom we share a love of the arts. They also belong to the music club, Music in Peebles. Philip is an artist, working in different media, a poet and an expert on music, frequently writing the programme notes for the chamber concerts we attend. Robina is a fellow-member of the U3A (University of the Third Age) and the local branch of the Lib Dem Party. They live in the High Street and are at the centre of the Peebles 'scene'.

The first battle was with Scottish independence. To combat this we joined the Liberal Democrats. This has been a very worthwhile, new experience for us: we feel we are doing our civic duty by belonging to a political party, even though we may not agree with all its policies. We have taken our membership seriously: we have delivered leaflets in different places, we have made financial contributions, and we have attended national (both UK and Scottish) conferences. Above all, we have campaigned to remain in the UK. I have even joined the campaign trail of the Conservatives on this issue having been invited by a local councillor to do so. We have also campaigned to remain in the EU: on this the Lib Dems have remained absolutely consistent, whereas Labour and the Conservatives have been split.

The second main battle has been with Galashiels Baptist Church. Because Dorle was baptised as an infant by her father, and not as a believer by immersion, she is not allowed to be a member of the church. We are great supporters of believer's baptism and respect those who wish to be re-baptised, but we also feel that those who feel that this is inappropriate should be respected and be allowed to join. As we are husband and wife and believe that we were brought together by the Lord, I will not join on my own, even though I am entitled to do so, having been baptised at the age of seventeen at Russell Park Baptist Church, Bedford. We were naive when we started attending Galashiels Baptist, because we did not realise that the majority of Scottish Baptist churches operate on the principle of Closed Membership: our experience of the Scottish Baptist system was at Hillhead in Glasgow, which had Open Membership. When we started attending Galashiels Baptist Church it was as if we were carrying on where we left off before joining the Anglicans at Neston. It felt, as I put it, like 'coming home'. We were much attracted to Arthur Hembling's ministry, and we supported him and his wife Wilma right up to his retirement. He instigated a discussion on Open Membership and there was a members' vote. The result was that a small majority was in favour of staying with the status quo, Closed Membership. However, we had to respect the vote as it was. What we did not do – and maybe should have done – is to let it be known that a majority vote against Open Membership would mean that Dorle would not be able to join, nor myself. Whether this would have changed the result I am not sure.

Nevertheless, we did eventually apply for membership, together. Our application was never put to the members. It was, however, considered by the Leadership, and two Leaders (as they were called then) visited us, which was the accepted, constitutional procedure. Dorle was asked if she was prepared to be re-baptised. She declined. There are other, very well-established people in the church who are in the same position. Our first official application was in 2014 and we have made no progress until now (2021). Each time excuses are found by the Leadership. We would have thought that we could have been transferred, having once been members of a Scottish Baptist church, or admitted out of respect for our previous service to the denomination in England, or even given a special compensation as Dorle was born in Germany where there are few Baptists. Compassion could have changed their minds, but the rules were apparently more important than human feelings.

Earlier, Dorle was appointed Treasurer of the church. She held this post for three years, although she was not officially part of the Leadership. She resigned at an AGM on the grounds that she was not acceptable for membership. This issue has been a source of great anguish for us both, and we find it very hard to accept that our experience (e.g. as leaders of a Baptist chapel in Kent, or in Dorle's case as a Sunday School leader and Deacon of a Baptist church in Essex) should be totally ignored. However, we have to accept that others – our brothers and sisters, with whom we have very good relations – think differently. Fortunately the Deacons have been discussing a change in the constitution, and are being advised by Rev Andrew Rollinson, who has written a paper on the issue. His recommendations for Open Membership were accepted in 2021.

The third battle was against the Eurosceptics. With our backgrounds – Dorle being a German national and retaining her German passport, and myself having lived for three years on the Continent and being a linguist – we are strong Europhiles. In addition, support for the EU was a central policy of the Lib Dems, which was the only party to be totally consistent on this issue. We joined a modest campaign organised by the Lib Dems in Galashiels on one occasion, but it was significant that the party who supposedly championed the EU cause, the SNP, did not join us. Later, after the referendum when the majority of Scots voters had voted in favour of remaining in the EU, the leader of the SNP, Nicola Sturgeon, shamelessly used the result of the vote to support her call for Scottish independence. We are against a second independence referendum, as (a) we respect the first, democratic, vote and (b) the latter caused a great deal of uncertainty, which would be detrimental to Scotland if it happened again. A federal United Kingdom might be the better solution. I believe in working together with people of different parties, languages and cultures, and I believe we are stronger together, whether in the UK or the EU.

KENNETH HALL

WE ARE A FUSION NATION

An Australian, about the country's identity

CHAPTER 23

Australia, again

In 2012 we went to Australia again. While we were in India an Australian couple, Garry and Robin Spry, took over our Kenton house on an exchange basis. They had spent a few months in England, but we had not completed the exchange by staying in their house in Queenscliff, on the western shore of Phillip Bay, south of Melbourne. We flew from Heathrow and stopped at a sports club in Singapore for a couple of nights on the way. Although we had flown overnight we went to an evening service at the Cathedral, held in a hall. It was an informal service with a band and dancers. The very forceful speaker from Malaysia was not brief. We had great difficulty staying awake! We continued our journey to Sydney, and took a connecting flight to Melbourne and a train to Frankston on the Mornington Peninsular, where Stuart met us. We stayed with Stuart for a week at Mount Martha, before taking the ferry across the mouth of Phillip Bay to Queenscliff. Vine was in hospital and was later transferred to a rehab home. We were introduced to the Sprys and took over one of their vehicles. We were given a choice: either a large van or a Mercedes automatic limousine. Dorle chose the latter. This was far smarter than our Ford Fusion! We hit it off with the Sprys, even though their style was very different from ours. Robin was a very skilled golfer, and Garry was interested in history and had done a course at Exeter University while they were in Devon.

Rachel, Stuart and Vine, Northcote, Melbourne, Australia

We visited Vine in hospital, with Stuart, and then on our own when she was resident in a home. She recognised us, but it was obvious that she was suffering from dementia and her mobility was somewhat limited. We took the ferry across, boarded a bus and then the very efficient train (almost like a tram) to the station nearest to the home. Vine was not released from the home, and this was the last time we saw her. She died in August 2017, aged 89. She was cremated at a local crematorium. Vine had requested that her ashes be scattered at Wilson's Prom and also into the River Ouse near where we used to live. We organised a memorial service for her on 04 November 2017. Through the generosity of our friends Stephen and Raynor Crow, we were able to use the Chancel of St Andrew's Church, Kimbolton Road, Bedford. Stephen and Raynor are members of this church. The venue was ideal, small enough to accommodate the number who attended and with a delightful chamber organ, which I played. They had a hall where we held the reception and they also had a regular caterer who provided our food, at a reasonable price. Neil scattered the ashes near the spot which, as teenagers, we used to call 'Our Place' and led the service. Martin and Robert and three of our grandchildren, Jemimah, Oliver and Emma, were present: Oliver and Jemimah read lessons and Emma distributed the orders of service. Dorle and I played a piece by Handel we had performed at Stuart and Vine's wedding, and Neil's son James showed a sequence of photographs of Vine and also recorded the service on video. There were friends of Vine's present and one or two local people who remembered her. It was a fitting farewell to a person loved by many. Personally Vine and I were close: her interest in music, and her strong support of performances in which I was involved, were an expression of our bond. This was no doubt a consequence of the family atmosphere under which we grew up: we were a unit of six, which was relatively rare even in those days, and profited from a sense of unity and solidarity.

Apart from visiting Vine, we had a very enjoyable stay at Queenscliff. The house was comfortable, and there was an upper floor with a balcony overlooking the bay. We enjoyed trips into town and shopping at unfamiliar supermarkets. We visited a wildlife exhibition, the Marine Discovery Centre in Swan Bay, and we also drove to other places in the vicinity, the most impressive of which was Geelong, which had a famous school, Geelong Grammar School, attended by Prince Charles and Prince William as part of their educational development. The main event of our stay at Queenscliff was a trip westwards along the Great Ocean Road, driven by Stuart. We stayed at a lodge. We saw the Twelve Apostles, a series of statuesque rocks along the coast. This spectacular coastline road certainly lived up to its reputation, and we were grateful to Stuart both for suggesting it and funding it.

On our way back to Heathrow we stopped again at Singapore and stayed in the same establishment as before. It was extremely warm. We went to a shopping centre and an artificial beach on Samosa Island, where we had a swim. We took a taxi to the latter and then boarded the regular, circular bus system. We were in Singapore again on a Sunday so we went to a confirmation service, in the cathedral itself this time, with fifty candidates. It was interesting to see how someone stood behind each candidate as they were confirmed, apparently in order to catch them if they fell backwards as they received the Holy Spirit. Such was the expectation of this Spirit-filled congregation! We received a welcome pack, which indicated that there were many activities going on at this place of worship.

*Bridge Encounter – Dorle and Stuart on a footbridge over the
Yarrow River in central Melbourne 2002*

KENNETH HALL

EXPLORE, DREAM, DISCOVER

Mark Twain 1835 - 1910

CHAPTER 24

Round the World

It is worth recalling here, even though it does not fit in chronologically, our second trip to Australia. This was in 2002 and involved a trip right round the world, in an eastward direction. It was only a year after the infamous 9/11 incidents in the USA, so air travel was still somewhat under a cloud. Our first destination was Bangkok in Thailand. We stayed in a Christian guesthouse recommended by my brother Neil and his wife Rosalie – they had stayed there when they were serving in Nepal. This was inspiring: there were people staying who were engaged in distributing Bibles, against the law, in communist countries. The tropical climate was extremely hot and mercilessly humid, particularly at night. Air conditioning in our room was essential. We explored the city, which was bustling with people and with an informal system of cabling which left wires hanging down on pavements, to be avoided at all costs. Traffic was heavy and general chaos reigned. Multiple boats plied the Chao Phrayer River as water travel was the best way of getting about. There were temples (or monasteries) everywhere – three hundred of them, according to the guidebook. Shortly after our arrival we foolishly engaged a tuk-tuk driver to show us the city. This was a grave error: inevitably, he took us to retail outlets where we felt obliged to buy something. I bought a ring for Dorle, but (as in North Africa) we resisted the pressure to buy a carpet, with even an offer of transportation to the UK.

We undertook a trip up the River Kwai after travelling on the infamous Death Railway. When we alighted we walked along a section where the track had been removed, and we visited the Commonwealth graves of those who died during its construction. This was a most moving occasion. We even inspected the huts where they were housed. We saw the famous bridge which straddles the river. We had booked a hotel on the river, and from there undertook a trip in a traditional boat upstream with a very un-traditional motor driving, with great force, a long shaft with a propeller on its tip. The river was in semi-spate so the current was fast. We landed at an elephant sanctuary and were given a ride, redolent of Rudyard-Kipling's colonial India, on a very compliant animal who was more interested in eating than in his passengers. We stopped again further upriver and descended into a very hot and humid stalactite-filled cave.

The next stage of our itinerary was Australia. We flew to Sydney and from there to Cairns, Queensland. From here we went further north to Port Douglas, in order to visit the Great Barrier Reef. We were ferried out there by boat and came to a viewing platform, from which we were able to swim in the sea and, armed with goggles and a snorkel, to see the wonderful variety of multi-coloured fish and corals. The freshness of the seawater and the vivid colours of what we witnessed through our goggles was an unforgettable sensation, worth all the trouble and expense of the trip. While we were in Cairns we had breakfast with birds in a large tent, and we engaged with board walks through the woods. From here we flew to Alice Springs, at the very centre of the Australian continent, in the Northern Territory. It was established as a staging-post for the overland telegraph line across Australia in the 1870s, and is on the Stuart Highway which crosses the country from Port Augusta in the south to Darwin in the north. Our accommodation was close to this main road and we could see the impressive truck 'trains' as they passed. Alice Springs is famous for its radio education and its flying doctor services, as the town is so remote. We visited the School of the Air, which provided classes for children in outback places without access to school – as we flew over Australia we were conscious how vast a stretch of land it is. Alice Springs was not a beautiful town, and the Aboriginals living there looked poor and neglected, despite their intricate, unique art. One of the reasons for going there was to see Ayers Rock, or Uluru, as it is called by the natives. The cost of guided coach trips was high, so we chose a cheaper company. The ride was bumpy but we did not mind. We stopped at a petrol station for a.toilet visit and, surprisingly, saw camels there. Apart from these, there were plenty of kangaroos along the way, many of them by the roadside. Ayers Rock and other outcrops were an unusual and awe-inspiring sight, and we could well understand why they had a special spiritual significance for the indigenous Aboriginals. We were allowed to climb part of the huge red rock – something which is now banned. It was very hot and utterly remote. The climax of the trip was an evening barbecue at some distance from the Rock, which glowed in the fading light. An unforgettable, 'once-in-a-lifetime' experience. On the way back to Alice Springs we passed many bush fires, burning alarmingly close to the road in the darkness.

We flew back south to Melbourne to stay with Vine and Stuart at their home in Mount Martha on the Mornington peninsula. Vine and Stuart had a large circle of friends and we were very happy to meet them. We visited a couple who ran a vineyard, and we were reminded how important the wine trade is to the economy of Victoria. We spent a night or two in a lodge on Wilson's Prom, the most southerly point of

Australia, a favourite holiday destination of Vine and Stuart. No permanent residents are allowed in this nature reserve and there are no towns or villages. Prominent here were the rosellas, very colourful parakeets. As expected, it was a peaceful paradise, unspoilt by too many human beings - 'far from the madding crowd'.

Continuing eastwards we flew to New Zealand. We passed over the spectacular Southern Alps: I was able to change places in the plane so that I could observe them from a window. We landed at Christchurch where we spent a night in a hotel. For the rest of our time on the South Island we hired a motor caravan – which is the most common way of touring for visitors. It was larger than our Volkswagen van and had its own bathroom. Driving on the ill-defined roads proved to be hazardous. Christchurch was founded as a Church of England settlement in 1851. As a city it lacks character, but it has a Neogothic cathedral and about a thousand acres of public parkland. We picked up the van on the Sunday morning. The night before, we ate in the hotel restaurant. We wanted to find a church for Sunday evening. We asked our waitress and she enquired what sort of church we wanted. We replied by saying we wanted a lively church in the neighbourhood. She said she would go and find out. She returned with the suggestion that we go to the local Baptist church, and she even gave directions. This was ideal. The service was held in a sports hall: it was obviously a church with a holistic approach towards its congregation; it also had a café. The preacher came from the Bethlehem Bible College, in Israel. His message was inspiring. It was just the sort of service we were looking for – and as we already had the van, we could drive there.

We drove in a westerly direction across the island. It was their spring, so it was quite cold. In fact we bought woollen nightcaps to wear in bed. As expected, there was a preponderance of sheep everywhere. As we approached the mountains, whose caps were gleaming white, the most startling feature we observed was the radiant azure colour of the lakes. We had never seen anything quite like this: it was almost artificial. I did some watercolour sketching, but I failed to reproduce that vivid colour. We crossed to Lake Tekapo, where we stopped for the night. We could see Mount Cook, at 12,316 feet the highest mountain in New Zealand, from here. We continued south to the town of Cromwell and then west to Queenstown, a tourist resort on Lake Wakatipu, where we camped again. We continued to Frankton and Kingston and stopped at Te Anau, before tackling the tunnel to Milford Sound along its lengthy approach road. On this road we stopped at one point and were visited by a Kea, a bird with a hook-shaped beak only found in New Zealand (mostly in the mountains), who insisted on nibbling our wing mirrors. No dissuasion would stop it, so we moved on quickly. There were no lights in the narrow tunnel and we entered hoping we would not encounter another vehicle. As it turned out, a bulky coach approached, travelling in the opposite direction. We were the smaller vehicle, so we had to give way. Backing without public lighting was extremely 'hairy'. I was very much afraid of hitting the sides of the tunnel which would not only have damaged our vehicle (tall enough as it was), but which would also have caused a dreadful hold-up. By some miracle (but with Dorle's help) I managed to back some distance till we reached a passing place, and all was well. Fortunately there was only one coach: seeing all the Japanese visitors at Milford Sound later, I realise it could have been a whole procession of coaches rather than just one.

We finally reached Milford Sound, a spectacular, glacier-carved inlet on the west coast. We had seen photographs of this fjord-like Sound, dominated by the immensely steep,

KENNETH HALL

Fijian Family in a village on Viti Levu near Suva

conical Mitre Peak (5551 feet high), and this was one of our chief tourist destinations on the island. Inevitably it was raining: Milford Sound is a very moist place, but we still managed to get some sensational photographs, enhanced by mist and drizzle. We were assailed by a swarm of midges. We took a boat trip down the Sound. Tumbling torrentially from vertiginous heights were white cascades, fed by the constant rainfall. Our boat had a lower deck from which we could view the underwater marine life. It was certainly a trip worth doing, fortunately not spoilt by the prevailing weather. We had a couple of nights here and used the facilities of the youth hostel at the site. We retraced our steps for the return journey, via Kingston and Frankton, and then struck west again to follow the coastal road to Haast Villeg, hoping to see some penguins. We discovered a deserted, pitiful fishing village which was really the back of beyond and reminded us how remote New Zealand is. This was obviously no longer a holiday destination. We found no penguins, and so we drove back along the coast northwards and took the road which led to the Fox Glacier. We reached Hokitika, a community which grew up during the gold rush of the 1860s. The beaches here were of no interest: they were full of flotsam and jetsam, washed up onto the shore by the westerly winds from the Tasman Sea. We camped here and then set off across the spectacular Arthur's Pass, which crosses the Southern Alps via the Otira Gorge, by road and rail. The views of the mountains from points along the route were temptingly photogenic. We stopped at a Maori museum. This brought us back to the east of the island, to Springfield and Christchurch, where we handed back the motor caravan.

Our next destination was Fiji. We flew to Auckland Airport, where we caught a transfer flight to Fiji. There were many Chinese at the airport. While we waited for our flight there was a tannoy announcement calling for Chinese passengers to join their flight. 'Will the following passengers please join their flight to ... immediately: Pong, Ping, Wong, Tong, Tung, etc. Quite spontaneously and unashamedly other passengers, including ourselves, burst out laughing at this monosyllabic, musical recitation of names. This was an unfair reaction, no doubt, as our own European names would have sounded just as strange to them! However, a sense of humour is perhaps a natural reaction whenever travellers have to endure the boredom of waiting in a departure lounge! We flew to Nadi International Airport on the main island of Suva. We were taken to our hotel by taxi: it was right by the beach behind a sugarcane miniature railway. Small trains passed regularly and made a tremendous racket when they passed. It was run by a Dutch couple. The Fijians were extremely friendly: two hundred years ago they would have cooked us in a pot and eaten us! Now, they rely very much on the tourist trade, which has become the chief industry. The climate was warm and very pleasant. We had a small pool at the hotel and we got to know the attendant who looked after it. He was a Christian and invited us to his Methodist church in the village nearby on the Sunday. We took the sugarcane train, which allowed passengers on board at certain times. At the service, in the corrugated-iron-covered church we did not understand the language, and some of the 'sermons' (or speeches?) were extremely long, but we appreciated the ardent singing of the choir. Afterwards our friend introduced us to his family when we visited their home. In our room there were geckos on the wall and ceiling: they made no difference to our comfort, mentally and physically. We much enjoyed swimming and snorkelling in the warm sea from the beach, where there were traders selling their goods. A young man offered to climb a palm and pick a coconut, for a fee. In various ways our Fiji visit was the highlight of our world tour: peaceful, relaxing activities amongst personable, hospitable people.

The return to Heathrow via Los Angeles, however, was tedious and frustrating. We found the staff at Los Angeles Airport aggressive and unfriendly, no doubt due partly to the fact that the 9/11 disaster was a fairly recent event. From Los Angeles we had to cross the whole of the USA and the Atlantic to reach the UK. It was a long journey! Originally we had asked to stop in Los Angeles, which would have broken up the earlier part of the journey, but we had run out of permitted stops within the travel agent's ticket price (six, in all), so we just had to grin and bear it. Returning to the UK in mid-winter was also a shock.

KENNETH HALL

THINGS TURN OUT THE BEST FOR THE PEOPLE

WHO MAKE THE BEST

OF THE WAY THINGS TURN OUT.

John Wooden 1910 – 2010,
American Basketball Player and Coach

CHAPTER 25

Lockdown

In 2020 the whole of the world was struck down by a plague, which changed our lives completely and caused widespread economic recession. It was originally called Coronavirus, but subsequently was referred to as Covid-19. In many ways it was like World War Two, but whereas humans had a big hand in the conduct and spread of that conflict, this was a secret enemy which wreaked its chaos willy-nilly. We do not know exactly where it came from, but early cases were centred on Wuhan, China. It was termed a pandemic, i.e. capable of spreading to all people. It struck with great force, causing respiratory problems, so that many patients had to be put onto a respirator. Various measures were recommended: people were urged to isolate themselves from others, to keep a distance of two metres away, to wash their hands frequently for at least 20 seconds, and to wear masks and, in some cases, visors. Vaccines were developed at record speeds, and these were being dispensed from January 2021, starting with the most vulnerable, the over-eighties, and quickly descending to those in their seventies. The figures for sufferers were given daily on the TV news, as were those for the hospitalised and the death rate: this was the main news item of every bulletin. The National Health Service featured heavily: in fact the main defence against the virus, apart from the vaccine, was the NHS. Special hospitals were set up. Certain areas of the economy were closed down: pubs, restaurants, gyms, public swimming-pools, sports venues, theatres and concert-halls could no longer operate. Transport was limited. A new method of 'attending' an event was born - Zoom. Important sports matches were staged without spectators. Most university lectures and school lessons were delivered online. A very different, 'virtual' world emerged. For some, there were advantages and unforeseen possibilities. It was possible to hold an event or meeting whereby participants could 'attend' from their own homes, even in their slippers and/or pyjamas! This impacted on the transport companies, particularly airlines. Funds for furlough arrangements had to be provided by the Government causing even greater strains on the economy, which was in its worst state for 300 years, we were told. This was worse than a World War. But, as in the latter, there were 'up-sides': generally speaking, people looked out for each other, and most complied with the daily briefings given by the UK and devolved Governments. One thing we did do as a communal exercise was to clap the NHS at 8 pm on Thursdays. We did this conscientiously and gratefully on most Thursdays, making sure that whatever activity we were doing that evening stopped early enough for us to do so. Mike and Sandra from opposite joined in, but the collaboration of the other nearby houses was significant by its absence! We felt we had a lot to be thankful for.

Initially the order was 'lockdown'. This is an American term which is used to indicate the confinement of all prisoners to their cells. Although this is a very negative concept, I welcomed 'lockdown' because (a) it was definite, meaning that we should not venture from our homes and (b) I was glad of the time released to tackle this autobiography: I had set 2020 as the year I would write it, but I was unsuccessful in finding the time. 'Lockdown' was a Godsend! We were extremely fortunate in having friends who would keep us supplied, both with our daily newspaper and our monthly prescriptions from Boots, and also Dorle was adept at ordering items online, notably our food from Sainsbury's. However, two things can only be done by personal contact: haircuts and podiatry. My hair became a terrible mess, but when total lockdown was relaxed I succeeded in getting an appointment at the barber's, and we managed to register with a podiatrist who would visit our home, suitably protected. We even drove out to a guesthouse for a Christmas meal, and called at the hotel opposite our home for another meal, consumed outside. This relaxation probably occasioned a resurgence of the virus infection, but it was useful for the purchase of Christmas presents. We also managed to buy a Christmas tree at a local garden centre.

Our meetings and church services have been by Zoom, which, although previously unfamiliar to us, has proved to be a replacement for physical human contact. The interregnum at our church has been an opportunity to bring in a number of visiting preachers on Sunday mornings, from different places, unhindered by distance. In fact, a medical couple serving in Bardai, Northern Chad, were able to visit us, 'virtually', in February of this year (2021) and give us a very graphic picture of their life in this inhospitable part of the Sahara. Zoom made their visit so much easier, as they were staying, on furlough, in Penzance, Cornwall. And another unexpected phenomenon has arisen - online *Alpha*, which is in many ways even more effective than before. One of the happiest occasions for us personally has been a regular games night with both our families, bringing them together although separated by many miles. There is a 'flip side' to every problem: on the one hand lockdown has split us apart, but. on the other, it has brought us closer together.

One interesting development from the pandemic has

Lane behind Balnakiel House, Galashiels, Scotland

been our participation in a research project. We have had regular visits from an employee of a research company, carrying out a survey on behalf of Oxford University. We are asked a series of questions relating to our health, and then we are given a Covid test - both the survey and the test are carried out under social-distancing rules. We have both had vaccinations from our GP surgery, and fortunately all our tests so far have proved negative.

When restrictions will end, we do not know. Trying to plan for the future is difficult, particularly for travel. We had planned to visit Siegfried (Dorle's brother) and his wife, Lotte, in Witten, Germany, last year but the pandemic put a stop to it. We shall try again next September, but, despite falling infection rates, we cannot predict whether we shall be allowed to travel. We are also planning to restart our camping in the early summer, but again we cannot be sure.

A PROBLEM IS A CHANCE TO DO YOUR BEST.

Duke Ellington 1899 – 1974

CHAPTER 26

Rowing Across the Sahara

When our missionary partners came to our church Zoom service on 21 February (2021), they told us about the need of a development facility in the x-ray department of their hospital at Bardai, Northern Chad, in the Tibesti region of north-western Africa. Before we teamed up with this couple, I was hardly aware of the existence of Chad. It is a former French colony which used to be known as Tchad. It has a very unstable history since independence in 1960, and had a period of one-party military rule. The hospital is situated in the Sahara desert in a very poor, inhospitable and dangerous highland area, subject to civil strife and gold prospecting.

We were told that the x-ray equipment was all set up in a suitable room, but there was no means of developing the slides, so it was useless. The cost of such a facility was estimated to be £25,000. I mentioned this at the next meeting of our church's Mission Core Group, indicating that I wished to raise the money myself. A member of the group who is a Scout leader, Tim Seabrook, suggested doing this via the *Kiltwalk,* in which his troop (at Earlston) took part. It was supported by the Hunter Foundation, of Edinburgh, who would increase the amount raised by 50%. To me this was a brilliant opportunity and I agreed to do it. The sum was reduced to £21,300 when I enquired at the BMS World Mission headquarters in Didcot, Oxfordshire. £7,800 had already been donated: this included £5,000 voted by our

church membership. In this way I decided to set a target of
£9,000, which, with the addition of £4,500 from the Hunter
Foundation, would bring the total to £21,300, the sum
required. I decided I would wear a Grant tartan kilt, as some
of my descendants (and my second name) were from this
family.

The *Kiltwalk* took place over three days, 23 – 25 April
2021. Our missionary medical couple suggested that I cover
the distance between Bardai and the nearest x-ray hospital in
Northern Chad, at the oasis of Faya, 410 miles away to the
south. That was a distance I could not walk in three days, or
at any time, so I would do it 'virtually' on my rowing machine,
which I used every day to keep fit.   As I wanted to relate the
'walk' to that distance I thought of virtually rowing it on Lake
Chad, to the south near the capital, N'djamena. However, the
dimensions of the ever-shrinking lake were too indefinite.
The couple proposed that I should 'row' that distance
overland instead. So, this is what I decided. However, if I was
taking part in a *Kiltwalk*, I needed a kilt, so Dorle ordered one
online for me and it was shipped from the USA. It took a very
long time to arrive. In order to complete my publicity, kindly
designed for free by Leander Paterson of Advanced Signs,
Galashiels (who had also done design work for our church), I
needed a Grant kilt. A man with the right garment was found,
through Sylvia Jones, a member of our church, and two
photographs of me wearing the kilt, one on the rower and one
standing, were submitted. We returned the kilt to its owner.
However, I was wearing it the wrong way round, and these
photographs had to be abandoned! Very fortunately, the
original kilt order arrived: we re-shot the photographs, and
passed them on to Leander. The resulting design was
brilliant. Printed copies were inserted into Easter cards and
sent to our friends, using our Christmas list and church

Kenneth wearing a kilt and on the rowing machine, April 2021

register. They were also delivered to our neighbours in our street. By mid-April the funds were well over £8,000, and I was confident I could reach my target. On one day the fund received £5 and £5,000. These are of equal status: the smaller amount came from someone on benefit, and the larger amount was anonymous. They were both very welcome and boosted my morale enormously. I also received many messages of goodwill. In all of this Dorle acted as manager and gave me sterling support.

The couple write:

Imagine arriving at a hospital with a broken leg or a chest injury and there is no x-ray department, and the nearest possible x-ray facility is 410 miles away. That is further than the trip from Galashiels to London, and there is no motorway. In fact there is no road. The trip normally takes 2 days.

The first day is 110 miles at 14 miles an hour on a track across the mountains climbing to 2500m/8000ft and then down to the sandy desert. The second day is 300 miles in 10 hours at 30 miles per hour across the sandy desert to the desert oasis of Faya, where hopefully, but not always, you could get an x-ray. For most people that is just not possible.

You might as well try and row across the desert – and that is exactly what Kenneth proposes to do.

The generosity of so many people was quite overwhelming. Many donations could only be described as 'sacrificial', although all amounts, large or small, were a reason for great rejoicing. By the beginning of the *Kiltwalk* (on Friday 23 April) I had exceeded my target by over £800, and the money kept coming in. My earlier fears, that I should not reach my target, were quite unfounded. One of the most felicitous donors, John Maddams, who was a fellow-member of Saffron Walden Baptist Church and an officer in the Boys' Brigade when Robert was in the company in the eighties -

with whom we correspond at Christmas - put my leaflet on his Facebook page.

Unfortunately there was a tragic coda to this saga. We had been informed that there were elections in Chad on 11 April, that the President, Idris Déby, was running for his sixth term, and that there was opposition to his re-election. In a prayer letter dated 20 April the couple wrote to say that the President had been killed in a battle with Chadian rebels who had entered the country from Libya on the night of the election. They are grouped under the French acronym of FACT (Front pour l'Alternance et Concorde de Tchad). The initial reports had said that they were stopped by the army, but there was fierce fighting on Saturday 17 April around 300 km from the capital, N'djamena. The British Embassy advised all its citizens to leave. There had been further fighting, but we were told that the rebel group appeared to be on the run. N'djamena was calm, but there was a heavy military presence there. Election results were released and showed that the late President had been re-elected with 79% of the votes. Colleagues in N'djamena and Bardai are now reported to be safe, but there is an uncertain future for Chad, as military rule has been established, with the son of the late President at its head. This will make life more dangerous for our friends at Bardai. Quite apart from this, there has been the problem of their return to Chad. They have had a couple of changes of plan, but, after their second Covid vaccinations, the latest (early June) departure date is 14 June, to France, where they will spend a fortnight. From there they will fly to N'djamena, where they will proceed to Bardai on a MAF (Mission Aviation Fellowship) flight on 12 July.

Other parts of the world, notably India, are in turmoil, even though the number of Covid cases is diminishing in the UK as the vaccination programme progresses. Here, in

Oil painting of Still Life – Mamhead, Devon

Scotland, life is beginning to turn the corner towards normality, with, for example, children back at school, but an aura of unease pervades our whole daily existence. In many ways our current global situation resembles that of the Battle of Britain in 1940, during the darkest days of World War Two.

However, my total at the point when the fund was closed stood at £10,180 and, according to the *Kiltwalk* website, was the highest amount of all the 'walkers' recorded this year. BMS World Mission has reported that they are confident that their workers will be able to return to Chad, once the political situation is clarified, and that they will be able to operate within tolerable limits. Our friends have put out the order for the x-ray facility, so that the money can be used for the purpose for which it was raised.

In the post I received a *Kiltwalk* medal, with a tartan on its ribbon. It was recognition that I had taken part. From my point of view, it was very much worth the effort. It was a crazy idea, but it seems to have caught the imagination of our family and friends. But, above all, it will have been worth it if the work of Bardai hospital is made easier and more effective. The ability to analyse the damage done by an accident or act of violence will be so much better. It will, I hope, assist the healing of wounds, but also the healing of relationships between different factions. It is, indeed, a statement of togetherness, which all civilisations need to learn. It is a statement of love, both of our neighbour and our enemy, which is at the very centre of our Christian belief. It is part of the process of 'beating swords into ploughshares'.[1]

---

1. This refers to Micah 4:4 and the text of the 3rd movement of the Cantata by Robert Hall *The Vine and the Fig Tree*, looking forward to a time when there will be no more war (*cf* Chapter 20).

It was the best of times,

it was the worst of times,

it was the age of wisdom,

it was the age of foolishness,

it was the epoch of belief,

it was the epoch of incredulity,

it was the season of Light,

it was the season of Darkness,

it was the spring of hope,

it was the winter of despair,

we had everything before us,

we had nothing before us,

we were all going direct to Heaven,

we were all going the other way .....

Charles Dickens 1812 - 1870:
A Tale of two Cities (1859)

CHAPTER *27*

To Each a Season

I love the passage in Ecclesiastes 3 about the time for everything. It was expressed brilliantly in a pop song by the Byrds in the sixties: *Turn! Turn! Turn!*[1]

To every thing there is a season, and a time to every purpose under the heaven: a time to be born, and a time to die; a time to plant, and a time to pluck up that which is planted; a time to kill and a time to heal; a time to break down, and a time to build up; a time to weep, and a time to laugh; a time to mourn, and a time to dance; a time to cast away stones, and a time to gather stones together; a time to embrace, and a time to refrain from embracing; a time to get, and a time to lose; a time to keep, and a time to cast away; a time to rend, and a time to sew; a time to keep silence, and a time to speak; a time to love, and a time to hate; a time of war, and a time of peace (vs. 1-8, King James Version).

I have experienced all of these phases, except the final one, death. We are all mortal: that is something that all human beings share, whether they are rich or poor, successful or smitten with failure. We all go through phases in our lives, as the wise writer of Ecclesiastes indicates. In the long run we are answerable for how we cope with the phases of life and, above all, how we share the given day that God has granted to us. Nowhere in the Bible is this more graphically expressed than in the three parables of Matthew 25:

(a) **The Wise and Foolish Virgins:** we must live as if the

Lord's return is just round the corner, like that of the bridegroom (vs.1-13). The bridegroom was a long time coming, and his arrival was sudden and unexpected: all ten virgins fell asleep. The five wise virgins had stocked up with oil and had enough to spare: their lamps were primed and ready to light as soon as the bridegroom arrived: the five foolish virgins were caught napping: they were unprepared and they panicked when the bridegroom arrived: they tried to borrow oil from their wise sisters, but they did not succeed. The wise virgins were welcomed to the feast; the foolish ones were exhorted to go to the shops to buy oil, but while they were away the door was closed and despite their protestations they were shut out: the bridegroom did not even recognise them.

(b) **The Talents:** we must use and develop to the full the talents that the Lord has given us (vs. 14-30). The owner of an estate went away and left three of his servants in charge. He gave them differing amounts of money, according to their ability. The first one used the money wisely and made a profit of 100%. The second did the same. However, the third, who had the least amount, buried it. When the owner returned he congratulated the first two servants and promoted them, but he was very angry with the third and even took away what he had allocated to him and gave it to one of the others. This servant was fired!

(c) **The Sheep and the Goats:** we must share the good things we have with the less fortunate: the generous are classed as sheep, the stingy as goats: we must be 'sheep' rather than 'goats' (vs. 31-46). This parable is about the King's judgement at the end of our lives. The people represented by sheep were congratulated. They were puzzled because they were unaware of what they had done. The King explained that every time they helped someone less fortunate than themselves, in terms of hospitality, providing clothing, visiting the sick and those in prison, the 'sheep' did it for him personally. And the opposite was the same with the 'goats': failure to help those in need was failing to help the King.

(Inasmuch as ye have done it unto one of the least of these my brethren, ye have done it unto me... Inasmuch as ye did it not to one of the least of these, ye did it not to me (vs. 40 and 45, King James Version).

These three parables indicate that we are responsible for the way we lead our lives. But in no way do they suggest that we can earn our right to go to heaven. What we need for this is a relationship with the Lord, which can happen if we dedicate our lives to him, as our Lord and Saviour, in a spirit of humility and recognition of our own unworthiness.

---

1 This song by Pete Seeger, the lyrics of which were adapted from Ecclesiastes in the Old Testament, was recorded by The Byrds on 9 October 1965 and reached number one in the charts in the USA. To quote the sleeve of the album, 'In late 1965, a time of division and rage' it was a 'much-needed voice of communion and reason'.

I HAVE TROD THE UPWARD

AND THE DOWNWARD SLOPE.....

AND I HAVE LIVED AND LOVED

AND CLOSED THE DOOR.

Robert Louis Stevenson 1850 - 1894:
Songs of Travel

CHAPTER 28

Requiem

Under the wide and starry sky,
Dig the grave and let me lie.
Glad did I live and gladly die,
And I laid me down with a will.

This be the verse that you grave for me:
Here he lies where he longed to be;
Home is the sailor, home from sea,
And the hunter home from the hill.

The words of this poem by Robert Louis Stevenson were carved on his gravestone. I am prompted to quote them because my friend Peter Naylor set them to music and dedicated the song to me[1]. His setting is supremely peaceful, with a vocal line which arches upwards, as if to heaven, and which, for a tenor, is a joy to sing. I empathise with the poet's sentiment about returning to a berth from a volatile sea, having located the near-invisible Fairway buoy and then wending my way along the delicate channel between the starboard (green) and port (red) marker buoys, as I have done on many occasions on my way to Exmouth Dock; however, I have no sympathy at all for hunting as a sport. At double the age of Stevenson when he died (i.e. in 2021, at the age of 88), I have to admit that I am not yet ready to lie 'down with a will'. There is still so much more that I would like to achieve and to experience, before I 'shuffle off this mortal coil', to quote another, earlier, poet[2]. I do, however, look forward to seeing the Lord at the end of this long journey, during which he has been my friend, and I look forward to being reunited with my family. What paradise will be like does not interest me, except that it will be 'heaven', or as Baudelaire called it (referring to human love), 'un goût de l'éternel' (a taste of heaven)[3] Music will be there in abundance, and this would for me include works of the greatest master of all, J S Bach. I hope I shall eventually be reunited with the one person with whom I have shared everything in my life since we met - my dearest, most wonderful wife Dorle. She and I are one person: the Lord brought us together, and we have shared everything, including our Christian faith. It has been a most exciting journey together, which will not end here and now, but last forever. Life on this earth has been worth living just to be with her. My love for her is unquenchable, everlasting, all-consuming. My story could equally be entitled, not *The Given Day*, but *The Given Wife*.

John Bunyan describes the end of earthly life as like crossing a river. I sincerely hope that it will not be an unpleasant experience, but, rather, a joyful one. I hope and pray that I shall approach it with supreme confidence. What I do believe is that the Lord will accept me and have a place already set out for me. I have in no way earned my place in heaven, because I do not believe that it is possible to do that, and because I do not claim any personal moral worth at all. I shall be there because of Christ's sacrifice on the cross for my inadequacies, as an act of forgiveness. His grace has already saved me, not my merit. My final wish is that others should learn that lesson and enjoy the 'more abundant life' while there is still time left.

Surely goodness and mercy shall follow me all the days of my life: and I will dwell in the house of the Lord for ever.
(Psalm 23 v. 6, King James Version)

1. *Cf* Peter Naylor Requiem YouTube for our recording of this song
2. Shakespeare, referring to the end of life on earth in Hamlet's famous monologue *To be or not to be*
3. From the *Mélodie Sérénade* by Gabriel Fauré (1845 – 1924)

Kenneth Hall

Appendices

Appendix 1 – Farewell to James
Appendix 2 – Reflections on the End of a World war
Appendix 3 – A Day in the Life of a Senior Volunteer
Appendix 4 – *Corporate Identity in Secondary Schools*,
Abstract of PhD Thesis

APPENDIX 1

Farewell to James

Chapter X THE HEAVENLY GARNER
of *White Unto Harvest*
By Raymond H. Belton (James's uncle)

The resumption of life at the cottage[1] had brought new hope to James and his parents that in time he would recover sufficiently to return to the work he loved, and take up again his Christian Union activities, in which he had been greatly missed. Writing to him while in hospital, a fellow student had said, 'G...'s departure and your temporary absence are a severe blow to our fellowship and witness'.

But before long further serious complications developed and within a fortnight it was decided that James must return to hospital. On his last Sunday at home he switched on the radio to listen to a broadcast service at which the Reverend G.B. Duncan was the preacher, and was thrilled to hear his baptismal hymn sung. 'O Jesus I have promised to serve thee till the end' had been the theme song of his life, and as he followed the familiar words he experienced again the exaltation of spirit that had been his on that sacred occasion.

Her was taken to Hammersmith Hospital by ambulance, where he accepted this new trial with the same faith and courage he had always exhibited. For his parents it was a bitter disappointment, hard to be understood.

In God's gracious providence the hospital was served by a Christian Almoner, who soon discovered in James a kindred spirit. Having free access to the ward, this young lady came to his bedside whenever she was free, to read and pray with him, a spiritual ministry which brought untold comfort to the patient. But if James was blessed, so was the Almoner, who in a letter to his parents wrote, 'I can't tell you what a help his testimony has been to me. I shall always remember those short times with him and with his Bible. They have been little oases of refreshment during a busy day – and it has been an inspiration to hear his comments on the passages we read together. A few weeks ago we read Revelation 7: 9 – 17, and he was thrilled to think what lay ahead for him, though at the same time most deeply concerned for other patients who are without Christ. I am sure that his brave and consistent witness will contrive to bear fruit in the lives of all who came in contact with him'.

James also found much comfort and assurance in a motto card sent to him by a friend of the family who had known him for a number of years. He was permitted to hang it at the head of his bed. Its message:

'I will never, never let go of your hand,
I will never, never forsake you'

was in his heart, and was part of his unfaltering witness. The secret of his brave conduct and uncomplaining spirit was the knowledge that his Saviour was always with him.

An associate at the Horticultural College, and a keen member of he Christian Union, sent James a card which he kept near him in his locker. It bore the words 'This day may you live so near to Jesus Christ that every life which touches yours may touch Him'.

James again had many visitors, and the testimony of all was the same: a blessing received rather than bestowed. The

Baptist Minister of Saffron Walden, the Reverend L.E. Addicott, who had become friendly with the family during their stay at Thaxted, wrote, 'I shall treasure the memory of my visit to James during the time he was in Hammersmith Hospital. We had an hour of real fellowship together. He asked me to read the story of Nicodemus and I remember thinking that he was not seeking mere words of comfort for himself. He wanted to hear the central note of God's amazing love. His gracious courage impressed and refreshed me more than I can say'.

'I felt that angels were round his bed' was the comment of one visitor. Said another, 'His courage through so much suffering was wonderful, and his faith and trust in the Lord Jesus was a source of challenge and encouragement to all who knew him.'

One visitor who brought him exceptional joy was a girl, now grown to young womanhood, who for several years when her parents were in India spent her holidays in his home. She had visited him previously, but on that occasion they had talked of the old days and things in general, but this time she had come to tell James that she had received the Lord Jesus Christ as her personal Saviour. Before making the visit she had said, 'Now I shall be able to talk about Christ.'

Besides those who actually visited James, were many others who took an interest in him. A baptismal candidate at Saffron Walden requested that the flowers be sent to him after the service, a kind gesture which greatly delighted him. Among churches pledged to pray for him were Shepherd's Bush Tabernacle and Thaxted Baptist Church, where the family worshipped during their stay at the cottage.

On the afternoon of March 8, 1955, James's parents were with him, taking tea at his bedside. He was cheerful, and his mind was clear and alert. He spoke in glowing terms of those who nursed him, and who, in their desire that no possible comfort might be denied him, carried him on bright days on to the balcony, that he might lie there in the sunshine.

'The Sister watches over him like a hawk', was the comment of the patient in the opposite bed.

James talked eagerly of the time when he would be well enough to come home, and mentioned his plans for the lay-out of the garden of the new house his parents had acquired in Bedford. He even chose, from the green of his counterpane, the colour of the decoration of his bedroom. Later the room was decorated as he had wished and named 'Bethany'.

As his parents were about to leave, James, with his accustomed thoughtfulness, urged them to take care and not to overtire themselves. 'Don't worry about me', was his parting admonition as with a radiant smile he bade them goodbye. It was his last word to them. The call for which he was so absolutely ready came suddenly and unexpectedly the next morning. His passing was utterly peaceful; he literally 'fell asleep in Jesus'. He had entered the eternal world which held no fear for him in life or death.

In view of the volume of prayer that had arisen for his recovery, it was difficult to understand why the answer was 'No!' James' name had been enrolled by someone at the City Temple, and at other healing centres with which he and the family had had not previous association. Groups at his Church, old school and college, at Oxford and Cambridge, where his brothers were undergraduates, as well as a group in the R.A.F. led by a member of James' home Church, were praying, not perfunctorily, but earnestly and intelligently, while someone had inaugurated a scheme whereby friends remembered him in prayer at 9.0 am and 9.0 pm each day. 'We are praying for you', was the theme of message after message that reached James or his parents.

'If ye have faith as a grain of mustard seed, ye shall say unto this mountain, Remove hence to yonder place; and it shall remove; and nothing shall be impossible unto you' was the passage uppermost in the mind of his father.

'Lord, my faith is bigger than a grain of mustard seed,' he pleaded, confident to the end that James would recover. But in his inscrutable wisdom God did not perform the miracle in James' case. He is Sovereign of life and death and He makes no mistakes.

Prayer was abundantly answered in other respects. James was enabled to bear an unsullied witness, and 'by his faith he still speaks to us today' (Heb. 11:4 Phillips).

'I could not tell you before,' wrote a close friend on hearing of James' passing, 'but when I prayed for his recovery I felt God was replying that he had something better for James than a return to life here. And so I changed my prayer and prayed that James would see God's will for him and be glad. And the prayer was answered in his serenity, his fine witness to the end and in his peaceful passage to Eternal Life.'

James' memory is perpetuated at Bethany School, Goudhurst, by the awarding of an annual 'James Hall Memorial Prize' for Scripture, and also a vase, suitably inscribed, which was presented to the School Chapel by his parents. It was at this School that he had discovered and had been encouraged to develop his gift for gardening, and he found joy and a sense of fulfilment in co-operating with the Creator in causing the earth to spring forth in beauty and usefulness. The same was true of his heart and life, in which, under the Hand of Heavenly Gardener flowers of rare beauty blossomed continually. At his Memorial Service, in the last public utterance to his memory, this thought was in the mind of the Reverend Gordon Smelling, who linked the fact that James was never happier than when in a garden, with the promise of Jesus, 'today shalt thou be with Me in Paradise' and pictured him walking with his Saviour in 'the garden of the King.'

1. In the grounds of Priors Hall, which housed the Thaxted Horticultural College, and which was also the home of Dr W.E. Shewell-Cooper, a well-know TV garden personality.

Reflections on the End of a World War

The Story of Wallace Orr and Siegfried Büttner
Written originally in 1995 to commemorate the 50th anniversary of the end of World War 2

.

In human relations black is seldom completely black, nor is white always as white as it may seem. In international relations this is even more so. Of course, it is easy to think of your enemy as totally evil because it implies that you are quite beyond blame. If there is a villain, then there must be a hero. But sometimes heroes and villains can be remarkably similar.

Wallace was a Scotsman. He trained as an artist and architect and in due course became a teacher. He was an elder in the Church of Scotland, an upstanding, gentle man. As a Christian he did not believe in fighting but was not lacking in courage, so when war came he enlisted in the London Fire Brigade. He experienced the terror and destruction of bombing from the receivers' end. But he was later to experience it from the other end. As the war drew on he felt he must do more to defeat the enemy and so he joined the RAF and became a rear gunner in a Lancaster bomber -- another brave act, as the survival rate in RAF Bomber Command was low: overall, typically, out of a hundred aircrew who served the full cycle of service only 24 would survive unharmed. The normal survival rate of the first tour was around fifty percent – in 1942 it was even worse: only three crews in ten could expect to survive their first tour.

On the night of 2nd/3rd January 1945 Wallace took part in a raid which destroyed the beautiful walled city centre of Nuremberg, one of the medieval and renaissance gems of Europe but also home to the infamous Nazi party rallies. On that night 514 Lancasters took part, with the loss of only four (although two also crashed in France). 1,838 people were killed on the ground and at least 50 were missing. A previous attempt to destroy the old centre on the night of 3Oth/3lst March 1944 had been a disaster: on that occasion 795 aircraft had been dispatched and 95 had gone missing, with a loss of 545 crew. This time, however, they fulfilled their mission with great thoroughness: the city of Albrecht Dürer, Veit Stoss and Hans Sachs, with its two famous hall-choir Lutheran churches, town hall and castle, had been almost completely destroyed. I am sure that Wallace, who stood for what the city represented in faith and art, would have considered such destruction an act of vandalism if it were not for the circumstances. He did what he had to do: for him there was no alternative.

Siegfried was a Lutheran pastor, the son of Moravian Church missionaries who served in what is now South Africa. He married Brunnhild, the daughter also of Moravian missionaries from the Transkei nearby. His first pastorate was in Neuötting, in Upper Bavaria, a strongly Catholic area, giving him a very scattered parish. Ironically enough, some of his flock were situated in Hitler's birthplace, Braunau, on the other side of the River Inn, in Austria. Inducted in 1934. it was a difficult time for Siegfried. He refused to support the Nazis or to become a 'German Christian', as Lutherans who decided to throw in their lot with the regime were called. It was a dangerous time, too. He would not keep quiet about Nazi atrocities and on one occasion he received a warning that he would be killed when he visited one of the towns in his parish. His next parish, from 1937, Ursheim, was in some ways more straightforward: it was a solidly Lutheran village, again in Catholic Bavaria, but the sort of religious island which was typical of the chequered history of the German-speaking peoples. Ursheim lies to the south of Nuremberg, another Lutheran enclave. Again Siegfried refused to remain silent or to curtail his activities. He and Brunnhild held a Bible class for adults, meetings for youth and Sunday School classes in their home and elsewhere, even though they were forbidden to do so. One day they received a visit from the Gestapo and were fined DM400, a large sum for them, which fortunately they were able to pay. Siegfried continued to speak his mind in church, despite the presence of a policeman taking notes. One of the issues he took up was the euthanasia of the inmates of the mental asylum in the next village of Polsingen. He warned that, as with the annihilation of the Jews, so the day would come for the Church as well. As a teacher of RE, Siegfried was not eligible for call-up. However this post was removed from him because of his subversive activities and in this way he was drafted into the army. He joined up as a radio operator in January 1943 and was trained in Coburg. That September he joined the German Sixth Army on the eastern front, on their retreat from Stalingrad. He was nevertheless able to witness the birth of their third child before he left. He sent letters home and wrote to his congregation. In 1944 he went missing in the Ukraine. He was never found but the place of his death is registered as Bertischew on 5 January 1944. When it was quite certain that he was not being held in a prison camp somewhere on the USSR, he was officially registered dead, but not until 1960. It is not known how he died but it is certain that he had.very little chance of survival. An NCO from his unit, whose life Siegfried had saved by carrying him to a medical station when he was wounded, sent his wife to Brunnhild (by chance he came from a nearby village) to inform her that the unit was a punishment detachment. In fact, as far as can be ascertained, none survived. Thus, Siegfried had no chance. Had he remained silent, he might have survived the war. Like Wallace, he was a reluctant combatant, but a courageous one.

Years of waiting and hoping, with three young children, was not easy. Brunnhild had seen the Pathfinder flares (they called them 'Christmas trees') on that fateful night in January 1945 and the red glow in the sky as the city burned. She had seen the hundreds of Lancasters flying overhead as they returned home (assuming that they took the same route as on the previous raid they would hove approached from the north and returned southwards before veering towards England), one of them, although she did not know it, carrying Wallace from his mission of destruction. The parishioners were good to her but it was difficult having to share the manse with another minister and his family. They got on well with the American occupying force: they were glad to have them, because above all they feared the Russians. In due course, in 1952, the family had to leave the manse and the village. She was given a small two-bedroom attic flat in a new development for ministers' widows in Nuremberg. Life was very hard: there was little money and the chances of work with three children were slim. She took in guests and did some seasonal part-time work. On some days they only had Quark (curd cheese) and potatoes to eat. Food was bought from the market and transported home in a handcart. The family used to visit different parts of the city, in order to acquaint themselves with it. One day they ventured into the old part and saw the terrible destruction. Brunnhild was so appalled she vowed not to return with the children -and this was over seven years since the bombing.

Wallace became Head of Art at Glasgow Academy. where I was appointed to my first teaching post. He designed and built, largely with his bare hands, a home on a stretch of moorland at Kippen, near Stirling, with a view towards the Trossachs. In due course he came to meet Brunnhild through her daughter Dorothea, who became my wife. They became friends and for several years one of his paintings hung in Brunnhild's home in the city he bombed. Having taken early retirement and then concentrated on painting, and having lost his wife. Wallace died in 1992. He wrote at Christmas 1991 saying that he had terminal cancer but was content to let nature take its course 'as I have been blessed with 84 happy and creative years'. The day before he wrote, he had delivered a set of paintings on the Life of Christ to St Giles Cathedral in Edinburgh: the previous week he had completed The Resurrection, which he felt was the climax of his career in art. He died the following February.

If Wallace had met Siegfried they would have found much in common, most of all their faith. I am sure, in today's custom, they would have exchanged the Peace. Fifty years to the day after the destruction of Nuremberg Wallace's son David exchanged the Peace with us all, including Brunnhild and Dorothea, at the dedication of our new home in Ness, South Wirral, Cheshire. It was a moving occasion: a symbol of reconciliation and a gesture of newfound hope in a united Europe.

Such reconciliation is not to deny what happened, nor to justify in any way the utterly despicable atrocities perpetrated by terrible regimes. It is quite understandable that those who suffered most, whether it be in concentration camps or on the

River Kwai, should be unable to forget and, in some cases, to forgive. We must remember: we must understand. However, while we rejoice in the outcome of the war and celebrate all the sacrifice made to bring down unjust and evil tyrannies, let us remember all who suffered, most of them innocently, and let us recall that there was goodness even amongst our enemies.

Postscript
Brunnhild died in 2008 at the age of 94 in her room in an old people's home, where Wallace's painting continued to hang. She is buried in the same cemetery as Albrecht Dürer. A cross is now placed every year, through the Royal British Legion, in the Field of Remembrance by Westminster Abbey, alongside thousands of other crosses representing the fallen of Britain and her allies, to commemorate Siegfried.

Kenneth Hall
Ness, Wirral, 1995, revised Clovenfords 2018

APPENDIX **3**

Abstract of PhD Thesis,
Liverpool University October 1995

Corporate Identity in Secondary Schools

*My thesis deals with three elements of organisations: **culture**, **identity** and **image**. By culture I mean the way an organisation operates; by identity, the way it projects its culture; by image, the way the identity is received. The thesis seeks to discover whether the practice of corporate identity, based on commercial models, in state secondary schools affects their success in recruiting pupils.*

The thesis starts with a general introduction defining the term corporate identity, and associated terms, and then explains its history and practice. A major diversion , by way of illustration, reviews the development of German history and contrasts the disparateness of the Weimar Republic with the imposed unity of the Third Reich.

The concept of corporate identity is then placed in the school context: a brief account of the development of state education is given and the events which led up to the management approach to school direction and to the current need for marketing, and hence the practice of identity creation. The literature pertaining to the topic and to associated topics is reviewed. There are no specific texts, only single chapters, or journal articles. The literature on school management is growing and since 1989 there is a small body of work on school marketing. That relating to commercial marketing is extensive, although the topic of corporate identity as such is still limited.

The first piece of primary research examines organisations other than schools, graduating from the fully commercial to the non-profit, such as higher education and charities. The thesis demonstrates that all organisations, unless they are of deliberately limited duration, carry on some form of marketing.

The main research is a survey of a one-third sample of secondary school in England and Wales. The survey shows that most schools market moderately but few take corporate identity seriously. Visits to over forty schools reinforced the findings of the survey and gave examples of good practice.

The third piece of primary research was a case study based on two Year 8 pupils in a Liverpool comprehensive. The pupils were observed in the classroom and were interviewed. Their teacher and parents were also interviewed. It was discovered that their choice of school was limited by social, psychological, educational and economic factors.

Success was measured against the school outside the survey, which contrasted with the case study school. It was discovered that **leadership** played a significant role in success, but this was combined with the best practice of corporate identity.

Finally, I give my findings from my research, state my own philosophical viewpoint and complete the thesis with my recommendations.

APPENDIX 4

A Day in the Life of a Senior Volunteer

As published in the Downning College annual alumni magazine and referring to our semester at Hebron School in South India in the summer/autumn of 2008

Our designation is 'Senior Volunteer'. There are five of us here at Hebron School, Ootacamond, known as Ooty, in the Nilgiri Hills, a hill station which was the former summer seat of the Madras government in the days of the Raj. Ooty is remote, being six hours by car (up 36 hairpin bends) from Bangalore and three hours from Coimbatore, the nearest big city. To call it a hill station is slightly misleading, in that it is highly populous, sprawling over a wide area and cascading down the slopes with terraces of houses, vegetable patches and tea plantations. The centre of Ooty is anything but Raj-style. It has lost almost all of its former rural charm and is now a hotchpotch of dusty, dirty, bustling and noisy streets, lined with mostly inelegant shops (although often providing an excellent service), and filled with jaywalking people and a few roaming goats, cows and horses. Yellow auto-rickshaws, cars, ancient-looking buses, polluting lorries and a multitude of motorbikes, ridden un-helmeted and often with a woman seated side-saddle on the back and sometimes with a child in front of the driver as well, ply up and down, vying for any available space which is claimed largely by hooting in as aggressive a manner as possible - the rule of the road here is that there are no rules! There are notices calling inhabitants and visitors to avoid litter and never to use a plastic bag, but neither the aural nor the visual environment seems to matter and the concept of Health and Safety appears to be totally absent. There are daily electricity cuts, fortunately restored by the school generator which cuts in after twenty seconds. Nevertheless none of this detracts from the sheer glory and beauty of the Nilgiri Hills, which you discover as you drive out just a few miles. Nor does it take away the affection which we feel for the Indian people.

We are: a lady musician from Australia, a Business Studies teacher from South London with his wife who does English and Special Needs, as well as Dorothea and myself, teaching German and French. In addition there is a group of International Guests, also volunteers, who are typically young people taking time off from their university studies or doing part of a gap year. Nearly all of us are here for a 5-month semester. All together there is a very large staff, with a very generous teacher-student ratio, and an enormous number of domestic staff. Teachers, including the Principal, are paid salaries which are described as 'sacrificial'. Nevertheless, all of us get our board and lodging free.

The day usually starts very early, partly due to insomnia. For some reason – maybe it's the altitude – we find it hard to sleep here. Around 5 am we may hear the Muslim call to prayer, especially in Ramadan, although it must be remembered that this is Tamil Nadu, a predominantly Hindu area. More prominently, at precisely 6 am, the whole neighbourhood receives its reveille call from a World War II siren - fortunately the 'all clear', when we quietly thank the Lord that the raid is over! Our own alarm goes off at 7am and we have the inevitable cup of tea. We are in a tea-growing area, as the climate is ideal, and a tea factory can be seen from our campus, up the hill opposite. Nilgiri tea is gentle, aromatic and delicious. It is drunk by the locals with warm milk and sugar. We have above us a dormitory of 11/12-year-olds who make their presence felt very early, especially on a Thursday, their inspection day. We call them the 'baby elephants'! From early on, too, lorries and other vehicles are straining up the steep hill which terminates opposite our building, so the chances of a lie-in, were we free to have it, are slim. We take our breakfast in our bed-sit rather than in the dining-hall, and some of the ingredients, such as milk and bread, are supplied free of charge. We have a 'traditional' English breakfast, with corn flakes and toast. We have managed to buy a toaster in town, and even marmalade.

Shortly after 8am two school buses arrive, depositing girls from their boarding house on the other side of town. These then return to pick up another two busloads The first obligation of the day, on 3 days of the week, having checked our pigeon-hole for messages or 'cover', is to attend assembly in the hall. This is always unapologetically Christian, as the Gospel is at the very heart of the school, which draws many of its students from Christian workers (who used to be called missionaries) in various parts of the world, mostly SE Asia. At least once a week there will be a speaker from the staff or outside. Frequently there will be a class-led assembly, put together and acted by the students, which from time to time can be very amusing! We invariably sing a hymn or worship song, the sound of which can be extremely moving. There are notices from prefects and staff and a true sense of family prevails.

At this time of year the mornings are invariably sunny and warm, without being hot. Frequently more senior groups can be seen sitting outside with their teachers. There are 8 periods of 40 minutes in the day, 5 in the morning and 3 in the afternoon. Our base is a staff workroom, down the hill, where we have a joint desk, in the main three-storey teaching block. Carting our books up and down the steep path keeps us fit. We take classes from Standard (year) 8 to Standard 13 (A level), the preparation and marking for which are a real challenge, largely because of our lack of recent school experience. We take lunch in the staff canteen, or sometimes with the students, and on sunny days quite often eat outside. The fare is usually South Indian, well spiced and mostly delicious. There are meetings and activities during the lunch hour. One of these is the school choir, which I direct. At the end of school there are frequently sports matches on the excellent dirt pitch or on the smaller grass area. Inter-school matches or athletics meetings are usually during class time. There is an abundance of activities of all sorts which frequently take groups of students to other parts, especially at weekends. The aim is to give an 'holistic' education and this includes the spiritual aspect. There was a huge Drama Festival in October, involving no less than seven separate productions, the senior of which was 'Blood Brothers', directed by the students themselves with amazing skill. On Sundays they all have to attend a service of some sort. The younger ones go to Union Church in Ooty, where the school usually organises the worship. Others can attend an 'alternative service' in the school chapel or go to the Anglican-style church in Ooty. There are also Christian activities run in the school, usually on a Sunday evening.

In the afternoon if we are free, Dorothea and I, in the current spate of warm weather, often manage a swim in the open-air pool, which is most refreshing. In the evenings we catch up with marking or preparation and frequently make a fire in our open hearth, using wood supplied by the kitchen. You cannot buy firelighters here but fortunately the oil-laden eucalyptus leaves from the abundant trees surrounding us, which are not native to these parts, burn enthusiastically. On one evening in the week we attend a Bible study group in the flat of one of its members and on another we go to a staff meeting, the greater part of which is spent in worship and prayer. There is a wonderful spirit of fellowship, mutual support and unity here amongst the staff, who come from traditions as different as Brethren to Roman Catholic. We have received many invitations to a meal in their accommodation. A part of the pastoral care is for our health and wellbeing. There is a sanatorium, called 'The Hoz', which not only provides beds for sick students and staff but also arranges appointments at clinics and hospitals. The nearest big hospital from here is at Coimbatore, which we have had occasion to visit twice, using a taxi hired for the day. Although you pay for it (at very moderate rates), the Indian health system is excellent.

We have made some memorable excursions at weekends, although our workload allows us relatively little free time. Our half-semester break took us to a Scripture Union family centre on the east coast near Chennai (Madras), which gave us warmth, peace and some fascinating outings. Part of the experience was a trip on the narrow-gauge rack-and-pinion 'Blue Train' through the spectacular Nilgiri hills, with an unscheduled halt of two hours due to a breakdown, to link up with the overnight Nilgiri Express to Chennai. A more local trip was by 'auto' up a very bumpy pot-holed road to the highest point in the Nilgiris, Dodabetta (8,600 feet), and a five-mile walk down to Ooty.

Our damp and dark bedsit has been rendered more habitable by an oil-filled heater giving constant background warmth. We wash in a bucket, as there is no plug for the basin which will fit, having drawn undrinkable water from the tap and heated it on a gas stove. For our teeth we have to use the filtered water which we collect every day from the kitchen. We are allowed three showers a week. These are primitive conditions, but luxury to many an Indian. We are happy to sink into our large double bed, suitably warmed up by an electric blanket, praying that we shall feel renewed and refreshed for another day as Senior Volunteers in the morning.

To call this 'the time of our life' would be an understatement. It is demanding, unexpected and enriching. We just thank God that we are given the strength to do the task to which we feel we have been called.

Kenneth Hall

Bibliography

BIBLIOGRAPHY

Bell, Les (1992) *Managing Teams in secondary Schools,* Routledge, London

Belton, Raymond H (1955) *White Unto Harvest, the Story of James Hall,* (Self-published), Bedford

Belton, Raymond H *Blacker than Coal, a Story for Children,* Pickering and Inglis, London, Glasgow, Edinburgh

Belton, Raymond H *Under New Management,* Pickering and Inglis Glasgow, Edinburgh, Manchester, London

British Petroleum (1989) *An Image for the Nineties,* BP International Limited, London

De-la-Noy, Michael (1999) *Bedford School, A History,* Bedford School

Dickens, C. (1859, reprint 1985) *A Tale of Two Cities,* Penguin Books, London

Downing College, Cambridge University, (2009) *College Magazine,* Downing College Alumni Association, Cambridge

Drucker Peter F. (1974) *Management*, Harper's College Press, New York

Drucker, Peter F. (1990) *The New Realities*, Mandarin Paperbacks, London

Drucker, Peter F. (1999) *Management Challenges for the 21st Century*, Elsevier, Amsterdam, Boston, Heidelberg, New York, Oxford

Elliott, Geoffrey & Shukman, Harold (2002) *Secret Classrooms*, St Ermin's Press, in association with Little, Brown (Time Warner Books UK), London

Firth, R. (1973) *Symbols*, Allen and Unwin, London

Figes, Orlando (2010) *The Europeans*, Penguin Books , London

Gumbel, Nicky *Questions of Life*, Alpha International, London

Hall, Kenneth G.M. (1995) *Corporate Identity in Secondary Schools*, PhD Thesis Liverpool University

Hampshire County Architects Department (1991) *Schools of Thought,* Hampshire County Council, Winchester

Handy, Charles (1996) *Gods of Management,* Oxford University Press, Oxford

Harper, Charles G. (1028) *The Bunyan Country, Landmarks of 'The Pilgrim's Progress'*, Cecil Palmer, London

Meyers, William (1984) *The Image Makers*, Papermac, London, Basingstoke

Stott, John (2019) *Through the Year with John Stott,* Monarch Books, London

Thompson Fred (1987) *Newport Free Grammar School, a Brief History,* The Old Newportonian Society, Newport, Saffron Walden, Essex

Thompson, Fred (Vol.1 1978) *Sons of Joyce Frankland 1588 – 1945,* The Old Newportonian Society, Newport, Saffron Walden, Essex

Thompson, Fred (Vol. 2: 1984) *Sons of Joyce Frankland 1946 - 76,* The Old Newportonian Society, Newport, Saffron Walden, Essex

Welby, Justin (2018, revised 2021) *Reimagining Britain: Foundations for Hope,* Bloomsbury Continuum, London,

White, Malcolm (2013) *Newport Free Grammar School, Essex, 1988 – 2013,* The Old Newportonian Society, Newport, Saffron Walden, Essex